Ethnic Armies

Polyethnic Armed Forces
From the Time
of the
Habsburgs
To the Age
of the
Superpowers

N. F. Dreisziger
Editor

Wilfrid Laurier University Press

Canadian Cataloguing in Publication Data

Main entry under title:

Ethnic armies

Papers presented at the 13th RMC Military History
Symposium held at the Royal Military College of
Canada in late Mar. 1986.
Includes bibliographical references.
ISBN 0-88920-993-6

1. Armies – History – Congresses. 2. Ethnic
groups – Congresses. 3. Sociology, Military –
Congresses. I. Dreisziger, N. F. (Nandor F.).
II. Military History Symposium (Canada) (13th :
1986 : Royal Military College).

UB416.E74 1990   306.2'7'089   C90-095416-7

(∞)

Copyright © 1990
Wilfrid Laurier University Press
Waterloo, Ontario, Canada
N2L 3C5

Cover design by Leslie Macredie

Printed in Canada

Ethnic Armies: Polyethnic Armed Forces from the Time of the Habsburgs to the Age of the Superpowers has been produced from a manuscript supplied in electronic form by the author.

CONTENTS

CONTRIBUTORS

Nándor F. Dreisziger is a professor of history at the Royal Military College of Canada.

Richard A. Preston is Professor Emeritus of History at Duke University and Honorary Professor in the Department of History at the Royal Military College of Canada.

István Deák is a professor of history at Columbia University and a former director of that university's Institute on East Central Europe. His history of the Habsburg Army is now being published by Oxford University Press.

Myron Echenberg is a professor of history and chairperson of McGill University's Department of History.

Bruce White teaches history at the University of Toronto's Erindale College.

Edwin Dorn is with the Joint Center for Political and Economic Studies in Washington, D.C. He is the editor of the recent volume: *Who Defends America? Race, Sex and Class in the Armed Forces* (Washington, 1989).

Teresa Rakowska-Harmstone is a professor of political science and a former chairperson of Carleton University's Department of Political Science.

Major John G. Armstrong has served as a historian with the Directorate of History at National Defence Headquarters and with the Department of History at RMC. He currently commands the Administration Training Company of the Canadian Forces School of Administration and Logistics at Canadian Forces Base, Borden, Ontario.

ACKNOWLEDGEMENTS

THE THIRTEENTH MILITARY History Symposium, held at the Royal Military College of Canada 20-21 March 1986, and the publication of its proceedings were made possible through the cooperation of numerous individuals and with the help of several institutions.

Grants to cover the cost of staging the meeting were received from the Social Sciences and Humanities Research Council of Canada, and the Multiculturalism Sector of the Department of the Secretary of State.

The then Commandant of RMC, Brigadier-General Walter Niemy, and his administrative staff helped with the myriad organizational chores involved in hosting the gathering. Professor Donald Schurman, the then Head of the History Department, as well as my colleagues in the department gave advice and encouragement. Professor Keith Neilson acted as symposium co-director. History Department secretary Mrs. Karen Brown shouldered most of the departmental share of the administration involved in the preparation and holding of the symposium. Mr. James Watt and his staff at the Royal Military College Senior Staff Mess, attended to the entertainment functions during the conference.

Several people helped with the preparation of the manuscript for publication. Mrs. Marilyn Pitre and Ms. Ann LaBrash put parts of the volume into electronic form. Ms. Anne McCarthy did some of the copyediting. Conference participant Professor Jean Burnet followed the book's progress with keen interest. She and the late Robert Harney gave advice on the use of terminology. They, as well as some of the volume's contributors, offered comments on the book's introduction.

This book has been published with the help of a grant from Multiculturalism Canada.

N.F.D.
Kingston, 1989

POLYETHNICITY AND ARMED FORCES: AN INTRODUCTION

N.F. DREISZIGER with R.A. PRESTON

MOST ARMED FORCES in the world today are multi-ethnic. They are composed of men and women of different races or cultures, often speaking different languages or dialects. This is true of the largest armed forces in the world, those of the USSR, the United States, China, and India; but the armies of such smaller countries as Yugoslavia, Switzerland, South Africa, Romania, and so on, are also mixed, racially or ethnically. Canada's own armed forces are composed of two major cultural elements, and a similar situation exists in a number of other countries, among them Belgium and Czechoslovakia, as well as in some South American states where native Indians co-habit with the descendants of Europeans.

Multi-ethnic armed forces have existed since ancient times. The armies of the ancient empires of the Middle East, of the Roman Emperors and the Mongol Khans, all tended to be conglomerations of diverse ethnic, religious, or racial groups. The immediate reason for this phenomenon was, for the most part, the fact that for rulers bent on conquest armies were often tools in which the soldiers, and in some cases the entire armed forces of subject nations, were compelled (or cajoled) to serve. But there was, and still is, another and fundamental reason for the existence of multi-ethnic armies in the past and the present. This is the fact that nations, from their earliest beginnings, tended to be polyethnic.

Polyethnicity in ancient and modern societies was the theme of three lectures that Professor William H. McNeill, one of North America's most distinguished historians, delivered at the University of Toronto in 1985. McNeill's main thesis was that, throughout history, the norm of societal existence was not nations made up of members of a single ethnic group but the opposite: states based on the coexistence of different ethnic groups. In ancient times, McNeill observed, "civilized societies" were multi-ethnic: foreign conquests, trade, and epidemics worked to make them so.[1] In the period between 1750 and 1920, as McNeill admits, a new ideal emerged that ran counter to this norm. This was the concept of a "nationalist base" for the political organization of society, and it favoured the

1

creation of nations that were made up of members of a single ethnic group. This ideal gained acceptance in Western Europe at a time when Europe was expanding overseas, and so initiating the mingling of races and cultures on an unprecedented scale.[2]

According to McNeill, the experiment in building homogeneous nation states began to be reversed after World War I, even though the worst outbreaks of militant chauvinism took place later. Since 1920, there has been a gradual return to the ideal of polyethnic society. Surveying the world today, McNeill sees the increasing mingling of peoples, the greater ease of international travel and migration, and the growing acceptance of the concept of multi-ethnic societies. Indeed, the only major industrial power that he could find as being an exception to this state of affairs was Japan, and in that country too McNeill saw the presence of forces that might make for developments similar to those taking place elsewhere in the world.[3]

Polyethnic states tend to have multi-ethnic armies. This axiom is true of both the ancient and the modern world. McNeill pointed out that in ancient times the constant need for new manpower, to replenish what classical societies lost in warfare (and the plagues that accompanied wars), required the admission of "an ever-widening circle of military recruits."[4] Even the armies of some smaller states tended to be multi-ethnic. In the early stages of the development of a city state, these armies were made up of "citizen soldiers" — though they undoubtedly included in their ranks many immigrants to the city. In the later stages of such a state's evolution, mercenaries were often hired to protect the state and its far-flung interests — and mercenary armies were notorious for their mixed ethnic composition.

The phenomenon of polyethnic armed forces is a complex one. A polyethnic army can be made up of two, three, or more nationalities or racial groups. A force can be both multi-ethnic (meaning that it is composed of more than one cultural group of the same race) and multi-racial. The extent to which armed forces can be polyethnic can also vary a great deal: in some armies or navies only a small portion of the members belong to a minority (or minorities), while in others there might not be a dominant ethnic group. This is true of forces made up of the members of several ethnic groups, each (or, at least, most) contributing a substantial fraction to the whole.

Further increasing the complexity of the situation is the fact that in some polyethnic armed forces the officer corps is made up of the members of an ethnic group (or groups) different from the "other ranks." In some of these forces we have an intertwining of class systems and the phenomenon of polyethnicity. Such superimposition of social "class" over the "ethnic" character of armed forces can be the result of deliberate policy (especially in societies with distinct caste systems or with traditions of racial or ethnic segregation), or it can be coincidental, that is, it can be the result of different ethnic groups within society having different propensities for entering military service.

What complicates an already complex situation still further is the fact that countries tend to use the "ethnic factor" in their armed forces for different purposes. More often than not, these purposes are political rather than military. A polyethnic armed force can be an instrument of racial or ethnic segregation and/or of oppression: it can be used to enhance the social and political position of one (or more) ethnic group *vis-à-vis* another ethnic group (or other ethnic groups). Conversely, the ethnic factor in armed forces can be used to appease a particular ethnic group (or more than one group) or, indeed, to promote national (ethnic or racial) integration and unity.

What usually determines the nature of the ethnic factor in a nation's armed forces, is the ethnic make-up of that country's society. On the whole, ethnic groups can be divided into dominant and subordinate types. The former tend to constitute majorities in their respective countries, but there are significant exceptions to this phenomenon. An obvious example is that of the Afrikaners of South Africa. In some countries two or more ethnic groups share political, social, and economic power, while the rest belong to the subordinate category or, in some cases, different subordinate categories. A case in point is Yugoslavia where the major ethnic groups (above all the Serbs, Croatians, and Slovenes), usually concentrated in their respective republics, share political power in the country, while other groups have less political influence (the Albanians of the autonomous Serbian province of Kosovo and the Hungarians of the province of Voivodina), and still others wield virtually none. Furthermore, in certain cases the situation of an ethnic group in society is not reflected in its position in the armed forces: some ethnic groups have played military roles that far exceed the influence they command within their state. The two groups that come to mind here are the Gurkhas and the Cossacks; indeed, the phenomenon of the utilization of a so-called "martial" ethnic group for state security has been referred to as the "Gurkha Syndrome."[5]

POLYETHNICITY OR THE "ethnic factor" in armed forces has been, and still is, a neglected subject in the literature of military affairs. The chroniclers of ancient and medieval military campaigns have usually been silent on the matter, probably because multi-ethnic armies were taken for granted as the order of the day. If a chronicler did comment on this aspect, his remarks were usually confined to a mere mention of an army's ethnic composition, rather than to a discussion of the question of communication within this army, or internal cohesion, or relations between officers and men, and so on. In pre-modern times (and in some parts of the world even today) the ethnic factor in armed forces was not seen as a serious problem worthy of detailed discussion because the soldiers' loyalty was not to the nation state, or to a particular ethnic community, but to a leader or monarch. Only since the second half of the eighteenth century, and in some parts of the world not even then, has this ethnic factor become an issue for the military, and a problem worth studying.[6]

One difficulty faced by those who attempt to study the phenomenon of polyethnic armies — indeed, polyethnic societies themselves — is the complexity and elusiveness of the terminology involved. Concepts such as *race, nation, nationality,* and the like, elude concise and precise definitions. This is especially true of *ethnic* (noun), *ethnicity,* and *ethnic group,* and *ethnic* (adjective). The meaning of these words tends to vary in space and time: they are often defined differently from country to country, and from one generation to the next. This applies to both general usage and academic language. Professors Alan B. Anderson and James S. Frideres, two Canadian students of ethnic theory, observed that all these terms have been continually "redefined" by social scientists.[7] Therefore, no definition of these concepts can be offered that will satisfy everyone. All that can be attempted here is the identification of those definitions that have been accepted by some careful and knowledgeable historians and sociologists in recent times.

Before the mid-twentieth century, the words most often used to describe a collection of individuals belonging to a certain cultural group were *race* and *nationality.* Social scientists, however, found these terms inadequate. As early as the 1930s, they applied the term *ethnic* to communities of individuals with distinct cultures.[8] Its rise to prominence in the English language was documented by the publishers of the *Oxford Dictionary.* The *Compact Edition of the Oxford English Dictionary,* published in 1971, still deemed the word *ethnic* "obsolete" and "rare" and said that it meant "heathenness, heathen, or superstition." The *Supplement* to the *Oxford Dictionary,* published the following year, however, produced a new definition: "ethnic character or peculiarity," with examples dating from 1953, 1964, and 1970.[9]

Closely related to the word *ethnic* is the concept of the *ethnic group,* a term which also defies easy definition. As many as four different schools of thought have been identified among social scientists who have attempted to define it.[10] In addition, a difference can be perceived between the way North American and European scholars use the term. Reflecting on these complexities, historians Jean Burnet and Howard Palmer, two Canadian students of ethnic affairs, remarked in a recent work that the concept "ethnic group" is "not wholly definable in objective terms, although it may have objective markers."[11] Nevertheless, these same scholars have found a definition they liked. It describes an ethnic group as "a collectivity within larger society having real or putative common ancestry, memories of shared historical past, and a cultural focus on one or more symbolic elements defined as the epitome of their peoplehood. . . ."[12] More recent than the terms *ethnic community* or *ethnic group* is the word *ethnicity*. In the early 1960s, sociologists Nathan Glazer and Daniel P. Moynihan, for example, began using this term in their discussion of cultural groups in New York City.[13] Since that time, the word has received widespread acceptance, as indicated by the number of publications that use it in their titles.

Though the word *race* is much older than either *ethnic group* or *ethnicity*, there is no agreement about its precise meaning. In international scholarly circles, however, there is general acceptance of the definition assigned to this word by physical anthropologists: "a specific group of people who could be phenotypically isolated. . . ."[14] It might be useful to add that, according to some scholars, a racial group can be an ethnic group within a larger society composed of members of another race (or other races), while an ethnic group is "not a race" in the opinion of students of ethnic and racial theory.[15] A few social scientists prefer to differentiate between race and ethnicity, that is between ethnic and racial affairs, suggesting, for example, that the interaction of whites and blacks should be discussed in the context of *race* and not *ethnic* relations.[16]

Other terms that often occur in works discussing ethnicity are *nation*, *nationality*, and *minority*. The first of these has not been equated by social scientists with either *race* or *ethnic group*. Membership in a nation is often determined in part by such political — rather than cultural or racial — attributes as birth and citizenship. A nation is not an ethnic group, yet the members of one nation living (as immigrants or displaced persons) in the land of another can be said to constitute an ethnic group. In Europe, where nations have often been dismembered as a result of wars or diplomatic settlements, groups of former members of one nation living within the boundaries of another nation-state are usually referred to as nationalities or minorities. To many European scholars and, as it is suggested by some authors in this volume, even to some North American students of European affairs, the terms *ethnic group* and *nationality* (or *minority*) are interchangeable. Canadian students of ethnic theory, however, make one qualification — which does not contradict the use of these terms in this volume. Anderson and Frideres feel that

the term *nationality* should be "restricted" to "politically significant" ethnic groups.[17]

Even a brief discussion of the terminology of ethnicity should
make mention of another word: *multiculturalism.* According to the
Oxford Dictionary, this word is even more recent than *ethnicity.* It
was listed for the first time in the second volume of the *Supplement*
which did not appear until 1976. The term was defined as meaning
"of or pertaining to a society consisting of varied cultural groups." It
is noteworthy that the examples given for it were almost all Canadian
or had reference to Canada, one of the most important being the
Royal Commission on Bilingualism and Biculturalism.[18]

While the United States and Canada have been the birthplace of
new additions to the vocabulary of ethnic studies, important differences remain in the way this terminology is applied in these two
countries. The most obvious difference is the usage of the word *race.*
In the U.S. the term is most often used to differentiate blacks from
whites, Indians from Europeans, and so on. In Canada, members of
the general public as well as many academics have, for generations,
been talking of the "British race" and the "French race." Much the
same, in Canadian public life as well as in some French-Canadian
scholarly literature, the term *ethnic* tends to be used in a peculiar
manner. It is assumed to be pejorative and, consequently, the British
and French in the country do not refer to themselves and are not
referred to as "ethnics." They constitute not *ethnic* but *charter*
groups because, as Burnet and Palmer explain, "they were the first
Europeans to take possession of the land."[19] This dichotomy in the
Canadian usage of the word *ethnic* is illustrated in the *Gage Canadian Dictionary* where the adjective *ethnic* is defined as "of or having to do with various groups of people and their characteristics, customs, and languages," but the noun is said to have a Canadian
"informal" meaning: "an immigrant who is not a native speaker of
English and French."[20]

In the scholarly literature of ethnic affairs in Canada the word
race is more likely to have its American or international meaning,
while the subject of "ethnic and race relations" is said to be composed of three main axes: the interaction between natives and non-
natives, between the English and the French, and between the "charter groups" and "other immigrants and their descendants."[21] It
appears then that, though English and French Canadians are not
"ethnics" in everyday Canadian parlance, they are treated as such by
Canadian students of ethnic affairs.[22] Furthermore, as they constitute
ethnic groups according to the definitions mentioned in this discussion of terminology, their interactions will be deemed to be part of
ethnic relations.

THE PURPOSE of the 13th RMC Military History Symposium, entitled "Race, Ethnicity and Armed Forces," held at the Royal Military College of Canada in late March 1986, was to provide a forum for the discussion of the question of polyethnicity in armed forces before a predominantly Canadian audience. In particular, the conference sought to highlight those aspects of the subject that are of special interest to students of Canadian military history and to officers of the Canadian Armed Forces. The conference consisted of seven presentations. In the first of these Richard A. Preston offered an introduction to the subject along with an overview of the Canadian experience of biculturalism in the military (for the latter see Chapter Six of this volume). This keynote address was followed by six specialized papers: two dealing with mainly pre-World War I examples of polyethnic armies, two with the problems of ethnicity in the military of the United States, and one outlining the ethnic question in the Soviet Armed Forces. The concluding paper returned to the Canadian experience with a case study of the fate of a black unit in the Canadian Expeditionary Force during the First World War.

Two of the specialized papers at the conference dealt with military forces no longer extant. Professor István Deák examined the armed forces of the Habsburg Empire, and Professor Myron Echenberg surveyed the story of France's colonial army in Africa. Although these forces disappeared after World War I and World War II respectively, their experiences are interesting as well as instructive both to students of military history and to specialists in ethnic affairs. Indeed, some of the lessons that can be learned from the history of these two polyethnic militaries are still meaningful for today's multi-ethnic or multi-racial armed forces.

If there ever was a truly polyethnic military, it was the armed forces of the Habsburg Empire. This state, situated in the very heart of Europe, as Professor Deák points out in his introductory paragraphs, was a hodge-podge of nationalities, acquired through centuries of conquest and marriage alliances. Before 1867 (when the Habsburg realm was reorganized into the "Dual Monarchy" of Austria-Hungary), the Habsburg Army and the imperial civil service were the Empire's only two supranational state institutions. After that year, the army became the sole such institution. Notwithstanding the transformation of 1867, the army's bewildering ethnic complexity continued.

This armed force, made up of more than a dozen different ethnic groups, carried the Habsburg Empire through the wars of the seventeenth and eighteenth centuries and then through the age of rising nationalism in the nineteenth century; and it was this military that survived the revolutions of 1848-49 and managed to save the Monarchy. The Habsburg Army underwent extensive reorganization after 1867. Subsequently its united element, the so-called "common army," faced the hostility of the Hungarian Parliament, as well as other political forces, which conspired to starve it of funds and recruits. Yet the Habsburg military, united by a loyalty to the Emperor-King Francis Joseph, persevered. The tribulations of this large and complex military establishment are outlined by Deák, with particular attention to the ethnic make-up of its various components and also to the problems of language and language-training for the men and officers.

As national strife increased in the Empire, especially after the 1880s, the situation of the Habsburg armed forces deteriorated. While career officers resisted the nationalistic fervour of the age, some reserve officers and a part of the rank and file became gradually but inevitably imbued by it. At the same time, nationalist politicians attacked the army which they justly considered to be the main pillar of the existing order. In peacetime, the army did its best to uphold this order, even when soldiers had to face demonstrators of the same nationality. But things began to change when peace gave way to war and the First World War turned into a prolonged, bitter, and cataclysmic conflict.

During the war, desertions and defections were common among some nationalities (such as the Czechs and Ruthenians), but other nationalities (above all the Germans, Hungarians, and Croatians) generally remained loyal to their Emperor and fought on. However, when the domestic front began to totter in 1916 and 1917, the army's situation also deteriorated, and when the Dual Monarchy disintegrated in 1918, what was left of the army was in no position to save it.

According to Deák, the failings of the multi-ethnic Habsburg Army were few. More could have been done to democratize it, but as Professor De k asks, how can democracy be introduced into an army whose loyalty is dynastic? The Habsburg Army might not have solved all or even most of the problems that face a highly multi-ethnic military, but it has to be kept in mind that, in the end, it was not this military that failed the Habsburg state. Rather, it was the political problems of that state that proved insoluble. The First World War immensely exacerbated these problems and caused the Dual Monarchy's disintegration. The bulk of the Habsburg Army, its soldiers by 1918 half-starved and in rags, continued to fight to the bitter end.

In the second essay on polyethnic forces no longer in existence, Professor Myron Echenberg examines the experience of the African *Tirailleurs* Army (ATA), a part of France's colonial military. In the century of its existence, this army of black Africans underwent several reorganizations and transformations. From an army of conquest in the last four decades of the nineteenth century, it became one of colonial occupation and, later, an all-purpose fighting force for France, deployed at various times in Europe, Africa, and Asia. It served France well, especially in her life-and-death struggles with Germany, on each occasion boosting French strength by some 100,000 men. Like the Habsburg Army, the ATA was dissolved not because of major military defects, but as a result of France's withdrawal from Africa as a colonial power.

The ATA was both a multi-racial (more precisely, bi-racial) and a multi-ethnic army, its African rank-and-file and some junior officers being conscripted or later recruited from many of the diverse French territories in West Africa. In his paper, Echenberg analyses three variables that determined the character of this force: race, ethnicity, and social class. Race (and racist theories that divided peoples into races suitable for leadership, soldiering, or other, non-military, activities) determined who was to be inducted into this army — who became the "ranks" and who served as officers. The ATA's officers were Frenchmen, though a few blacks were admitted to junior ranks. The rank and file were members of the diverse black ethnic groups, such as the Bambara and Mossi. Caucasoid African populations were excluded from service in the regular units of the ATA — they were not considered "martial races." Racial tension did exist in this military, Echenberg concludes, but it was "no worse" than that found in West African civil society.

The ethnic variable within this army was more significant: it touched the vast majority of its members and affected its relationships with African society at large. Ethnic tensions, such as rivalries for influence among soldiers and aspiring junior officers of different ethnic background, co-existed with racial tensions between Europeans and Africans. To this was added the variable of social class, further complicating a complex situation within this highly polyethnic fighting force. Interestingly enough, while service in the ATA often reduced social distinctions among the rank and file, ethnic differences tended to remain.

In his conclusions Professor Echenberg stresses the lasting legacy that the ATA bequeathed to the lands where it had existed. During its existence and, especially, during the post-World War II period when it went through its last, "Africanization," phase, it had affected the economic, social, and political development of West Africa. The ATA and its institutions, ranging from military schools to veterans' associations, had made their mark on African society and left an ambiguous legacy that continues to benefit or plague, as the case may be, the nations of this part of Africa to this day.

Professor Bruce White's study, "The American Army and the Indian," covers a subject that is both similar to and different from the case of the polyethnic armies discussed by Professors Deák and Echenberg. The major similarity is that in the Native Americans serving in the U.S. military we have an example of members of a subjugated ethnic group being a part of the armed forces that had conquered them. In the Habsburg Army, all but the German element had been similarly defeated groups, even though by the late nineteenth century a few other groups had come to share power and influence in the Habsburg state and its forces.[23] In the ATA, all black soldiers were members of "conquered" peoples. The major difference between the American Indians and the ethnic groups serving in the other two forces under discussion is that the former were always a small minority in the U.S. military. Professor White, then, discusses the case of a quite marginal (both in terms of numbers and influence) ethnic group in the military of a state. What he makes clear is that the extent and character of the participation of such a group in an armed force is determined very much by the attitudes that prevail in society at large toward that particular ethnic group. The issue of the relationship between the American Indian and the U.S. military, then, is very much a question of the inter-relationship of "white" American society and the native peoples of North America. Appropriately, Professor White begins with an analysis of white attitudes toward native people from the time of total war for European survival in North America, to the period when the Indian "problem" became "only" a frontier issue. He next examines the attitudes of the U.S. Army towards American Indians, both those that were part of that force and those that existed outside of it as friends, foes, or neutrals.

In the second part of his study, Professor White turns to the Native experience in dealing with white society and its armed forces. In this regard, for nearly three centuries after the European discovery of North America, the situation for its indigenous population was the opposite of what it was for the colonists. For Native Americans, first came skirmishes on the edge — or frontier — of Indian settlement, which only later turned into a total war for the cultural and physical survival of their race. In this war, or, more precisely, intermittent warfare, some Indians were drawn into the colonists' armed forces as allied irregulars or auxiliaries. Later, when the importance of the Indian wars became dwarfed by other struggles, Indians also fought in the white man's conflicts — in the Civil War and then in America's wars abroad. Professor White discusses explanations for Indian enlistment in the American Army. One of these cites ethnic "marginality" — the cultural "rootlessness" of Native people as well as their increasing dependence on white men.

The legacy of Indian warfare, and an exaggerated emphasis on the Indians' so-called "special martial qualities," have influenced the American Army's use of Native soldiers and their units. To some extent, Indians were victims of the Gurkha syndrome, much as were the Croatian-Slovenian *Grenzers* in the Habsburg Army, or the Bambara in the ATA. The results were predictable. In many battles, particularly in the two world wars, Indians were sent on life-threatening assignments because of their real or supposed "special" abilities, often with fatal consequences. In reality, the Native Indian had few special skills, though in many campaigns good use was made of those he had (we need only to refer to the ability of Indian "communication specialists" to put radio messages into instant "code" by using their own native tongues). More common than these special skills were the difficulties that Native soldiers encountered after induction into the army. Service in the white man's military brought culture shock, and its long-term consequence was often the disruption of the cultural and social life of the Indian soldier (and veteran), with similar effects on the lives of their communities.

In his study on the American blacks in the U.S. armed forces, military affairs specialist Edwin Dorn points out that the society that had emerged from the War of American Independence was racist both in practice and in law. This racism survived the Civil War and the emancipation of blacks, and affected both non-white and white ethnic minorities. It also tended to determine the extent and nature of the participation of ethnic groups in the American military. This was certainly true in the case of the blacks.

The participation of blacks in America's armed forces had been circumscribed in a multiplicity of ways from the earliest days of the Republic to the middle of the present century. The rules restricting their entry into the forces, and progress through the ranks, were bent only in times of dire need for manpower. Otherwise blacks were confined to auxiliary roles and segregated units, and their ascent to higher ranks was almost invariably blocked. One reason for these policies was, according to Dorn, the fear of American white society that a fuller participation by blacks in the defense of America would invoke calls for a more dignified place for them in American society.

Change began to take place in this situation only after World War II. Interestingly enough, when it came, it took place faster in the military than outside of it. Measures to render the armed forces less racist tended to be implemented more effectively than steps designed to decrease racism in American society at large. And when the volunteer principle replaced conscription in the U.S., the stage was set for still further changes in the nature and extent of black participation in the military of the Republic. Black under-representation in the military was replaced by over-representation in some of its elements, particularly the enlisted ranks. The cause of this change probably had to do with the social and economic marginality of much of the black population. The lack of opportunities in the civilian economy, according to Dorn, might have driven many blacks to enlistment. Matters of ethnicity have helped to determine the blacks' under-representation in the American military before the 1970s, while they contribute to their over-representation since then.

Service for blacks in the U.S. armed forces has, and will likely continue to have, an important impact on them and their community. Dorn suggests that it will help to equip many blacks for meaningful civilian economic pursuits. On the other hand, the fact that participation is mainly for the "best and the brightest" of black youth, deprives those who cannot qualify for service of the chance to escape economic and social marginality. The implications are important for both the black community and American society at large. The solutions to these and many other problems relating to blacks in the American military will require time and, as Dorn emphasizes, statesmanship.

The ethnic factor in the Soviet Armed Forces (SAF) is the subject of Professor Teresa Rakowska-Harmstone's paper. The inclusion of a study on the Soviet military in the program of the 13th RMC Military History Symposium was highly appropriate since the SAF are truly multi-ethnic forces, reflecting the demographic situation of the USSR: Russians make up only one half of that country's population, while the other half is composed of close to a hundred ethnic groups. In the military of such a society the importance of the ethnic problem is not surprising.

The military of the Soviet Union was born in the turmoil of revolution and civil war. Its progenitor, the Imperial Russian Army, was also a polyethnic force, but one that shunned the induction of certain non-Christian and non-Slavic minorities. The SAF's immediate predecessor, the Red Guard of the revolutionary period, was even more multi-ethnic than the tsarist army had been. Ethnic elements played a disproportionately large role in this force, and they were joined by various Central European groups that were recruited by the Bolsheviks from tens of thousands of Austro-Hungarian prisoners of war.[24]

During the bitter and lengthy Civil War (1918-21), out of this motley force of ethnic soldiers an efficient army was forged. Contrary to what might be expected, however, this was not to become a military force representing a coalition of more or less equal nationalities; it remained an instrument of a state controlled by the dominant Russian ethnic group. Consequently, in the SAF, as Professor Rakowska-

Harmstone points out, no significantly autonomous units of the nationalities were allowed (except very early, and even then only at a basic level). During the Second World War, however, manpower requirements and military expediency compelled their acceptance.

One of the enduring characteristics of the Russian military, both in tsarist and post-revolutionary times, is the use of the armed forces as an instrument of societal integration, more precisely, as a means of imposing an official culture and world-view upon Russia's various nationalities. Under tsarist rule this meant spreading the triad of Orthodox religion, political conservatism, and the Russian language. In the post-revolutionary era, Marxist theory and Leninist political practice have replaced the religious and political overtones of the earlier days; but promotion of the Russian language and culture continues. Professor Rakowska-Harmstone explores in depth the use of the SAF as an instrument of assimilation. Other themes she discusses include the ethnic make-up of the various branches of the Soviet military; the ethnic antagonisms that have existed and continue to exist in its ranks and their impact on the perceived reliability of the SAF's various components; and Soviet attitudes to education, indoctrination, and language problems in the military.

The Russian military (both the SAF and the tsarist army), like the Habsburg forces, the ATA and, in certain respects, the American Army, is the product of historical processes that had seen the subjugation of numerous ethnic groups by one particular ethnic group. In this sense, the Russian military is the instrument of a conquest state – and here we do not mean to ignore the fact that some of Russia's conquests were engendered by outside aggression. As such, it is a military whose inner dynamics are determined by perpetual concerns of state security and threats against the hegemony of the dominant ethnic group both from within and outside the country. As Professor Rakowska-Harmstone points out, Russians distrust their nationalities and believe they need to maintain their dominion over them. These facts make the ethnic factor most vital in the SAF.

Of the previously discussed polyethnic forces, the Habsburg Army, in its genesis and complex ethnic make-up, most reminds us of the SAF and, especially, their tsarist forerunner. There are, however, crucial differences. In the Imperial Russian Army, as in the SAF, there was (or is) only one dominant ethnic group. In other words, in the Imperial Russian Army there was not (the Cossacks were not such a force), and in the SAF there is not, a Ukrainian or Moslem equivalent of the Dual Monarchy's *honvéd*, looked after by a fiercely particularist parliament in Kiev or Alma Ata.

Of course, the SAF are a modernized descendant of a dynastic army. The Soviet military has gone through a revolutionary metamorphosis, and it has successfully survived the supreme test of total war. These trials strengthened it and have brought to it technological and organizational modernization. Yet some of the problems that faced the Habsburg military still confront the SAF, including a threat posed by the centrifugal forces of local particularisms and by the uneven demographic development of the USSR's Slavic and non-Slavic populations. As the example of the Habsburg Army shows, these and other problems need not unduly weaken a military, except possibly in the event of prolonged total warfare. Whether these problems will overwhelm Soviet society itself is a more pertinent question; but an attempt to answer that query is beyond the scope of this collection of studies.

THE CANADIAN EXPERIENCE in polyethnicity in military forces is examined in the last two papers in this volume. The size of the Canadian forces and their "strategic weight" in the international power balance would hardly seem to justify a discussion of them in a volume of essays on some of the world's large and powerful polyethnic armies. However, the experience of Canada in bicultural institutions is almost unique, and this does invite an examination of the way "biculturalism" is reflected in the Canadian military.

Canada's armed forces, like all the other militaries discussed in this volume, have a conquering army as their progenitor. In the Canadian case, this was the British Army (and Navy) which had conquered New France in the Seven Years' War (1756-63) and which thereafter served as an army of occupation in Canada for decades. At the same time it should be emphasized that Canada's present-day military is further removed from the army-of-conquest-and-occupation stage of development than any of the other forces considered in this volume. It was less than a century and a half ago that the Habsburg Army occupied re-conquered Hungary (after the Hungarian War of Independence of 1848-49), the American Army fought a protracted frontier war in the West, the French embarked on their conquests in Africa, and the Russians expanded into Central Asia. By that time, in British North America a political partnership between the French and English elements of the population was already emerging, making possible the genesis of a Canadian confederation based on sharing political power. While the Canadian Confederation of 1867 did not bring complete equality to French Canadians in all or even most aspects of Canadian existence, it did give them a share in the political decision-making process.

While French Canadians became partners in the political and even, to some extent, the economic affairs of post-1867 Canada, they were not equal partners in its military institutions. As Professor

Richard Preston pointed out in his keynote address to the conference (and in his paper in this volume), French-Canadian participation in the young country's militia, and later in its small professional force, was barely marginal. The reasons for this were complex, but they had much to do with the fact that the Canadian military modelled itself on the British Army. The use of Canadian units in British imperial wars at the end of the nineteenth century also served to alienate French Canadians from what was then predominantly an English-Canadian institution. Concurrent political conflicts in Canada between French and English also contributed to an atmosphere in which French Canadians preferred to dissociate themselves from Canada's armed forces. Efforts to reverse this situation began in earnest only after World War II and resulted in the creation of a Canadian military that is increasingly a bilingual and bicultural institution.

In some respects this new Canadian military differs from the militaries of most other polyethnic countries in the world today. According to Professor Preston it cannot be considered as an instrument for the preservation of an existing political balance (more precisely, imbalance) between the country's major ethnic groups. Rather, the Canadian Armed Forces are the means to build and preserve a cohesive Canada.

While the major issue of ethnicity in the Canadian Armed Forces is the question of English-French relations, still another "ethnic factor" ought not to be forgotten. About a third of Canada's population is of neither French nor English ancestry. In fact, it could be said that Canada has been a polyethnic nation from her very beginnings. Since the start of European settlement of Canadian soil, Native peoples coexisted and even cohabited with the French. Afterwards they shared the country also with British populations. Still later, immigrants began arriving from parts of the world other than those that had provided the country's "founding peoples." Most of these were Europeans, but there were also Asians among them, as well as a sprinkling of blacks from the United States. By the second half of the twentieth century Canada had become a polyethnic and, to some extent, multi-racial country.

The participation of these "other" Canadians in the armed forces dates back to the country's very beginnings. Canada's Native population played an important part in many of the campaigns that the British Army fought in North America in the late eighteenth and early nineteenth centuries. Furthermore, among early immigrant ethnic groups that might be considered neither anglo- nor francophone, the Scots had provided many soldiers, as well as entire military units, for British North America's colonial military. There were also soldiers from German or Polish lands, or from elsewhere in Europe, as well as a few blacks — descendants of black "loyalists" or escaped slaves from south of the border. Later, tens of thousands of immigrants of other than Anglo-Celtic-French stock arrived and many joined Canada's forces. This was a slow process. In the First World War many of these groups were not welcome in the Canadian military: people who had been born in enemy countries were not allowed to enlist even if their sympathies were clearly with the Allied Powers. For instance, Czechs, Slovaks, Serbs, Romanians, and Ukrainians from the Dual Monarchy were rejected. Furthermore, Orientals were, on the whole, not welcome in Canada's forces until after World War II.[25]

The contribution of these "other" Canadians to the country's military development, and to the defence of Canada in her wars, has not yet been examined in adequate depth and detail by historians. Few studies touch the subject, and only minor aspects of the story have been uncovered.[26] For these reasons the program of RMC's 13th Military History Symposium included a case study dealing with this subject. Major John G. Armstrong's paper examines the tribulations of a small unit of mainly Nova Scotian blacks that served in France during the First World War. While the contribution made by this unit was ignored at the time, it gave both inspiration and legitimacy to later black claims for a more dignified participation in Canada's institutions, including her armed forces.

IN CONCLUSION it might be asked whether and to what extent the experiences of other polyethnic armed forces are instructive for Canada's armed forces. No categorical answer can be given. It has been indicated that the Canadian polyethnic military experience has been almost certainly unique. As a result, it is likely that lessons from the experience of other forces, that would be quite relevant for other militaries, are only a little or not at all applicable to Canada's armed forces. Yet Canadians may possibly draw some important lessons from the broader comparative histories of other polyethnic armed forces.

In its origins and early evolution, the ATA was most unlike the Canadian military. Professor Echenberg's study of this army revealed how extensive the impact of a military, and of service in it, can be on the communities whose members make up that military. This "lesson" of the ATA's experience is particularly applicable to societies in which the armed forces play a preponderant role. It is applicable to Canada only on a lesser scale since this country's military, especially the peacetime military, plays only a limited though not unimportant role in political, social, and economic affairs.

The lessons offered by the experience of the Soviet Armed

Forces are also only marginally relevant to the Canadian military because Russian traditions and Soviet political practices differ greatly from those of Canada. Yet one of these lessons is useful to all militaries. This is that the use of the military as a means of maintaining and extending the hegemony of one ethnic group over others, and of promoting one culture at the expense of others, tends only to exacerbate ethnic conflicts and to increase centrifugal tendencies in the whole of society as well as within the armed forces. As long as no such use of the Canadian military is attempted, these dangers remain low. Canadian history, however, does provide examples that approximate the utilization of military forces for the imposition of one ethnic group's political will over that of another. One can refer to the Second Riel Rebellion of 1885 and, with less certainty, to the FLQ Crisis of 1970. In view of these precedents, the possibility of such use for the military in Canada must be deemed real.

The experiences of the Indians in the United States Army and of blacks in the various services of the American military are also worthy of Canadian attention. After all, as Major Armstrong pointed out in his paper, "marginal" ethnic groups have existed (and continue to exist) in Canada. For their members – and for their "ethnic" communities – service in the Canadian military has sometimes been, and might in the future be, just as disruptive and traumatic as was service in the U.S. Army for American Indians. It is also evident from the American experience that the terms and character of such service for socially and/or economically marginal minorities would likely be determined by the attitudes of society at large toward such groups. In a racially tolerant Canada, one could expect the acceptance of the "ethnic soldier" as an equal member of his or her unit; but if the country were to become intolerant, equality of treatment would become unusual or even unlikely.

The experience of the Habsburg military is in some ways very different, and in others very similar, to that of Canada. If we look at the tensions and rivalries between the Dual Monarchy's two dominant ethnic groups, the Austrian Germans and the Hungarians, we are reminded of similar tensions and rivalries between English and French Canadians. Yet there are few marked similarities between the positions and experiences of the Hungarian *honvéd* army and Canada's 22nd Regiment. However, were the French-Canadian elements of the Canadian military to develop closer ties with the government of the Province of Quebec (perhaps under some scheme of sovereignty association), the kind of rivalry that existed between Budapest and Vienna over military affairs could surface between Quebec City and Ottawa. But the most important lesson of the Habsburg polyethnic military experience for Canada is something

different. The example of the turn-of-the-century Habsburg Army
demonstrates that a multi-ethnic army has difficulty in being an effective fighting force in an era of growing nationalism, ethnic intoler-
ance, and its resultant inter-ethnic tensions. The implications of this
"lesson" for the Canadian Armed Forces are clear. A bicultural Canadian military can be expected to prosper only in a Canadian society
that is at least tolerant toward and, at best, enthusiastic about other
bicultural institutions in Canada.

Another lesson from the experience of the Habsburg military (as
from that of still other polyethnic forces) is even more fundamental.
The survival of armed forces and their ability to fight as a cohesive
entity in a prolonged war is, to some extent at least, determined by
the ability of society as a whole to remain united in war. As has been
mentioned, neither the Habsburg Army, nor the ATA – nor even the
Russian Imperial Army in early 1917 – caused its own demise by failing to remain a relatively cohesive force in time of war. Each collapsed, or was dismantled, mainly for political rather than military
reasons. In the case of the Habsburg Army, the country it defended
had already disintegrated, and in the case of the tsarist Army, the
regime it served had disappeared. According to the experience of the
three armed forces in question, the ability of a society to remain
united in time of crisis is vital for the survival of the military which
serves that society. For Canada then, national unity, i.e., political
harmony between the two major Canadian ethnic groups, is of vital
importance. And if the building of a truly bicultural Canadian military
can help to enhance that political harmony, this endeavour assumes
greater than military significance.

Notes

1. William H. McNeill, *Polyethnicity and National Unity in World History*
   (Toronto, 1986), p. 33. This idea constituted the thesis of Professor McNeill's
   first lecture in this series held to honour the memory of historian Donald G.
   Creighton. The lecture was entitled "Empire and Nation to 1750." See ibid.,
   pp. 3-29.
2. Ibid., p. 36.
3. Ibid., p. 70.
4. Ibid., pp. 23f. The same point is made by Professor Cynthia H. Enloe in her
   Ethnic Soldiers: State Security in Divided Societies (Athens, Georgia,
   1980), p. 210.
5. Enloe, chapter 2. Enloe's description of the Cossacks as off-shoots of the
   Tatar ethnic group (p. 43) is likely to be questioned by historians of Russia
   and the Ukraine.
6. For a Canadian survey of this subject see Richard A. Preston, "Ethno-cultural
   Pluralism in Military Forces: a historical survey," in *Policy by Other Means:
   Essays in Honour of C.P. Stacey,* ed. Michael Cross and Robert Bothwell
   (Toronto, 1972), pp. 19-49. For mention of further literature see Professor

Preston's paper in this volume, as well as Enloe's book, particularly under the sub-heading, "Militaries and Theories of Ethnicity" (especially p. 9).

7. Alan B. Anderson and James S. Frideres, *Ethnicity in Canada: Theoretical Perspectives* (Toronto, 1981), p. 36. While some social scientists keep redefining the terminology of *ethnicity*, others don't define the terms at all. Wsevolod W. Isajiw complained in the journal *Ethnicity* that of the 65 relevant studies he had examined, the authors of 52 had provided "no explicit definition [of the term *ethnicity*] at all." Isajiw's paper, "Definitions of Ethnicity," is reprinted in *Ethnicity and Ethnic Relations in Canada: A Book of Readings*, ed. Jay E. Goldstein and Rita M. Bienvenue (Toronto, 1980), pp. 13-25.

8. Anderson and Frideres, p. 36.

9. The *Shorter Oxford English Dictionary*'s 1972 revised reprint defines an *ethnic* as "A Gentile, heathen, pagan," adding that in modern usage the word meant, "the religions of the Gentile nations or their common characteristics."

10. Anderson and Frideres, pp. 47f.

11. Burnet, p. 4.

12. R.A. Schermerhorn, quoted ibid., p. 4.

13. Nathan Glazer and Daniel P. Moynihan, *Beyond the Melting Pot: The Negroes, Puerto Ricans, Jews, Italians, and Irish of New York City* (Cambridge, Mass., 1963). See also a volume edited by the same, *Ethnicity: Theory and Experience* (Cambridge, Mass., 1975).

14. Anderson and Frideres, p. 14. One important exception to the acceptance of this definition will be mentioned below.

15. Ibid., p. 36.

16. Information from Professor Jean Burnet and the late Robert Harney, in letters to the author dated 27 July and 1 August, 1989, respectively.

17. Anderson and Frideres, p. 28.

18. *Oxford Dictionary, Supplement*, 1976.

19. Burnet, p. vi.

20. *Gage Canadian Dictionary* (Toronto, 1983), p. 405. The editors add in small print that, "This use of *ethnic* has become established in Canada and is spreading to the United States, though many people consider it unacceptable. While the word is useful in that it recognizes that different nationalities have individual qualities and customs, it becomes insulting if it is used to refer scornfully to people not of English or French descent."

21. Raymond Breton, in the *Canadian Encyclopedia*, 2nd ed. (Edmonton, 1988), vol. 2, p. 723.

22. Anderson and Frideres, p. 39. John Porter, in his study "Ethnic Pluralism in Canadian Perspective," devotes several paragraphs to the discussion of French-English relations. See Glazer and Moynihan, *Ethnicity*, pp. 265-304.

23. Even those nations of the Habsburg Empire whose land had been acquired through diplomacy (or, more likely, through a marriage alliance) can be regarded as "conquered" peoples as their attempts to liberate themselves from Habsburg rule were put down through the use of military force. Yet, after 1867, some of these same nations — the Hungarians in particular (and within the "Hungarian" half of the Dual Monarchy, the Croats; and in the "Austrian" half, the Poles) — enjoyed privileged positions.

24. Samuel R. Williamson, Jr., and Peter Pastor, eds., *Essays on World War I: Origins and Prisoners of War* (New York, 1982). See, in particular, Professor Pastor's essay in this volume.

25. Roy Ito, *We Went to War: The Story of the Japanese Canadians Who Served During the First and Second World Wars* (Stittsville, Ontario, 1984).

26. On the contribution of the Scots see George Stanley, "The Scottish Military Tradition," in *The Scottish Tradition in Canada*, ed. W. Stanford Reid (Toronto, 1976), pp. 137-60. Most of the other volumes appearing hitherto in this series, *Generations: A History of Canada's Peoples* (published by McClelland and Stewart in collaboration with Multiculturalism Canada and the Department of Supply and Services), touch on this subject but often say disappointingly little. The Ukrainian contribution during World War II is covered in Thomas M. Prymak, *Maple Leaf and Trident: The Ukrainian Canadians during the Second World War* (Toronto, 1988), and in Bohdan Panchuk's memoirs, *Heroes of Their Day: The Reminiscences of Bohdan Panchuk*, ed. Lubomyr Y. Luciuk (Toronto, 1983); while the Polish contribution is outlined in Aloysius Balawyder, *The Maple Leaf and the White Eagle: Canadian-Polish Relations, 1918-1978* (Boulder, Colorado, 1980). The Japanese-Canadian story is told in Ito's book, cited above. George Stanley has touched on the contribution of the Indians to the defences of Canada in early colonial times in several of his works. See, for example, his *Canada's Soldiers: The Military History of an Unmilitary People*, rev. ed. (Toronto, 1960).

An important addition to this literature has appeared after the editing of the papers in this volume. It is the study by James W. St.G. Walker, "Race and Recruitment in World War I: Enlistment of Visible Minorities in the Canadian Expeditionary Force," *Canadian Historical Review* 70 (1989), pp. 1-26. This work outlines how the "Western ideology of racism," which penetrated Canadian society in the decades before World War I, led to the rejection of the "domestic experience" (of using blacks and Indians in the Canadian forces) and resulted in the belief that the conflict that broke out in 1914 was "a white man's war." In World War I, Canada pursued a recruitment policy that shunned the enlistment of visible minorities. "Canada's war effort," concludes Walker, "was [thus] impeded by prejudices for which there were no Canadian foundations."

THE ETHNIC QUESTION IN THE MULTINATIONAL HABSBURG ARMY, 1848-1918

ISTVÁN DEÁK*

THE SUBJECT OF this essay is an army that changed its name, its organization, and its recruitment and promotional systems more dramatically than any other major armed force during the relatively short span of 70 years between 1848 and 1918, all in an effort to accommodate the rapid changes in the political system it served. Throughout this process, however, at least one element remained constant in the armed forces of the Habsburg Monarchy: the complex ethnic composition of the rank and file and of the officer corps. Of all European armies, only the Ottoman was similarly multinational in make-up, but the army of the Sultan was unified by a single religion, Islam, while the multinational and multiconfessional Habsburg forces shared no common creed other than loyalty to their Supreme Commander.[1]

In 1848, when our story begins, the Habsburg state was known as the Austrian Empire, and its military as the Imperial-Royal Army (*kaiserlich-königliche Armee*, or *k.k. Armee*). In 1918, when our story ends, the collapsing state was called Austria-Hungary, or the Dual Monarchy, and its armed forces were composed of three autonomous parts: 1) the Common, Joint, or Imperial and Royal Army (*kaiserliche und königliche Armee*, or *k.u.k. Armee*), which included, incidentally, the entire naval establishment; 2) the Austrian National Guard (*kaiserlich-königliche Landwehr*, or *k.k. Landwehr*); and 3) the Hungarian National Guard (*königlich ungarische Landwehr*, *k.u. Landwehr*, or, in Hungarian, *magyar királyi honvédség*). Despite their differences in name and territorial base — the Common Army recruited its rank and file and officers from the

* I wish to express my thanks to the International Research and Exchanges Board (IREX) and the U.S. Department of Education Fulbright-Hays Research Program, whose combined grants enabled me to do research in the Vienna and Budapest archives for several months in 1984 and 1985. I am also indebted to the Woodrow Wilson Center for Scholars in Washington, D.C. for its grant in 1985 which allowed me to begin writing a monograph on the social and political history of the Habsburg officer corps.

Monarchy as a whole, and the two National Guards from the Monarchy's Austrian and Hungarian halves, respectively — the three parts gradually became equal in equipment, training, and combat value, and together made up the armed forces (*österr.-ung. Wehrmacht*) of His Majesty, the Emperor and King. In World War I, over one million members of that force laid down their lives in defense of their prince.[2]

To illustrate further the sweeping changes that took place over the seven decades, it is sufficient to note that in 1848 the Austrian army was based on limited conscription but after 1868 filled its ranks through universal military service, and that whereas in the first half of our period the officers were all professionals, during World War I civilians in uniform — i.e., reserve officers — vastly outnumbered their professional colleagues. But at all times, both rank and file and officers of the Common Army and of the two National Guards hailed from varied German, Hungarian, Czech, Slovak, Polish, Ruthene, Slovene, Croatian, Serbian, Romanian, Italian or other ethnic stock. Nor was the confessional make-up of the armed forces any less bewildering: one encountered there Roman Catholics, Greek Catholics, Armenian Catholics, Greek Orthodox, Calvinists, Lutherans, Unitarians, Jews, and Muslims. Finally, because the boundaries of the Monarchy's historic kingdoms, principalities, duchies, margravates, counties, baronies, and lordships practically never coincided with the linguistic boundaries within Austria-Hungary, members of the same unit were more likely than not to speak several different languages. Just before World War I, of the Common Army's 329 independent units (regiments, ranger battalions, etc.) only 142 were made up of men who spoke the same language. In 163 units two major languages were in use, and in 24, three or more. In only 31 units (12 infantry regiments, 12 artillery regiments, three cavalry regiments, and four ranger [*Jäger*] battalions) did the vast majority of the rank and file speak German, which meant that only in this small segment of the Common Army were the officers and NCOs able to instruct their men exclusively in the official language of command and service.

For its part, the Austrian National Guard had only 19 units in which a single language — not necessarily German — was spoken, and 44 units with two or more officially recognized tongues. Finally, in the Hungarian National Guard, where, in contrast to the other two bodies, the language of command and service was Hungarian rather than German, and where no official recognition was accorded to any other languages spoken by the rank and file, the ethnic admixture was equally complicated. Thus, while 91 percent of the men in the 1st Budapest *Honvéd* Infantry Regiment were Hungarians or at least Magyar speakers, 85 percent of those in the 15th Trencsén

(Trentschin, Trenčin) Infantry Regiment were Slovaks, and very few members of this Hungarian "national" unit spoke or even understood Hungarian.[3] Paradoxically, the only part of the armed forces where the men formed a solid monolingual group was the Croatian-Slavonian National Guard (*Hrvatsko-Domobranstvo*), an autonomous subdivision of the Hungarian *honvédség* whose language of command and service was Serbo-Croatian. Even this relatively small force was divided, however, by the confessional and cultural differences between its Serbian and Croatian soldiers.

If anything, the ethnic distribution of the officer corps was even more complicated since officers of the Common Army, unlike the men, were assigned to units not on the basis of territorial origin but of a variety of other considerations. It is true that in the two National Guards, officers were drawn from their respective half of the Monarchy (although Hungarian officers were often assigned to the Croatian-Slavonian Guard and vice versa), but, as I have suggested already, territorial origin had precious little to do with language or nationality in the case of such enormous territories as "Austria" or the Kingdom of Hungary.

An explanation should be added here on geographical terminology. Because the official name of the Austrian half of the Monarchy was "The Kingdoms and Lands Represented in the *Reichsrat*" (*Reichsrat* or Imperial Council was the name of the Parliament in Vienna), and that of the Hungarian half: "Lands of the Hungarian Holy Crown," contemporary parlance substituted "Cisleithania" and "Transleithania" for these impossibly cumbrous designations. The Leitha, a small river east of Vienna, separated the Austrian half (Cisleithania) of the Dual Monarchy from the Hungarian half (Transleithania). Rather than using these anachronistic names, I have opted here for the terms "Austria" and Hungary. Awkward as they may seem, the quotation marks next to the word Austria are necessary in order to distinguish between Cisleithania and what I shall be calling German-Austria, the so-called Hereditary Provinces within Cisleithania which after 1918 would form — more or less — the Austrian republic. German-Austria included the provinces of Lower Austria (capital: Vienna), Upper Austria (capital: Linz), Salzburg, Styria, Carinthia, Carniola, the Tirol, and Vorarlberg.

In order to better appreciate the ramifications of the ethnic question in the armed forces of Austria-Hungary, it is worth emphasizing the overwhelming importance of the armed forces in the history of that state. Even well before 1867, the army was the major institution holding together what historians and contemporary observers liked to call "the Ramshackle Empire," and after the Compromise Agreement of 1867, the Common Army functioned as the

sole remaining supranational institution within the new Dual Monarchy. (The "common" Foreign Service concentrated its attention, by
definition, on things outside the Monarchy.)

The Habsburg Monarchy had virtually never had a central government or unified civil service. Rather, before 1848 there existed
several more or less autonomous provincial administrations, manned
by local notables, and just a handful of all-monarchical central offices
in Vienna, chief among them the *Hofkriegsrat* or Court War Council, which was charged with administration of the military. In the
upheavals of 1848, the several major kingdoms and provinces of the
Monarchy attempted to set up sovereign governments of their own,
retaining only tenuous links to Vienna. These attempts were subsequently crushed, however, by the Austrian army; building on this military triumph, Francis Joseph tried, in the 1850s, to create a unified
and centralized modern state. This attempt failed as well, however,
due in large part to the Monarchy's disastrous foreign wars in 1859
and 1866. As a result, in 1867, the Emperor-King was obliged to pre-
side over the division of his Monarchy into two sovereign halves,
"Austria" and Hungary. At more or less the same time, Galicia in the
Austrian half and Croatia-Slavonia in the Hungarian were also
granted specific subordinate autonomies.

The Compromise Agreement greatly reinforced the pre-existing
national and particularistic currents within such all-monarchical institutions as the Catholic Church and the great landed nobility. Bishops
and aristocrats now came to represent more of a challenge to the
Monarchy's integrity than a support for it. Francis Joseph himself,
having sworn in 1867 to uphold both the Hungarian and the Austrian
constitutions, became as much a symbol of the monarchy's disunity
as of its unity. Hereafter, only as supreme commander of the armed
forces and as the maker of foreign policy could the Emperor-King act
as an effective representative of all-monarchical interests. It was,
therefore, his Common Army — representing the bulk of the armed
forces — which constituted the mainstay of the Dual Monarchy. However because, according to the new army laws of 1868, the vast
majority of conscripts served for just three years (and, after 1912,
only two years) a period of time manifestly insufficient to imbue
German-Austrian, Hungarian, Slavic, Romanian, and Italian youngsters with an all-monarchical, supra-national ideology, it was actually
the career officers and NCOs of the Common Army who became,
after 1867, the Monarchy's sole important supranational body. What
makes the history of these career soldiers so fascinating is the fact
that they managed to perform their integrating function with so very
little violence, at least between the nationalist, democratic revolu-

tions of 1848-49 and the national, democratic, or socialist revolts of 1918.

Origins and Early Ethnic Problems of the
Multinational Army

LIKE OTHER EUROPEAN armies, the Habsburg armed forces stemmed from several diverse sources: mercenary companies, noble levies, regiments of conscripts created by order of provincial diets, and assorted volunteer formations. Soldiers came from every corner of the Habsburg family possessions, but also from German lands which recognized the Habsburgs as their elected emperor and not as their territorial prince, and from Spain, the Swiss cantons, Sweden, Italy, and other lands.[4] No less importantly, from the mid-16th century the Habsburgs disposed of a permanent militia force on the southern confines of their possessions, facing the Ottomans. Gradually consolidated, this Military Border, manned by a militarized free peasantry and directly subordinated to Vienna, came to represent one of the Habsburgs' greatest military assets. Although the Border was later extended into Southern Hungary and Transylvania, it was the Croatian-Slavonian Military Border, with its 11 territorial infantry regiments, which made the Border Guards, known as *Grenzer*, feared and respected everywhere. Fiercely loyal to the Emperor, whom they justly considered their benefactor, the *Grenzer* were nevertheless a national army in the making, for they spoke various dialects of the same Serbo-Croatian, were led mainly by native officers, and were united by the desire to maintain their special privileges. Fortunately for the Habsburgs, when the age of nationalism dawned early in the 19th century, the wrath of the *Grenzer* was directed not at them but at Hungary, which, as constitutional suzerain of Croatia-Slavonia, claimed the right to reincorporate the Military Border into the Hungarian Kingdom.[5]

The bitter experiences of the War of the Austrian Succession and the Seven Years' War between 1740 and 1763 led Empress Maria Theresa to perpetuate the standing army, and to standardize its organization, supply, armaments, and uniforms, and the education, training, and pay of its officers. The latter continued to be recruited from all parts of Europe and, in any case, the ethnic origin of the soldiers was of so little consequence at that time that Frederick II of Prussia did not once mention ethnic problems in his voluminous writings on Maria Theresa's possessions. And yet, in the Hungarian Noble Guards, created by the Empress in order to win over Hungary's penniless lower nobility, the first murmurs of national sentiment could already be heard, and when Maria Theresa's son, the passionately modernizing and centralizing Joseph II died in 1790, the

Hungarian Diet clearly expressed its desire to set up a separate Hungarian national army under the king. The latter may have been an expression more of estate particularism than of modern nationalism, but the French revolution was soon enough to bring unambiguous nationalist ideology into Central Europe. While the French revolutionary and Napoleonic wars initially silenced particularistic tendencies, it was not long before nationalism began to flourish within the Monarchy. Cultural and linguistic in its early stages, German, Hungarian, Slavic, Romanian, and Italian nationalism grew more and more truculent under Metternich's conservative rule, and it came to affect even the officers.

Well before 1848, minor Italian and Polish conspiracies were unmasked in the Habsburg officer corps, but more significant was nationalism's negative effect on the army. In Polish-inhabited Galicia, in the Protestant parts of Hungary, and especially in Venetia and Lombardy, the army lived as in enemy territory. Shunned by the better families in these provinces, the officers turned inward, cultivating an *esprit de corps* that in turn isolated them even more from the public. Nor did it help matters that regiments were almost permanently on the move, a unit being transferred to a new garrison on an average of every two years. There are no comprehensive data on the ethnic composition of the officer corps in Metternich's time, but there can be no doubt that it was as cosmopolitan as ever, with a hefty admixture of foreigners, particularly from Great Britain.[6]

The army obliged its officer candidates to learn at least one of the Monarchy's languages besides German, and newly assigned officers were also required to learn the regimental language or languages of their unit, but aside from such practical concessions to ethnicity, the army continued to ignore the nationality question. The ethnic background of officers was not even considered worthy of statistical inquiry, at least not until 1897, and the officers' voluminous personal records (*Qualifikations-Listen*) never contained any designation of the individual's ethnic background. The army remained staunchly Austrian, in the dynastic rather than national sense of the term.

The Revolutions of 1848-1849

THE SPRINGTIME OF the Peoples came as a nasty surprise to all in the officer corps but a handful of politically conscious individuals. Within a few days in March, soldiers had been driven out of Vienna, Venice, and Milan, and were subjected to abuse and ridicule in Budapest and other cities by demonstrators shouting incomprehensible slogans. As central authority collapsed and various local governments and national committees extracted sweeping concessions from the feeble-minded Emperor-King Ferdinand, the officers suddenly confronted terrifying dilemmas. Those who happened to be stationed in Hungary were made to take an oath to the constitution sanctified by the King, those in German-Austria were told that the Hereditary Provinces would soon merge with the new unified German state, and that the officers' loyalty was to the Frankfurt Assembly, not to Austria.[7]

Yet it was one thing to swear loyalty to a newly constituted legal authority, such as the Hungarian, and quite another to be told that, because the Serbian population and Serbian *Grenzer* battalions in Southern Hungary had revolted against the constitutional Hungarian government, one had to lead regular Habsburg troops against those "rebel" troops who also proclaimed their loyalty to the Emperor-King. The situation grew even worse in September 1848, when the Commanding General and Governor of Croatia-Slavonia, Josip Jelačić, invaded Hungary to "restore order there." Now the Hungarian government ordered a Habsburg general to march against another Habsburg general and against the latter's loyal Croatian troops. In the confusion, some regular officers in Hungary attempted to remain neutral; others joined the "rebel" Jelačić; still others decided to make a stand against him and effectively stopped the Croatian invasion at the end of September near Budapest. The subsequent truce "between the Royal Hungarian and the Imperial-Royal Croatian forces" symbolized the catastrophe that had befallen an army which had known no other loyalty than that to the Emperor-King. Meanwhile, in northern Italy, Habsburg regulars of every conceivable nationality fought the Lombard and Venetian rebels as well as Piedmont, a foreign invader. Thus there was a civil war or, rather, a series of civil wars, but also a foreign war, and in all these events various units of the same army fought on either side as bitter enemies. Because the two line battalions of each regiment were mostly in Italy, while the third, or reserve, battalion was generally at the regiment's home base, it was not uncommon for the line battalions of Hungarian, Serbian, and Croatian regiments to be comrades-in-arms in Italy while their reserve battalions were firing on one other at home.

Finally, such determined generals as Radetzky, Windisch-Graetz, and Jelačić took matters into their own hands, and suppressed the upheavals one by one, often in defiance of Ferdinand's written orders and against the legally constituted authority. By late fall 1848, the national movements in Vienna, Prague, and Milan had been crushed, and Piedmont had been defeated. The Venetian revolutionary republic held out against the Austrian army until August 1849, and a major war between Austria and Hungary came to an end only in early

October 1849. The Hungarian national army had been constructed on the foundation of regular Habsburg units and, with only a few exceptions, all of the command posts in Louis Kossuth's army were given to Habsburg officers. Altogether about 1000 career officers, 10 percent of the Habsburg officer corps, fought in the Hungarian *honvéd* Army. The vast majority of these officers were there because fate had placed them in units stationed on Hungarian soil, and because the Emperor-King had instructed them in the spring and summer of 1848 to obey the orders of the Hungarian minister of war. Changing to the Austrian side meant disobeying the Emperor-King's command, at least until October 1848. In that month, an imperial-royal manifesto outlawed the Hungarian parliament and national assembly, but it then became even more difficult to change sides, not only because the Hungarian authorities forbade such a thing, but also because one risked severe punishment by the Austrians for not having changed sides earlier. Many officers took the risk nevertheless, meeting with various fates; others, about 1000 strong, stayed on the Hungarian side to the bitter end and were punished drastically afterwards.

Far from all of the rebel officers were of Hungarian nationality. According to the computation of the Hungarian military historian Gábor Bona, of the 830 field-grade and general officers of the *honvéd* army (the vast majority of them Habsburg regulars), 571 or 68.8 percent were Magyar, 129 or 15.5 percent German, 35 or 4.2 percent Polish, and 31 or 3.6 percent Serbian and Croatian.[8]

Of the 14 Hungarian rebel commanders tried at Arad after the war, 13 of whom were hanged or shot, one was a German from outside Austria, one a German Austrian, one a Serb, and one a Croatian. The other nine were Hungarian citizens, but several of the latter were in reality Germans, and not even all of the genuine Magyars were able to speak or understand Hungarian. All the generals had been junior or field-grade officers before the war; none had participated in politics. It can be demonstrated that a few had been driven by patriotic or democratic convictions; the majority, however, had simply obeyed the orders of the legally constituted authority until it was too late. All enjoyed the brilliant career opportunities offered by the Hungarian national army, which allowed them to exchange the command of platoons and companies for the command of brigades, divisions, and army corps.[9]

There is considerably less documented evidence concerning nationalist sentiments among the rank and file in the revolutions of 1848-49. On a few occasions, troops did rebel against officers who attempted to switch sides in a way that contradicted the national interests of the men. Alan Sked and Robert Nowak have also documented that disaffection and desertions ran high in the Italian regiments of the Habsburg army stationed in Northern Italy, and that Radetzky lost 17,000 men out of 62,000 because of desertions.[10] There can be no doubt either regarding the nationalist enthusiasm of some Croatian, Serbian, Polish, Romanian, and Hungarian units. And yet, most of the regulars ended up fighting to maintain the unity of the Empire. If one trait characterized the army rank and file as a whole in 1848-49, it was bewilderment. Consider, for instance, the plight of several Italian battalions caught in the Hungarian war who, by the will of their commanders, found themselves alternately on the Hungarian and the Austrian side. The soldiers could do no better than to obey their superiors, especially as disobedience was punished most severely in both camps. No matter how one looks at it, nationalism was a matter for the educated classes in 1848, and would remain so for many decades to come.

The Multinational Army under Francis Joseph

POST-REVOLUTIONARY ABSOLUTISM began where Metternich had left off early in 1848, except that it was even more absolutist and far more centralistic than the old regime. The army had saved the Monarchy and, as a result, the officer corps dominated politics in the 1850s, to the point where the real decision-maker in the state became General Count Grünne, the Emperor's First Adjutant General. For the soldiers, this meant even stricter discipline, the constant movement of regiments, more parades and drill, and — paradoxically — less and less preparation for war. But war came in 1859, against Piedmont-Sardinia and France. The Army High Command assumed that the Italian, Hungarian, and even the Croatian troops were disaffected (the Croatian leaders had had none of their nationalist ambitions satisfied as a reward for their loyalty in 1848-49) and, indeed, hundreds of Italian and some Hungarian soldiers deserted during the Northern Italian campaign. Ever since, it has been an article of faith among Austrian and other historians that the defeats at Magenta and Solferino were due, not only to a lack of provisions and the unspeakable stupidity of the generals, but also to the disloyalty of some ethnic elements. Elsewhere I have tried to demonstrate that this was not quite the case.[11] True, many Italian soldiers from Lombardy did desert during the war, but this was small wonder, given the fact that they were on home territory and could easily melt away among the civilians. Hunger, fatigue, and brutal discipline may have motivated the other nationalities to follow suit, but they had nowhere to go. As a result, the overwhelming majority of the Hungarian units fought bravely or at least obeyed their superiors. Enthusiasm for the Italian Risorgimento or for Kossuth's attempts to liberate

Hungary seem to have played as little a role in all this as did loyalty to the dynasty. When an even greater war came, against Prussia in 1866, and the Habsburg army suffered one of its worst defeats, there were no desertions at all, perhaps because the nature of the campaigns was different. Ironically, we are told that the Hungarians and other ethnic groups fought unflinchingly in that war. Yet what better reason did the peasant-soldiers have to die on behalf of the Emperor at Königgrätz than they had had at Solferino?

The Königgrätz disaster led to a public outcry, demands for a complete overhaul of the military establishment, and much soul-searching among the officers. The overhaul was largely accomplished in the years after 1867, in conjunction with liberal reforms in the newly constituted Dual Monarchy. Universal conscription was introduced, a reserve officer corps — to which only young men with a high-school education could aspire — was created, the training of career officer candidates was reorganized, and the teaching of liberal arts in the military schools was raised more or less to the level of civilian high schools (the new educational requirements put an end to the commissioning of ordinary soldiers, but the sons of NCOs were actively encouraged to choose an officer's career). Admission to the General Staff was made dependent on ever more rigorous competitive entrance examinations and on extensive training; the Chief of the General Staff was put in charge of the entire armed forces, thus weakening the separatist tendencies manifest in the Hungarian National Guards; and the archaic institution of regimental proprietorship was turned into a purely symbolic affair. The purchase of promotions in the officer corps had already been forbidden; now promotion was no longer to be within each regiment but within a general rank list encompassing an entire service branch. Promotions were standardized so as to eliminate glaring inequalities; healthier barracks, hospitals, and veterans' homes gradually replaced the decrepit old converted monasteries that had once housed the soldiers; the cantonment of the cavalry on the rural population was abandoned; officer's pay improved considerably, as did the provisioning of ordinary soldiers. The Military Border, by then a historical anomaly, was dissolved, and the entire Border was incorporated into Hungary or Hungary's subordinate kingdom, Croatia-Slavonia. The incessant wanderings of the regiments was slowed down until, in the 1880s, it was decided to keep most regiments at their home base, a measure which contributed to the territorialization of the Common Army. Finally, great efforts were made to modernize armaments and the training of soldiers.[12]

All this was not easy, given the traditionalism of the Emperor and the officers and the hostility of the liberal Austrian and Hungarian parliaments toward the "reactionary" and "feudal" officer corps. The Hungarian deputies in particular did their best to starve the Common Army of funds and recruits. The Hungarian political elite were not at all satisfied with the military concessions they had won in 1867. Rather, they hoped ultimately to reduce relations with "Austria" to that of a mere personal union. The *sine qua non* of this new relationship would have been the division of the Common Army into two "national" armies. As a first step, the Hungarians demanded that Hungarian be adopted as the language of command and service in all regiments originating from Hungary. The Hungarian political leaders were unable to have their way, however, and the Common Army remained just that, with German as its *lingua franca*, but in the first decade of the 20th century, the Hungarian government did succeed in wresting so many minor concessions from the High Command as to foreshadow the coming dissolution of the Common Army. Had the World War not intervened, it is difficult to see how a showdown with the Hungarians could have been avoided. Caught in the vortex of nationalist politics – for the Hungarians were not alone in demanding concessions in military matters – the officers of the Common Army grew ever more dynastic and a-national. They held on stubbornly to their specific code of honour, which, with its medieval, knightly ideology, further widened the gulf between the political parties and the army. The institution of a reserve officer corps in 1868, a step aimed at least in part at "softening" the army, actually benefited the career officers more than the liberal politicians: the new reserve officers on the whole hastened to embrace the ideology and behavioural code of the career corps, at least during their period of active service. Universal conscription did not mean that all able-bodied young men were actually inducted. On the contrary, financial considerations made it impossible to provide full-time military training to any more than one out of five men of military age.

The military statistical yearbooks published for the years 1870 to 1911 contain precise statistics on the ethnic make-up of the Common Army's rank and file. But the statistics (and the Vienna War Archives) provide no indication as to how these figures were arrived at. Chances are that the unit commanders were asked to provide the necessary data, and that the method they were instructed to use was that of the Austrian Statistical Office. While Hungarian census takers inquired about a person's mother tongue, the Austrians were interested in *Umgangssprache*, the language most commonly used in everyday affairs. Thus, while the combined Austrian and Hungarian census data on the general population reflect two different approaches to the question of ethnicity, the Common Army's statistics probably reflect only the Austrian approach. To complicate mat-

ters further, the Austrian and Hungarian civilian statistical compila-
tions allowed for "other nationalities" alongside the standard ones.
But army statistics recognized no such category. Surprisingly,
though, the latter diligently accounted for the Monarchy's far-from-
numerous Bulgarians. Following the emancipation of the Jews in
1867, Austro-Hungarian statisticians no longer treated them as a separate nationality; consequently, the Jewish population came to boost
official counts of those nationalities into which Jews tended to integrate most frequently, namely the Germans, Czechs, Poles, and, most
importantly, Hungarians.

Statistics indicate that all nationalities – willingly or not – "did
their duty" to the Monarchy. The somewhat elevated proportion of
German and Hungarian enlisted men relative to the representation of
these groups in the general population may well reflect a lesser willingness to use the many loopholes available to those who wished to
avoid military service. The opposite may apply to the Poles and Italians. In view of the small number of men actually inducted, the army
could afford to be choosy; still, the poverty and poor health of the
Galician population must be ruled out as a factor in the relative scarcity of Polish soldiers, as the even poorer Ruthenes (Ukrainians)
were not under-represented. Since the statistics tell us nothing of the
army's possible bias against one or another ethnic group, let us turn
to an examination of the ethnic distribution among the various
branches of service. Certainly, some branches such as the *Jäger*
(Rangers), the cavalry, and the artillery, were held to be more desirable and respectable than the lowly infantry or transports. Note, however, that unlike Russia, Prussia, or Great Britain, the Habsburg Monarchy never established the institution of elite Guards Regiments.

The uneven ethnic representation in the service branches was
the result of variations in the recruiting area, tradition, and educational requirements. The infantry, for example, took in mostly young
peasants – hence the over-representation of such a "peasant nationality" as the Romanian. The elite *Jäger* recruited primarily in the
Western provinces of the Monarchy – hence the enormously high
proportion of Germans and Italians. The latter, inhabiting the South
Tirol for the largest part, tended to be drafted into the four regiments
of the famous Tirolian *Kaiserjäger*. The cavalry drew a dispropor-
tionate number of recruits from Hungary (*Husaren*), Galicia (Polish
and Ruthene *Ulanen*), and Bohemia-Moravia (Czech *Dragoner*). By
contrast, the mountain-dwelling Slovaks, Slovenes, and Italians
scarcely figured on the cavalry lists. The artillery (and engineers)
favoured the better educated and technologically trained Germans
and Slovenes and looked askance at the generally less well educated
Serbs, Croats, and Romanians. The Hungarians, many of them famil-

iar with horses, were vastly over-represented in the transportation corps, and Germans provided one-third of the effectives in the sanitation corps (medics). All in all, it can be argued that, far from being motivated by ethnic bias — as its critics pretended — the Common Army distributed its recruits among the various service branches on the basis of practical considerations.

Reserve Officers

UNLIKE THE RANK and file, officers were not recruited at all evenly from the various national groups. Whereas the number of German, Hungarian, Czech, and Polish enlisted men closely approximated their proportional representation in the general population, the number and proportion of the officers reflected the varying class structure, wealth, education, dynastic loyalty, and military tradition of each group. They might also have reflected the ethnic bias of the army leadership.

It should be recalled that the reserve officer corps had been established in 1868 in order to provide the mass army of universal conscription with an intelligent leadership for times of emergency as well as to link the new bourgeoisie more closely to the army. The corps drew its members exclusively from among the one-year "volunteers" (a euphemism, of course), young men with a high-school diploma or its equivalent who served twelve months instead of the customary three years. The "volunteers" enjoyed a rather privileged existence while on active duty, and were given an opportunity to complete reserve officers' school during this period. Following release from active service and participation in a few summer manoeuvres, they could be considered for a reserve officer's commission. This depended, however, on a candidate's possession of an adequate income and/or profession worthy of an officer (petty shopkeepers, for example, were automatically disqualified), and on his acceptance by the officers of his regiment. Here, then, was ample opportunity for the exercise of national, religious, or social bias. Of social prejudice there can be no doubt: a candidate who had married below his station, for instance, was almost never commissioned.[13] Of political or religious bias, however, there was scarcely a trace in a reserve officer corps which — unlike the Prussian — commissioned even Social Democrats, and in which the proportion of Jews surpassed their share in the general population four- or even five-fold.[14] In fact, the proportion of Jewish reserve officers closely approximated their representation among high-school graduates, and thus among the one-year volunteers. It is another question, however, why Slovaks, Poles, Ruthenes, Croats, Serbs, and Romanians were so grievously under-represented among the reserve officers.

Even if we consider that the proportion of educated youngsters among the Monarchy's Germans vastly surpassed that of the other ethnic groups (except for Hungarians, Czechs, and Italians), one must still search for an explanation why Ruthenes, to give only one example, were virtually nonexistent in the reserve officer corps (0.5 percent in 1911, a total of 50 individuals).[15] Certainly, a much higher number of Ruthenes than that had finished high school and thus qualified for one-year volunteer service. Ethnic prejudice could be a partial answer, although such an explanation is contradicted by the enormous over-representation of Jews in the corps. After all, unlike the official statistics, many officers certainly viewed the Jews as a separate, alien, and less than attractive ethnic group! Rather than ethnic bias, then, the explanation for the scarcity of Ruthenes and others is probably the following: 1) the eagerness of the educated elite in such lower-class or peasant nationalities as the Ruthenes, Romanians, Serbs, and even Croats, to "pass" as Poles in Galicia or Magyars in Hungary; 2) the great advantage enjoyed by the Jews and the Czechs – almost all spoke German – over the educated Ruthenes, Croats, Serbs, and Romanians, whose second language was likely to be Hungarian, Czech, or Polish; 3) the increasingly dynamic nationalism, by 1910-11, of the Slavic, Romanian, and Italian social elites, which led them to shun military service or, if that could not be avoided, to shun an officers' commission. It must be remembered that it was a strong political statement on the part of an educated Ruthene in Galicia not to call himself a Pole, just as it was for educated Slovaks, Serbs, or Romanians not to identify themselves as Magyars in Hungary. Others of their national group had long embraced the notion of assimilation to the locally dominant nationality. The situation in Bohemia was different since the Czechs had become, for all practical purposes, the dominant nationality there. Hence, the relatively large number of self-confessed Czech nationals in the reserve officer corps. Finally, it must be remembered that in Austria-Hungary, unlike the German *Reich*, a reserve officer's commission (*Leutnant in der Reserve*) was not indispensable for landing a good position, nor did it enjoy universal respect.

The ethnic distribution of reserve officers among the several service branches displays as many divergences as the distribution of enlisted men. German reserve officers, like the German enlisted men, were heavily represented in the elite *Jäger* battalions, and there were proportionally more German reserve officers in the mounted – and hence more elegant – field artillery than in the stationary fortress artillery. Both Hungarian enlisted men and reserve officers constituted a major presence in the cavalry but, surprisingly, there were also a significant number of Hungarian reserve officers in the *Jäger*.

The situation was less comforting from the point of view of the Czechs, who were seriously under-represented in the cavalry; their proportion in the field and mountain artillery was only a bit over one-fourth of that in the fortress artillery. On the other hand, one out of every four reserve officers was a Czech in the less than glamorous cart-driving transportation corps. (Jews accounted for an amazing 30.3 percent of the reserve officers in that branch!) Croats and Serbs were heavily represented in the infantry as well as in the special Bosnian-Hercegovinian infantry and *Jäger* (in the latter, 58.4 percent of the reserve officers were Serbs or Croats). The number of Slovak, Ruthene, Slovene, Romanian, and Italian reserve officers was so small as to defy generalization. By contrast, there were 63 Jewish reserve officers in the aristocratic and terribly expensive cavalry! But then these Jews reported or counted as Germans, Hungarians, Czechs, or Poles. The same consideration applies, to many a reserve officer of Slovak, Ruthene, Romanian, or Italian extraction.

Career Officers

ALL THESE MEDITATIONS cannot obscure the fact that at least one-half of the Habsburg reserve officer corps consisted of Germans. If we are to believe the military statistics and the historians, the proportion of Germans in the career officer corps was even higher. According to *official* statistics, four out of every five career officers were Germans, and their proportion was growing. All other nationalities were badly under-represented, although the Hungarians had made some headway between 1897 and 1910. The proportion of Czechs, Poles, Croats and Serbs was declining, and the other nationalities were barely represented at all. Can this be true? If it were, then the multinational Habsburg army was — as its anti-German critics and its later Nazi apologists claimed — just another German-led force, different from that of the German *Reich* only insofar as the majority of its rank and file consisted of subject races. Historical evidence, however, does not support these official statistics.

Throughout its history, the Habsburg army was opposed to any manifestation of nationalism. It recruited its officers from all the provinces of the Monarchy (after 1867, the number of foreign-born officers began declining rapidly). Officers born in German Austria were certainly not grossly over-represented. In any case, place of birth was not decisive in a corps in which one-third came from military families, that is, from families in which the father was likely to have served in a remote garrison. Altogether, two-thirds of the officers were born to fathers in public service. True, in 1867, all public services were divided between "Austria" and Hungary and, thereafter, only members of the Common Army served throughout the Monarchy. Still, it did little for a boy's national identity when, to give one example, his railway official father was transferred from Italian- and Croatian-speaking Trieste to Romanian-, Ukrainian- and Yiddish-speaking Bukovina. Both places were "Austria." In any case, the son might well have left home at the age of ten for a military school located, for example, in Hungarian- and Slovak-speaking Kassa (Košice, Kaschau) in Northern Hungary. The fact is that an enormous number of Common Army officers had, for all intents and purposes, no nationality.

In Franz Theodor Csokor's popular drama, *3 November 1918*, published in 1936, a group of ill or wounded officers are recuperating at the end of the war in the mountains near Austria's Italian front. There they learn from a passing revolutionary of the collapse of the Monarchy. The news brings joy to some reserve officers who have suddenly discovered their special "ethnic roots"; it brings fear to a Jewish reserve officer who is the only true "Austrian" among the civilians in uniform, and it completely destroys the morale of the foremost professional among them, an army colonel. When asked about his nationality, the colonel invokes his regiment and, at the end of the play, he shoots himself. Csokor's dramatic presentation is corroborated by hundreds of memoirs, letters, and other documents. Although to a lesser extent than in the first half of the nineteenth century, as late as 1918 many career officers viewed the Monarchy as their extended family and the regiment as their immediate one. Having been brought up in a regimental town, they served as cadets in some other part of the Monarchy, and were then assigned to active duty in still another province. At all times, they were taught to view any expression of national sentiment as unbecoming of an officer or even as treasonous. Only the aristocratic Polish and Hungarian cavalry regiments represented an exception to this rule. In service, as in the mess hall, the officers used German and, consequently — unless their non-German ethnic identity happened to be particularly strong, as it was increasingly among Hungarians — they must have reported, when asked, that German was the language they used most frequently. Indeed, German was the officers' *Umgangssprache*.

In my attempt to analyze the social history of the Habsburg career officers, I have collected detailed information on 1000-odd individuals grouped in two cohorts, those who were career lieutenants in 1870 and those who were in 1900. Since the first generation was born generally between 1840 and 1850 and the second between 1870 and 1880, the careers of the two groups embrace the greatest part of the period under investigation here. A random selection was made of every tenth lieutenant in each group, as culled from the rank lists of officers in the *Militärschematismen* for the years 1871 and 1901. The result was a representative sample of approximately 500 (486 and 516, to be precise) career lieutenants from each cohort. I was interested among other things in the name, birthplace, legal domicile, religion, linguistic skills, travel, and, whenever available, family origin of the officers. All of this and much more is to be found in their personal record. On the basis of my research,[16] I have concluded that in 1870 only 20.8 percent of the career officers were born in those provinces which, after World War I, became the Austrian republic. Their proportion in 1900 was 24.9 percent. Contrast this with the general population of the German-Austrian provinces, whose not-at-all-purely-German-speaking inhabitants constituted 14.5 percent of the Monarchy's total population. It is true that more career officers were born in Bohemia, Moravia, and Austrian Silesia (32.9 percent of the 1870 cohort, and 32.8 percent of the 1900 cohort), with their heavy admixture of Germans, than in the Austro-German provinces, and that an absolute majority (54.4 percent in the 1870 cohort and 60.9 percent in the 1900 cohort) of the officers born in these "Czechoslovak" provinces were of German nationality. It is also true that an inordinate proportion of career officers were recruited from the German "diaspora" in Hungary, Transylvania, and Galicia. Still, I have been able to determine that of all the officers in my sample, only 52.0 percent qualified as German in the 1870 cohort and 55.0 percent in the 1900 cohort. If we add to this those officers of mixed nationality, the proportion of Germans and half-Germans amounted to 62.6 percent in 1870, and 70.3 percent in 1900. These are very considerable proportions, but still well below the figures indicated (77.7 percent of the 1897 cohort and 78.7 percent of the 1910 cohort) in the official statistics. The fact is that the military statisticians did not know how to handle the question of ethnic background.

While there can be little doubt that Germans constituted an absolute majority of the career officers, others, especially Hungarians, Czechs, and Serbo-Croats, were also fairly well represented. When it comes to the ethnic distribution of career officers in the various service branches — the reader will be spared the details here — it is clear that not only Germans but Hungarians, Poles, and Czechs as well were over-represented in those formations which required a considerable private income (cavalry), scientific training (artillery, engineers), a combination of both (field artillery), or good social and official connections (*Jäger*).

Career and Nationality

EVEN IF WE assume that the Habsburg army was truly "ethnic-blind" in recruiting its career officers — every single military memoir insists that this was indeed the case and no archival evidence indicates the contrary — the question still remains whether the majoritarian Germans did not enjoy a distinct career advantage over the others. As a first step, I have decided to examine the military careers of my statistical sample in each half of the Monarchy.

One is struck first of all by the low proportion of officers born in Hungary but also by the remarkable success of this group in reaching higher ranks. While an absolute majority of those born in "Austria" were still first lieutenants after 14 years of service, an absolute majority of the Hungarian-born officers had made it to captain or higher. Furthermore, not all those born in Hungary enjoyed such an advantage but only those among them who could speak Hungarian.

Clearly, the highest pay and, by implication, the highest ranks belonged to those who had been born in Hungary and were also of Magyar nationality or, at least, spoke the language. Non-Hungarian speakers from Hungary did not fare any better than those born in "Austria," and officers born in "Austria" who were familiar with the Hungarian language (probably because of service in a Hungarian regiment) did worst of all. Statistical data on the 1900 cohort indicate an even more favourable situation for Magyar-speaking Hungarians.

The reason for this is not difficult to determine. The *honvéd* army, created in 1868, aimed its recruiting efforts precisely at those officers who had been born in Hungary and spoke Hungarian. To counteract this drive, the Common Army offered improved career opportunities to its Magyar officers. In addition, those Magyars who remained in the Common Army were probably more talented and more dedicated to their vocation than those who went over to the far less prestigious *honvéd* with its virtual guarantee of rapid promotion. Certainly, the *honvéd* army commanders complained repeatedly about the reluctance of the best qualified Magyars in the Common Army to join the Hungarian National Guard.[17]

If being a Magyar represented a definite career advantage in the Common Army (despite the Hungarian parliament's insistent assertions to the contrary), the situation was less clear regarding other nationalities. Certainly, those born in the German-Austrian provinces — who were probably mostly Germans — were generally better educated and took more advanced training courses after being commissioned lieutenants than did those born in other parts of the Monarchy. This is all the more significant given the fact that by 1870, and even more by 1900, a good military education and advanced "post-graduate" training were the single most important, if not the only key to a truly successful military career.

In the Common Army, as in all late nineteenth-century European armies, enormous importance was attached to attending the "right" military schools and taking the "right" continuation courses (for example, those offered by the War College [*Kriegsschule*]). As my analysis of the 1870 cohort shows, those who completed one of the elite military schools and subsequently attended some of the more prestigious advanced training courses had a 53.4 percent chance of reaching the rank of captain or higher after 14 years of service. In the 1900 cohort, the statistical chances of members of this select group reaching a high rank was an amazing 94.3 percent, meaning that virtually all those with an elite education and elite post-graduate training were rapidly promoted. Those who attended one of the less prestigious military schools and took lower-level continuation courses moved ahead far more slowly. In fact, by the turn of the century, it was widely recognized that those who had gone to a *Militär-Realschule* (equal in quality to a *Gymnasium*) and subsequently attended one of the two military academies (as opposed to the much more numerous *Kadettenschulen*) had a distinctly superior chance of gaining admission to the *Kriegsschule* and then to the General Staff from which generals were ultimately selected. True, there were many dramatic exceptions to this rule, but they remained exceptions.

My examination of the education and training of the officers in the two cohorts indicates that place of birth *did* make a significant difference in terms of elite or non-elite education and training.

In the 1870 cohort, exactly one-half of the officers born to soldier-fathers in German-Austria attended elite military schools; in the 1900 cohort, the proportion was 41 percent. At the other extreme, only 14 percent of those in the 1870 cohort born in the South-Slav provinces of Croatia-Slavonia, Dalmatia, Slovenia and (after 1878) Bosnia-Hercegovina attended elite military schools. In 1900, this figure had increased only slightly to 22.7 percent.

Let us now turn to the "post-graduate" training courses. Of those officers from military families in the 1870 cohort who were born in German-Austria, 75 percent attended elite continuation courses. This proportion diminished marginally to 66.7 percent in the 1900 cohort. Conversely, among such officers in the 1870 cohort who were born in the South Slav provinces, only 26.3 percent attended elite training courses and, in the 1900 cohort, a more respectable 45.5 percent.

What explains these differences? No doubt legendary German diligence and industry, the higher educational level of the German population, and the fact that the native tongue of these officers was the army's official language all had something to do with this phenomenon. The ethnic biases of those who decided on admissions to the military academies and elite training courses may also have been a factor. To be sure, ethnic bias must probably be ruled out in the first part of the selection procedure for admission to the *Kriegsschule*, because the written tests submitted by applicants at this stage were identified only by a number. The second, oral test was another matter. In any case, the very low participation of the South Slavs in elite education and training requires some additional explanation. I would argue that the unfavourable situation of this group was due not so much to ethnic discrimination as to the peculiarities of their background.

Until the gradual dissolution of the Military Border in the late 1870s and early 1880s, most Serbian and Croatian officers hailed from the Military Border and went back to serve in Border Guard regiments. This was reflected, among other things, in the extraordinarily high proportion of Serbian and Croatian officers who had been born into military families: in the 1870 cohort, 78.1 percent of the Serbs, and 66.7 percent of the Croats. Almost invariably of peasant origin, the average *Grenzer* (Border Guard) officer was content to remain in his own regiment and lacked the ambition needed for a great career. At least so we are told by the memoir-writers and the collectors of military anecdotes. The *Grenzer* officer was "Kamerad Krawatowitsch," a simple-minded but fiercely loyal soldier. Certainly, the majority ended a life of service as junior captains or even lieutenants.[18]

Of course, not all South Slav officers ended their careers as lieutenants or captains. One of the principal Austrian commanders in the wars of 1848-1849, General Jelačić, was a Croat; a highly popular general in the army of Francis Joseph, Mollinary, was the son of a Border Guard family; the occupation of Bosnia-Hercegovina in 1878 was directed by a South Slav, General Philippovich; and the 1882 uprising in that same province was suppressed by another South Slav, General Jovanović. There were many great South Slav military dynasties and Croats and Serbs were very well represented among the generals.

Some further evidence may be adduced to demonstrate that the Habsburg army was more "ethnic-blind" than biased. Of the Dual Monarchy's 387 actively serving generals on November 1, 1918, 166 could be considered Germans, 94 Hungarians, 64 Czechs and Slovaks, 25 South Slavs, 24 Poles, nine Italians, one Romanian and four classified as "other." It should be noted, however, that the source of this data, the Austrian statistician Wilhelm Winkler, based his computations mostly on the generals' legal place of residence, a somewhat doubtful procedure.[19] Similarly, of the Monarchy's nine active field marshals during the Great War, Friedrich, Eugen and Joseph were Habsburg archdukes; Conrad and Rohr German-Austrians; Böhm-Ermolli, born in Ancona, part German, part Italian; Kövess, who had a Hungarian name and was born in Hungary, German; Krobatin, born in Moravia, Czech; and Boroević, a South Slav.[20] Needless to say, however, all the field marshals viewed themselves as Austrians above all else, and their unconditional loyalty was to the Emperor. After the war, only the former Chief of the General Staff, Conrad, claimed to be a Great-German nationalist, while Archduke Joseph paraded as a Hungarian patriot. Most of the field marshals, like the great majority of the other career officers, never admitted to a specific nationality. Nor should we insist too much on assigning one to them.

National Strife in the Habsburg Army

IF THE CAREER officer corps as a whole refused to be nationalistic (and with good reason, since the survival of the multinational monarchy was, for them, a bread and butter issue), the same could not be said of individual soldiers, to say nothing of the politicians. The history of the Monarchy, particularly between 1867 and 1914, was largely one of national strife, kept within limits by the silent agreement of the leading politicians not to destroy a system whose existence and growing prosperity were beneficial even to its domestic enemies. This strife, consisting mostly of the attempt by national leaders to enhance their own position and influence, spilled over into the rank and file of the armed forces and even affected some of the officers. We have already noted the revolutionary activity of a few Polish and Italian officers before 1848 and the near-dissolution of the army during the Springtime of the Peoples. These events were followed by several decades of relative ethnic peace, but in the 1880s and 1890s national strife erupted again. Hungarians began clamoring louder and louder for virtual independence in a Personal Union with "Austria"; Czechs yearned for a constitution similar to the one obtained by the Hungarians in 1867; Croats strove for their emancipation from Hungarian tutelage; Serbs demanded autonomy within Hungary and within (or in union with) Croatia-Slavonia; Ruthenes wanted autonomy in Galicia, the Romanians in Transylvania, and so on and so forth. Finally, a great number of German-Austrians looked to the Second *Reich* for assistance against Slavic and Italian attacks on German national integrity. Again and again, army units confronted nationalist mass demonstrations, often staged by members of their own nationality. Particularly painful to the officers were the German demonstrations, such as those in Vienna and Graz in 1897 during the socalled Badeni Language Riots. German-speaking officers confronting the demonstrators were accused of being in the pockets of Czech politicians or, alternatively, of an international Masonic-Jewish and Catholic conspiracy.[21]

The troops as a whole did their duty. There were, however, individual cases of disobedience and, especially after 1900, a fair number of desertions. These infractions were committed less by officers, among whom mutiny, desertion, or espionage remained a rarity, than by the rank and file. My study of the military court records in the Vienna War Archives for the period 1896-1915 reveals that, of all the criminal investigations involving officers in 1896, only 0.6 percent could be classified as "political"; in 1912-13, the proportion was 2.4 percent, and in the Fall of 1914, 1.8 percent. Moreover, the great majority of political cases concerned reserve officers. Moreover, those under investigation were, with only a few exceptions, officers of junior rank. It is true, however, that *Feldmarschalleutnant* (two-star general) Nikolaus Cena, a retired officer of Romanian nationality, was arrested at the end of July 1914 on suspicion of espionage on behalf of Romania. He was released almost immediately, however, although he later became a Romanian national leader. The notorious Colonel Redl, who killed himself in 1913, had spied on behalf of Russia, but for money, not political reasons.

Only the briefest mention can be made here of political unrest among the troops. Almost invariably, such an unrest was occasioned by an international crisis in which the Monarchy's actions were considered detrimental to the interests of one or another nationality. Such episodes were invariably preceded by strong nationalist agitation among the civilians. In 1908, for example, when partial mobilization was declared on account of the international crisis over the Monarchy's annexation of Bosnia-Hercegovina, and after Czech politicians had violently protested the annexation, Czech soldiers of the 36th *k.u.k.* Infantry Regiment and of the 10th *k.k. Landwehr* Infantry Regiment refused to obey the orders of their superiors. They had no desire to fight, they declared, against their brother Russians and Serbs.[22]

The 1908 mutiny was suppressed with relative ease, but not so the Pardubitz Mutiny of Czech soldiers in November 1912, which involved the reservists of the 8th *Dragoner* (cavalry) Regiment. About to be transported to Galicia to face the Russians during the great international crisis caused by the First Balkan War, the reservists suddenly refused to board the train. Forced in to the wagons nonetheless, they battled intermittently (with no serious casualties) against loyal troops all along the unit's route from Bohemia to the cavalry barracks at Auschwitz. Similar but less violent events took place somewhat later among the reservists of the Czech 18th

Königgrätz Infantry Regiment. The trial of the mutinous *Dragoner* concluded in 1913 with the sentencing of 38 men to prison terms ranging from one month to eight-and-a-half years.[23] Characteristically, the same Balkan crisis had provoked an outburst of pro-war enthusiasm among the Hungarian population.

World War I

THAT NATIONAL DISCONTENT did not yet represent a mortal danger to the Army or at least that its effects could be postponed was proven by the successful general mobilization of 1914. The tremendous losses suffered by the Habsburg army during the first few months of the war should not be attributed to the disaffection of certain nationalities but to poor generalship and, even more, to material unpreparedness.

Since the career officer corps and well trained rank and file were virtually annihilated in 1914, the rest of the war was fought by and large by underage recruits and older or untrained reservists, often under the command of hastily trained reserve officers. This was no longer a truly professional army but a civilian militia. In the course of that war, more than eight million Austro-Hungarians were pressed into uniform, and casualties numbered in the millions.

The wartime performance of the various nationalities was definitely uneven, although, once again, it should be stressed that the great majority of troops performed their duty irrespective of ethnic affiliation. The Army High Command treated the Ruthenes, Romanians, Czechs, and Serbs with great suspicion, and the latter sometimes responded in kind by going over to the other side. There were even a few notorious cases of entire regiments — mostly Czech ones — surrendering to the enemy. By contrast, the performance of the Germans, Magyars, Slovenes, Croats, and Bosnians was justly held to be impeccable, and the Poles, Slovaks, and Italians stood somewhere between the two extremes.

Losses were also unevenly distributed among the nationalities, a fact which had as much to do with the peasant character of certain groups (and their consequently higher representation in the infantry, which shouldered about 90 percent of all casualties) as it did with the policy of the Army High Command to send the most reliable units — Germans, Hungarians, Croats, and the like — to the most endangered sectors of the front. The greater or lesser reluctance of various nationalities to die for the Monarchy can also not be discounted entirely here.

Whatever the reasons for the discrepancies, it has been calculated that the rate of deaths resulting from combat was 29.1 per thousand in the purely German-speaking districts of "Austria" and 28.0

per thousand in the purely Hungarian- or mixed Hungarian-and-German-speaking districts of Hungary. At the opposite extreme, the rate was 16.2 per thousand in the purely Polish-speaking districts of "Austria" and 11.9 per thousand in the primarily Ruthene-speaking districts of Hungary. It should be noted, however, that the last two figures reflect, among other things, the fact that much of Galicia and parts of northeastern Hungary were occupied by the Russians in 1914/15, precluding the possibility of raising troops from these regions during that period. One final comparison: in German-speaking Pettau in Styria, 196.2 of out of every 1000 inhabitants were killed during the War, while in Italian-speaking Rovigno, only 5.7 per thousand perished.[24]

The difficulties facing the reserve officers who commanded most of the platoons and, often, even the companies cannot be overemphasized. Among other things, they had no time to learn any of the languages spoken by their men. A Common Army officer relates how he once spent an entire week alone in a foxhole with a Hungarian liaison officer from a *honvéd* battalion; the two were unable to exchange even a single intelligible sentence.[25]

By 1916-1917, the Monarchy was facing acute shortages of food, clothing, rolling stock, fuel, and weapons. The poverty, terrible casualties, seeming endless character of the conflict, and the outbreak of the Russian revolutions all contributed to disaffection among the troops. Thousands deserted, some out of nationalist convictions, others to avoid further suffering and death, and still others as a result of revolutionary socialist agitation. By 1917, South Slav deserters had formed partisan units in Croatia; Czech legions had been formed from POWs in Russia and Italy; and increasing numbers of mutinies were occurring, not so much at the front as in the hinterland. It had become very difficult to dispatch replacement units to the front.

The situation reached its worst in the spring and early summer of 1918; still, the front held fast, and until the last day of the war, no enemy soldier set foot on Austro-Hungarian territory.[26] Indeed, a sufficient number of loyal troops could be found up until the end of October to crush industrial strikes and military mutinies. In that month, when combat soldiers were literally starving and dressed in rags, the Army still disposed about half a million combat troops on the Italian and Balkan fronts. Some regiments even went on fighting for several days after the dissolution of the Monarchy at the end of October. A cease-fire was signed with the Italians on November 3 but, as a result of some confusion over the time it was to take effect, the Italian army was able to capture an additional 436,000 Austro-Hungarian troops. It turns out that these post-cease-fire POWs included no Hungarians (they had been previously recalled by their own government), and only a small minority of German-Austrians. The rest consisted of Czechs and Slovaks, Croats, Slovenes, and Serbs, Poles, Ruthenes, Romanians, and Italians, all of whom were now theoretically allies of Italy, as citizens of the newly created Romania, Poland, Czecho-Slovakia, and the South Slav state. Nonetheless, the Italian High Command held them in open-air camps, where some 30,000 of them died.[27]

The disappearance of the Monarchy did not mean an end to national strife. On the contrary, a whole series of local conflicts broke out almost immediately.

Conclusion

THE NATIONALITY PROBLEM in the Habsburg Monarchy was insoluble. No matter what the Ruler did to address it — and the Compromise of 1867 was but the last of many such attempts — it was bound to disappoint many of his subjects and leave even its intended beneficiaries less than satisfied. It has often been said that the Compromise represented the triumph of the German bourgeoisie and the Hungarian nobility, yet no groups were more critical of the Compromise than they, and none worked more effectively to undermine it. The aggressive demands of the German and Hungarian nationalists after 1867 were met in turn by the increasingly aggressive demands of the others. The so-called "un-historic" nationalities, who had never had a native elite or had lost it at some point in the past, gradually developed such a leading stratum, composed of priests, journalists, lawyers, and businessmen, whose ambitions inevitably clashed with those of the elites of such "historic" nationalities as the Germans, Magyars, and Poles. No federalist solution, no matter how generous and circumspect, could ever have reconciled this congeries of conflicting and overlapping ambitions. One could only delay, not prevent, the ultimate dissolution of the Monarchy, and this task was shouldered primarily by the Common Army. The efforts of the latter were not wholly without fruit, however, for the grace period they granted to the peoples of East Central Europe provided the region with an opportunity for unprecedented economic growth and cultural flourishing.

It is rather useless to debate whether the Army could have acted otherwise than it did. At no time in its modern history, except perhaps in 1848-49 and again in the 1850s, was the Army master of its own fate. It was forced to adjust to the political changes imposed from above and strove hard to do so, not always unsuccessfully. The most significant blow to the Army's a-national dynastic ideology was the formation in 1868 of two (actually two-and-a-half) National

Guards. The Hungarians subsequently pressed hard for a complete
division of the armed forces into an "Austrian" and a Hungarian half,
but is difficult to see how this could have improved matters: each half
would simply have confronted an even more vicious nationality problem within its own ranks. The Army had made a unique concession to
national sensibilities – and practical considerations – by obliging its
officers to instruct the men in their own languages. Had it truly
"nationalized" every one of its units – a solution very different from
the one demanded by the Hungarians – then the army might well
have become unmanageable. Nor would it have satisfied the various
nationalist politicians, whose true concern was not with the language
of command but with gaining control over the military. A truly multinational army, divided along ethnic lines down to the platoon level,
would still have had to represent a unified will, or else it would have
ceased to be an army. But who could have imposed this unified will
on such a divided force?

Perhaps the officers should have done more than simply learn
the languages of their men. A more democratic training might have
allowed them to communicate better with the recruits, cultivate a
genuine camaraderie, and develop a sense of common purpose. But
what, ultimately, was this purpose to be, and how could one have cultivated democratic values in an army whose loyalty was dynastic and
whose ideology was feudal? Giving up these pre-modern values would
have involved a surrender to nationalism, the very force that
threatened the existence of the Monarchy and, hence, the Army.
There was no way out of the vicious circle; one could only employ
the tactics of delay. Meanwhile, there were colourful uniforms,
parades, prancing horses, flying banners, and, at the end, there was
death.

Notes

1. Some of the main sources on the Habsburg army's multinational composition
   are Joh. Christoph Allmayer-Beck and Erich Lessing, *Die k.(u.)k. Armee,
   1848-1918* (Munich-Gütersloh-Vienna, 1974); Wilhelm Czermak, *In Deinem
   Lager war Österreich: Die österreichisch-ungarische Armee, wie man sie
   nicht kennt* (Breslau, 1938); Alfons Danzer et al., *Unter den Fahnen: Die
   Völker Österreich-Ungarns in Waffen* (Prague-Vienna-Leipzig, 1889); István
   Deák, *Beyond Nationalism: A Social and Political History of the Habsburg
   Officer Corps, 1848-1918* (New York, 1990); Maximilian Ehnl, "Die öst.-ung.
   Landmacht nach Aufbau, Gliederung, Friedensgarnison, Einteilung und
   nationale Zusammensetzung im Sommer 1914" (Vienna, 1934); this essay
   forms Supplement [Ergänzungsheft] nr. 9 to *Österreich-Ungarns letzter
   Krieg*, ed. Edmund Glaise von Horstenau and Rudolf Kiszling, 7 vols. (Vienna,
   1930-1938); Fr. Fenner von Fenneberg, *Österreich und seine Armee*
   (Leipzig, 1842); Béla K. Király, ed., *East Central European Society and
   War in the Era of Revolutions, 1775-1856* (New York, 1984), especially the

essays of Raimondo Luraghi and István Deák; Béla K. Király and Nándor F. Dreisziger, eds., *East Central European Society in World War I* (Boulder, Colorado and New York, 1985), particularly the essays of Tibor Hajdu, Gunther E. Rothenberg, István Deák, and Richard G. Plaschka; Rudolf Kiszling, "Habsburgs Wehrmacht im Spiegel des Nationalitätenproblems 1815 bis 1918," in *Gedenkschrift für Harold Steinacker* ("Buchreihe der Südostdeutschen Historischen Kommission, 16"; Munich, 1966), pp. 240-53; Richard G. Plaschka, *Cattaro-Prag. Revolte und Revolution* (Graz, 1963); Richard G. Plaschka, Horst Haselsteiner and Arnold Suppan, *Innere Front: Militärassistenzen, Widerstand und Umsturz in der Donaumonarchie 1918*, 2 vols. (Vienna, 1974); Gunther E. Rothenberg, *The Army of Francis Joseph* (West Lafayette, Ind., 1976) and, by the same author, *The Military Border in Croatia, 1740-1881: A Study of an Imperial Institution* (Chicago, 1966); Alan Sked, *The Survival of the Habsburg Empire: Radetzky, the Imperial Army and the Class War, 1848* (London and New York, 1979); Adam Wandruszka and Peter Urbanitsch, eds., *Die Völker des Reiches*, 2 vols. ("Die Habsburgermonarchie, 1848-1918," III; Vienna, 1980); Samuel R. Williamson, Jr., and Peter Pastor, eds. *Essays on World War I: Origins and Prisoners of War* (New York, 1983); Wilhelm Winkler, *Der Anteil der nichtdeutschen Volksstämme an der öst.-ung. Wehrmacht* (Vienna, 1919), and, by the same author, *Die Totenverluste der öst.-ung. Monarchie nach Nationalitäten* (Vienna, 1919). Statistical data on the ethnic composition of the armed forces are provided by the extremely thorough *Militär-Statistisches Jahrbuch, 1870-1911* (Vienna, 1872-1912). Unfortunately, Habsburg military statisticians became interested in the ethnic origin of officers only beginning in 1897. The ethnic breakdown of the rank and file was statistically reported from 1870 on.

2. See "Die Verluste der kriegführenden Heere im Weltkrieg," in Glaise and Kiszling, vol. VII, Beilage 37.

3. Ehnl, pp. 14, 84, and 87.

4. On the early history of the Habsburg army, see specially Joh. Christoph Allmayer-Beck and Erich Lessing, *Die kaiserlichen Kriegsvölker von Maximilian I bis Prinz Eugen, 1479-1718* (Munich-Gütersloh-Vienna, 1978), and, by the same authors, *Das Heer unter dem Doppeladler. Habsburgs Armeen, 1718-1848* (Munich-Gutersloh-Vienna, 1981) as well as Herbert St. Fürlinger and Ludwig Jedlicka, eds., *Unser Heer. 300 Jahre österreichisches Soldatentum in Krieg und Frieden* (Vienna-Munich-Zurich, 1963), pp. 1-214.

5. The best modern study on the early history of the Military Border is by Gunther E. Rothenberg, *The Austrian Military Border in Croatia, 1522-1747* ("Illinois Studies in the Social Sciences, vol. 48"; Urbana, 1960). The later period is described in Rothenberg, *The Military Border in Croatia, 1740-1881.*

6. On foreigners in the Habsburg army under Metternich, see Fenneberg, pp. 96-98 *et passim.*

7. On the crisis of the Habsburg army in 1848-1849, see the essays by István Deák, Aladár Urbán, Raimondo Luraghi, Zoltán Bárcy, and István Kovács, in Király, *East Central European Society and War in the Era of Revolutions, 1775-1856*; also Sked, Parts I and II, as well as Rothenberg, *The Army of Francis Joseph*, chapter III, and Rudolf Kiszling, *Die Revolution im Kaisertum Österreich, 1848-1849*, 2 vols. (Vienna, 1948).

8. Gábor Bona, *Tábornokok és törzstisztek a szabads gharcban, 1848-49* [Generals and field-grade officers in the (Hungarian) war of independence, 1848-49] (Budapest, 1983), pp. 67-68 *et passim*.

9. István Deák, *The Lawful Revolution: Louis Kossuth and the Hungarians, 1848-1849* (New York, 1979), pp. 331-33.

10. Sked, chapter 3, and Robert Nowak, "Die Klammer des Reichs. Der Verhalten de elf Nationalitäten Österreich-Ungarns in der k.u.k. Wehrmacht 1914-1918," 4 vols., unpublished manuscript [1964] Vienna, Kriegsarchiv, B/726, nr. 1, vol. I, p. 80.

11. István Deák, "Defeat at Solferino: The Nationality Question and the Habsburg Army in the War of 1859," in *The Crucial Decade: East Central European Society and National Defense, 1859-1870*, ed. Béla K. Király (New York, 1984), pp. 496-516.

12. The re-organization of the Habsburg army in and after 1867 is discussed, aside from the authors listed in Note 1, by Antonio Schmidt-Brentano, *Die Armee in Österreich: Militär, Staat und Gesellschaft 1848-1867* (Boppard am Rhein, 1975), and Walter Wagner, *Geschichte des k.k. Kriegsministeriums*, vol. II, 1866-1888 (Vienna-Cologne-Graz, 1971). The first volume, published in 1966, covers the period 1848-1866.

13. One-year volunteers and the reserve officer corps are discussed in Anton Triulzi, *Der einjährig Freiwillige und k.k. Reserve-Officier in der österreichisch-ungarischen Monarchie* (Vienna, 1872); Anton Kainz, "70 Jahre Reserveoffiziere in Österreich," in *Militärwissenschaftliche Mitteilungen*, 68 (1937), 350-70; and Rothenberg, *The Army of Francis Joseph*, pp. 83, 108, 127, and 151.

14. In 1911, when the proportion of Jews in the Monarchy as a whole was 4.4 percent, Jewish officers constituted 17 percent of the reserve officer corps. Early in the twentieth century, their proportion had been even higher. See *Militärstatistisches Jahrbuch*, 1911, p. 145, and pp. 184-87.

15. Ibid., pp. 184-87.

16. All statistical work on my representative sample of 1000 career officers was prepared, programmed, and processed by Drs. Antal Örkény and András Ungár, two young scholars at the Department of Sociology of the University of Budapest, Hungary. My intellectual debt to them is immeasurable.

17. See Bona, chapter 2, and Tibor Hajdu, "A tisztikar társadalmi helyzetének változásai, 1849-1914)" [Changes in the social position of the officer corps], *Valóság* (Budapest), 87/4 (1987), pp. 55-80.

18. The documented near-total unfamiliarity of these officers with French and English, mastery of which was a mark of gentlemanly distinction, bears testimony to the group's lower-class background and limited education. In 1870, for instance, only one out of twenty Border Guard officers (not just those in our sample) spoke French, and only two individuals out of a total complement of 996 spoke any English. (Because the Border Guard regiments had ceased to exist by 1900, it is impossible to determine whether humanistic education had made any headway by then among the Serbian and Croatian officers.) These figures contrast sharply with those for the almost equally unprestigious infantry officer corps, where one in five knew French and 2.29 percent knew English, and even more with those for the cavalry, where two out of five officers spoke French and 8.29 percent knew English. See *Militär-Statisches Jahrbuch für das Jahr 1870*, Part I (Vienna, 1872), p. 222.

19. Winkler, *Der Anteil der nichtdeutschen Volkestämme an der öst.-ung. Wehrmacht*, p. 3.
20. See Georg Zivkovic, *Heer and Flottenführer der Welt*, 2nd ed. (Vienna, 1980), p. 76.
21. See Berthold Sutter, *Die Badenischen Sprachenverordnungen von 1897*, 2 vols. (Graz-Cologne, 1965).
22. A particularly valuable contribution to the Habsburg army's ethnic problems is Nowak, "Die Klammer des Reichs," a massive manuscript in the Vienna War Archives. The 1980 Czech mutinies are described in vol. I, pp. 192-95.
23. Nowak, vol. I, pp. 204-29, and Rothenberg, *The Army of Francis Joseph*, p. 170.
24. Winkler, *Die Totenverluste der öst.-ung. Monarchie*, pp. 7-8 and 12-16 and Glaise and Kiszling, vol. I, pp. 44-45.
25. Georg Nitsche, *Österreichisches Soldatentum im Rahmen Deutscher Geschichte* (Berlin-Leipzig, 1937), p. 263.
26. Some of the major sources on the military collapse of the Monarchy, and on the nationality problem in the armed forces during the last months of the war, are Emil Ratzenhofer, "Der Waffenstillstand von Villa Giusti und die Gefangennahme Hunderttausender," in Ergänzungsheft [Supplement] nr. 2 (Vienna, 1931) to Glaise and Kiszling, *Österreich-Ungarns letzter Krieg*; Karel Pichlik, "Der militärische Zusammenbruch der Mittelmächte im Jahre 1918," in *Die Auflösung de Habsburgerreiches: Zusammenbruch und Neuorientierung im Donauraum*, ed. Richard G. Plaschka and Karlheinz Mack (Vienna, 1970), pp. 249-65; and Czermak, *In Deinem Lager war Österreich*. See also István Deák, "The Habsburg Army in the First and Last Days of World War I: A Comparative Analysis," in Király and Dreisziger, *East Central European Society in World War I*, pp. 301-12.
27. See Ratzenhofer.

RACE, ETHNICITY, AND SOCIAL CLASS IN THE FRENCH COLONIAL ARMY: THE BLACK AFRICAN *TIRAILLEURS*, 1857-1958

MYRON ECHENBERG

No LESS A personage than the Sun King, Louis XIV of France, was said to have greeted one of his royal officers of African descent in the following manner: "Prince Anabia, il n'y a pas de différence entre vous et moi que du noir au blanc."[1]

The ambiguity was no doubt intentional, for Louis knew full well the differences not only between king and courtier but also between white and black in the eighteenth century. The King's statement is also interesting for its confirmation of the early presence of African military officers in French service. Before examining this point further, it may be helpful to situate black African soldiers generally within the French Army as a whole. Members of the French Colonial Army, black African soldiers have been commonly labelled *Tirailleurs Sénégalais* after the Regiments of that name first created by Governor Louis Faidherbe in 1857.[2] The term is somewhat misleading since these regiments, soon after their founding, began incorporating Africans from the interior territories as well as from Senegal itself. Thus the term "African *Tirailleurs*" (or ATs) seems a more appropriate designation; by extension, the term "African *Tirailleur* Army," or ATA, is preferred for the totality of black African units in the French Colonial Army at any given time. Though the ATs were a major component of the Colonial Army, other largely segregated units were the Malagasy *Tirailleurs*, the Algerian *Tirailleurs*, the Moroccan *Tirailleurs*, and several other more specialized units.[3] The French *Armée d'Afrique* on the other hand, while part of the Colonial Army, consisted of men of European origin recruited from among the so-called *colons*, or settlers living in French-controlled North Africa. The *Armée d'Afrique* in particular should not be confused with the ATA, since African subjects were not allowed in this exclusive force. Lastly, no inventory of French forces should omit the

50

ubiquitous Foreign Legion, most decidedly also a part of the Colonial Army, though consisting by definition of men who were neither French citizens nor subjects.

In contrast to the Colonial Army, the French Metropolitan Army refers to the territorial regiments of metropolitan France, as well as to special units officered by men who held commissions as officers of the Metropolitan Army. It should also be noted that although black Africans did serve as junior officers in the ATA, the ATA was commanded predominantly by French officers often known collectively as *La Coloniale*.

It would be an error to see these divisions exclusively on racial lines, though race was clearly a factor. Most of the rank and file in the Metropolitan Army was white, and in the Colonial Army, non-white. The Foreign Legion and the *Armée d'Afrique* were the exceptions in the latter force; in the Metropolitan Army, a handful of French citizens of colour from the French Antilles and Réunion, for example, enlisted as a rule in French territorial regiments. So too would a Frenchman of colour born and raised, for example in Toulouse. The citizens of the four communes of Senegal were a puzzle in this regard. Unless as officers, they could not normally serve in the ATA. Senegalese who were French citizens and studying or working in France, as was Léopold Senghor when mobilization occurred in 1939,[4] were assigned to territorial regiments.

Not surprisingly, the ATA underwent dramatic change over the course of its one hundred years of life. Most ATs in 1857 were still being issued muzzle-loaders, while some of their successors a century later included AT paratroopers who had jumped into the inferno of Dien Bien Phu in 1954, or into Port Said during the ill-fated and ill-advised Anglo-French operation at the Suez Canal in 1956. To illustrate some of these changes it is useful to sketch the development of the ATA over four phases of its existence, each one marked by what might be termed a different Army.

The Conquest Army lasted from 1857 to 1904.[5] Basically a mercenary force, it consisted of slaves and others drawn from the lowest social ranks, together with a few military leaders from among the notable families of African societies. Recruitment was overwhelmingly involuntary, and little ideology bound men to their duties. Most of the officer corps was French, and usually from the *Infanterie de Marine*, perhaps the least prestigious branch of the French armed forces of the day. Ties between officers and men were of a personal nature, and crossed racial and ethnic lines. Compensation consisted of a tiny *per diem* wage, augmented by spoils of war.

After France's colonial possessions were largely secured south of the Sahara by 1904, the ATA entered a transitional phase, that of an occupation army, which lasted from 1905 to 1918.[6] This period saw important structural changes, such as the introduction of a partial conscription bill in 1912 to augment recruitment of ATs for the conquest of Morocco, as well as the fixing of wages, pensions and other benefits as the era of conquest subsided. Most importantly, the size of the ATA increased dramatically. Whereas a force of some 5,000 had been sufficient to conquer black Africa, by 1914 France required some 14,000 ATs to occupy its vast colonial territories.[7] The dramatic events of the First World War were to bring still larger demands to France's African subjects. Heavy recruitment drives in 1915 and especially in 1917-18 brought the standing ATA to over 100,000 men by 1918.[8] Despite these huge levies, little effort was made to transfer an ideology to the African troops.

The third and longest phase of the ATA stretched from 1919 to the end of the Second World War in 1945. This period was inaugurated by a peacetime Conscription Law of 1919 which greatly elaborated on the mechanics of recruitment, while reducing the overall size of the ATA.[9] The army was fixed at roughly 50,000 men, two-thirds of whom were to be three-year conscripts drafted by means of a universal lottery for all African males in their twentieth years. The annual intake was to range between 10,000 and 12,000 men. The ideology of French Republicanism was becoming more important as well. Differential perquisites to the families of soldiers such as exemption from the head tax, as well as better access to medical and educational benefits, combined to differentiate soldiers, veterans and their families from the peasantry as a whole. Gradually, the francophone African military took on the features of a petty bourgeoisie in the emerging class structure of colonial French West Africa. At the outbreak of war in 1939, lower peacetime levies of troops ended in favour of a mass mobilization which saw some 100,000 Africans enter the ATA in 1939-40, many just in time to participate in the disastrous events of May and June of 1940.[10] Before the war was over, twice that number had served in one or another of the various French armies of the day. Relative to other communities making up the French empire, the black African share of the military burden was higher during the era of the Conscript Army than at any other time. At one point, the 50,000 ATs constituted 10 percent of the entire French Army; combined, colonial soldiers made up full 50 percent, or 250,000 men in an Army of half a million.[11]

The fourth and final phase of the ATA lasted from 1946 until the coming of Independence in French West Africa (hereafter FWA) after 1958. This was the era of the Professional Army, reflecting the sharp decline in conscripts as opposed to career soldiers. These years were characterized by much smaller annual intakes of 5,000 men on average to reflect the vastly changed nature of warfare.[12] The ATA now sought men with higher educational and skill levels, and, most importantly, more Africans as officers. Elaborate officer-training programs were designed and implemented at such centres in France as Fréjus, Saint-Maixent, and Coëtquidan to tempt bright young Africans into a military career.[13] Such programs succeeded for the most part in transferring to what would be the first generation of independent African army officers the French military way of seeing the world and their vocations.

Without question, France militarized its African colonies to an unprecedented degree in modern Colonialism. The ATA became at one and the same time the army that conquered and controlled Africans, and the force in which sons, brothers, husbands, uncles and fathers served. Over the course of its century-long existence, this major institution of French colonialism was designed to exercise four major functions. Initially, it had been an instrument of conquest. Next, by means of its garrisons of territorial regiments in each colony, it became an Occupation Army. Third, the ATA served as an expeditionary force in other parts of the French Empire and even beyond. Finally, during two World Wars, Africans in large numbers were employed in the defence of the mother country.

THE VARIABLES OF race, ethnicity and social class help us understand the changing relationships of men serving within the ATA. Attitudes towards race have certainly played a part in the ATA's history. In the late nineteenth century in particular, misapplication of Darwin's theories led French military authorities to put forward a series of racial stereotypes regarding allegedly "warlike" peoples, *les races guerrières*.[14] Indeed, Charles Mangin, the architect of the modern ATA, argued the superiority of the "Black Force" as he called his proposed army, on the grounds that black Africans were the most disciplined, loyal and "warlike" soldiers in the entire French Empire.[15] A passionate paternalist who had great affection for his African troops, Mangin, in addition to being ruthless and callous in regard to high casualty rates, shared with most Europeans of his day an essentially racist world view. He based his notions on the premise that military qualities were genetically transmitted on racial lines. Where he differed from other French officers was on which races were "innately warlike," and, more significantly, where he had empirically observed colonial troops in action. Mangin felt that North Africans made good soldiers but their loyalty to France was divided by appeals of Islamic and Arab Nationalism. Other French officers such as De Torcy and Azan, who had commanded North African troops, disagreed, holding that their troops were superior to black

Africans.[16] Nevertheless, Mangin's views prevailed politically as well as militarily for much of the colonial period. As for other peoples in the French Empire, Mangin argued that Malagasys were third-rate soldiers because of poor physical condition and a lack of discipline, while Indochinese were the most intelligent and quickest to learn but too frail to stand up to the punishments of modern warfare.[17] He saw their role as stretcher bearers and ambulance drivers. After Dien Bien Phu and the First Indochina War generally, many French observers had learned otherwise, but old ideas died hard. A French officer in 1956 went through this same sort of stereotyped analysis on the grounds that while the French may have been wrong about the Vietnamese, the generalizations still held for the rest of the colonial peoples![18]

Race was also a factor within the ATA. Most soldiers were recruited from the black African agricultural population living in sub-Saharan Africa. But French West Africa also included such Caucasoid pastoral peoples of the desert and sahel zones as the Moors, Tuaregs, and Berbers. These populations were exempted from conscription into the ATA on the grounds that they served in specialized desert units such as *goums* and *spahis*; that is, camel and cavalry corps. In reality, the French were concerned with two factors: the costs of conscription in far-flung desert constituencies; and the racial tensions that would result within the ATA should desert peoples find themselves under the command of a black African sergeant or native officer. The desert peoples held strong racial ideologies stemming from centuries of slavery and the slave trade. In the colonial period, many pastoralists continued to keep black slaves and clients, and would not accept to be commanded by people they regarded as racially inferior.[19]

Race relations between predominantly white officers and their black troops was yet another variable of behaviour. Tensions undoubtedly existed between officers and men, as in any armed force, but in the ATA no bloody equivalent of an Indian Mutiny ever sullied its reputation or gave the French planners serious pause. To be sure, incidents of rebellion did occur. One peculiar mutiny took place in 1899 in the Lake Chad region, when two European officers, Captains Paul Voulet and Jules Chanoine, ordered the ATs under their command to shoot down Colonel Klobb, a superior officer sent out to reprimand them and remove them from command of an ATA military expedition. After obeying their rebellious officers and killing Klobb, the ATs had second thoughts. Under the command of an African sergeant, Souley Traoré, the ATs rallied to the cause of France.[20] The second set of incidents occurred in the winter of 1944-45 and can be properly labelled soldiers' protests rather than mutinies; they were the result of harsh wartime conditions and a sense that France was ungrateful for all the sacrifices made by the war-weary ATs.[21]

Race was also at issue at the officers' level. Louis XIV's remarks to Prince Anabia suggest the presence of African officers in French regiments of the *ancien régime*.[22] Although there is no continuous line forward to the twentieth century, various French governments did allow for Africans as officers. In the middle of the nineteenth century, Governor of Senegal Louis Faidherbe, a believer in the Jacobin ideology of assimilation and a democratic army, made his thinking clear when awarding the commission of second lieutenant to one Alioun Sall, a Senegalese soldier who had distinguished himself in the ATA:

> Ce poste a été crée spécialement pour recompenser les nombreuses preuves de dévouément que M. Alioun Sall nous a données depuis le commencement de la guerre. Cette nomination a, en outre, une signification plus générale: elle montre que, même en ce qui concerne les positions élevées de notre hiérarchie sociale, la couleur n'est plus une cause d'exclusion et c'est dans ce sens que la population noire doit la comprendre . . .
>
> La carrière sera ouverte à eux comme à tous les autres, et aux mêmes conditions. Les plus capables arriveront seuls. Ceux qui s'obstinent à préférer l'ignorance à la civilisation resteront dans les rangs infimes de la société, comme cela a lieu dans tous les pays du monde.[23]

While the tradition of having Africans as officers certainly distinguished the ATA from British and other colonial armies, it should not be concluded that the officer corps was a model of integration. For one thing, no African advanced beyond captain until the 1950s. Most officers were designated as "African officers," a separate and inferior designation. Such men were invariably promoted from the ranks of non-commissioned officers and usually had very low educational qualifications. At most, they would have received one year of officer training at Saint-Maixent or Fréjus. At the time of independence, Sangoulé Lamizana in Upper Volta and Jean-Bédel Bokassa in the Central African Republic represented this type of officer. Nor were African officers numerous. Until after the Second World War, only fifteen or twenty African officers, each commanding ATA infantry companies, could be found in the entire French colonial army.

After 1945, dramatic changes occurred as the pressure for reform and decolonization mounted. In response to demands from newly elected African politicians, the French Army led the way in Africanization. Using the slogan *"mêmes sacrifices, mêmes droits"* Africans were able to appeal to fellow veterans in France and obtain legislative support for reforms, even from otherwise conservative

Gaullists. These reforms affected all aspects of service, pensions, benefits, and promotions.[24] Perhaps the best known of several new African officers to receive higher education in France was Ahmadu Fall, born in Saint-Louis, Senegal to an African merchant family. Fall became a Major and then a Colonel just before independence in 1958, and came to command white as well as black troops.[25]

Entrance into French military academies, however, required sound *lycée* preparation, and was extremely competitive throughout France and its overseas territories. To enable Africans to qualify for officer training, a special *"Promotion Africaine"* was created at Saint-Maixent and Fréjus, no doubt because very few were succeeding in the tough competition for places in St Cyr. Some Africans resented a route they recognized as inferior, but it certainly produced results, with several hundred professional officers trained by the eve of Independence in 1958. Officers like Moussa Traoré of Mali and Mathieu Kérékou of Bénin, later to become military Presidents as the result of military coups, followed this route. Above all, Africanization of the officer corps helped establish and preserve strong bonds to France and the French military way in the decades after Independence.[26]

As in so many other respects, conditions within the ATA tended to mirror conditions in the larger society. Thus, racial tensions certainly existed in the ATA, but they were certainly no worse and often less sharp than those in civilian society.

ETHNICITY RATHER THAN race was the more significant variable within ATA units. Captain Marceau, an experienced French officer writing in 1911, estimated that two-thirds of all recruits were by this time Bambara speakers.[27] The Bambara *Tirailleur*, wrote Marceau, was "un rude gaillard qui complète toutes les fortes vertus guerrières, mais qui n'éclaire malheureusement pas un très vive intelligence."[28] In short, he was a compliant, stolid peasant soldier obedient to his new French masters. In contrast, the Wolof soldier was spoiled by his long association with France and had become "un snob de la caste" towards other Africans whom he regarded as "sauvages": "C'est un negre des 'Droits de l'homme'; c'est un citoyen sans cité; c'est un électeur qui dédaigne nos uniformes: il n'est plus guère bon pour 'faire tirailleur.' Aussi, même au régiment de Saint Louis, trouve-t-on peu de Ouolofs."[29] Marceau believed that from the ranks of the Tukolor came the best officers and sergeants: "C'est un guerrier d'essence. C'est un soldat de vocation qui ne se plie malheureusement pas toujours de bonne grace à notre discipline militaire."[30]

Apart from their subjective basis, what is so remarkable about such opinions is that they were so enduring, in part no doubt because they were self-fulfilling. As late as the 1950s, officers were repeating the homilies of Marceau and of Mangin regarding "warlike races."[31] Mangin, for example, doubted whether people of the forest regions of Africa had the discipline and physical stamina to make good soldiers.[32] His strong influence on ATA recruiting policy, together with the fact that forest zones were the last to be conquered and occupied by the French, meant that only after 1919, when universal male conscription became systematic, did forest peoples begin to be a modest minority within the ATA.[33]

As Bambara came to dominate the ranks and non-commissioned grades, the Bambara language became, alongside the *petit-nègre* French that the military insisted upon, the ATA's vernacular language. New recruits from Bambara and related Mande-speaking regions of the West African savanna came to find the army a more hospitable institution than did, say, Agni speakers from the forests of southern Ivory Coast. Thus patterns established in the formative years were to hold sway decades later.

Although leading exponents of the ATA in France, in particular Mangin, argued strenuously for the recruitment of mercenaries from among the traditionally "warlike" peoples of the savanna, his preferences and those of the French military generally did not prevail. Military service became the burden of virtually all sedentary populations of French West Africa, and of parts of French Equatorial Africa as well after 1919. Despite the granting of exemptions and dispensations, conscription served to spread the burden of military service more or less uniformly. While this meant that larger ethnic groups like the Bambara and the Mossi would provide more soldiers, neither community constituted a majority within the ATA. In time therefore, French rather than any vernacular language became the primary means of communication. Nevertheless, Bambara remained as a second language, particularly useful when, as often was the case, the French officers could not speak it.

By and large regional variations in the pattern of recruitment helped create a multi-ethnic ATA. These regional patterns were more evident for career soldiers than for conscripts. While conscription was applied evenly among the sedentary populations of FWA, re-enlistment decisions were based on the relative popularity of military service when measured against other economic opportunities in the various regions.

Both in relative and absolute terms, men from Senegal were under-represented in the ATA.[34] Because the French used total population as a general principle for recruitment, Soudan and Upper Volta had the largest contingents in the ATA. In addition, young men from

Senegal had several practical opportunities to avoid military service unique to their colony's special situation in the French colonial system. A minority of Senegalese, those born or living in the Four Communes, were recognized as French citizens after 1917 and served in units of the regular French army, not in the colonial ranks.[35] Also, Senegalese subjects lived in closer proximity to the centre of patronage in the Federation, the city of Dakar and its neighbourhood. This gave them better access to schools and jobs in the private and public sectors, and better access to military deferments and even exemptions.[36] Finally, annual conscription in West Africa took place first in the colonies of the interior, during the months from January to March in any given year. Only after the results were complete did conscription begin in Senegal, usually in April and May. This allowed the colonial authorities to adjust the Senegalese quota downward should colonies of the interior have exceeded their quotas. The converse was never true; colonies of the interior always at least met their quotas, so it was never necessary to make up deficiencies in Senegal.[37]

Still more under-represented than Senegal were the desert fringe colonies of Niger and Mauritania. Both areas had the highest rates of absenteeism during the annual recruitment campaigns, one clear indication of dissatisfaction with military recruitment.[38] The two colonies were also very thinly populated, and therefore marginal to the overall process of recruitment so that a strict enforcement of the conscription law was simply not worth the trouble.

Conversely, military service seemed least unpopular in Guinée, Ivory Coast, Upper Volta, and parts of Soudan, again judging from absentee rates. On the level of district or *cercle*, the areas with the lowest rates of absenteeism were often regions remote from the district or colony capital, places where other opportunities to earn cash income were lacking. A sampling of these *cercles* would include Beyla and N'Zérékoré in Guinée, Kong and Assinie in Ivory Coast, Tougan and Batié in Upper Volta, and San and Koutiala in Soudan.[39]

Some regions saw the popularity of military service rise and fall, depending upon political, social, and economic factors. In the case of Dahomey, military service grew unpopular in the late 1920s, in the aftermath of political repression of Dahomean intellectuals.[40] More important for its impact on conscription was the new legislation of 1926 which called for the mobilization of the hitherto inactive *deuxième portion* into labour brigades, in uniform and under military discipline, to be handed over to private contractors.[41] The unusually high rates of absenteeism from the annual draft were the responses of Dahomeans to the very well-founded rumour that the *deuxième portion* was about to be activated. It is significant that this protest by Dahomeans proved effective. Under this pressure, the French prudently decided to abandon plans to activate this group, and in the early 1930s Dahomean responses to military recruitment became more favourable. Conversely, labour brigades were indeed activated in Soudan, the only colony where this occurred.[42] So horrific were conditions on the work sites of the *Office du Niger* irrigation project and other places where the labour brigades were assigned that this produced two effects on conscription. First, the rates of volunteers increased; this guaranteed an able-bodied young man that he would at least serve in the orderly conditions of the active colonial army. Second, absentee rates soared among those who preferred to remain outside either the ATA or military labour units entirely.[43]

Some *cercles* and colonies might be said to be bell-wethers of general conditions with regard to conscription and military service. Dahomey is a good example of such a colony, and Casamance, in Senegal, such a *cercle*. Because it was a border *cercle*, Casamance continually presented potential conscripts with the opportunity for escape across the frontier to Portuguese Guinea. When absentee rates in Casamance were low, this suggested that conditions of pay and military service in general were acceptable, and terms and risk of overseas service tolerable. High rates of absenteeism conversely indicated low pay in relation to economic opportunities at home, combined with high risks of service abroad.

AFTER RACE AND ethnicity, social class is the third variable under examination in this essay. Once a civilian colonial government was established for FWA after 1904, all ATs, whatever their social origins, became salaried employees of the state. Wage earning was the marker for new social relations based on class, however difficult it is to define the African soldier's class membership. By one measure, the common soldier stood below the unskilled labourer since his starting wage was set at roughly one half the common day labourer's.[44] On the other hand, two potential benefits were extended to African troops which day labourers could never enjoy. First, the soldier and his family were exempt from head taxes as long as he was in service.[45] The second perquisite was often more apparent than real. It consisted of a pension, granted by the decree of 1889, but only to those Africans who served in the ATA for twenty-five years. Not until 1904 did a second decree allow a proportional pension for those ATs with fifteen years of service.[46] While such stringent rules limited benefits to a small minority, in 1910 some 303 soldiers, or 3 percent of the 12,000 man ATA, had twelve years or more of seniority and were likely to qualify eventually for a proportional pension.[47]

One of the most important privileges for the African military was access to education for themselves and their families. In the early years, African soldiers received the bare minimum of training necessary to carry out their military tasks, which were largely those of infantrymen, the unskilled labourers of modern armies. After 1945, however, political pressure for more African officers coincided with the Army's need for more technically-skilled men to open up educational opportunities for young African soldiers. Special training facilities in France formed an important part of the ATA's new look, what in time came to be called the "Africanization" of the ATA officer corps.[48]

For the sons of soldiers, special primary schools were created in the 1920s. Called *Ecoles des Enfants de Troupe*, or EETs, there were three such military academies, at Saint-Louis in Senegal, Bingerville in Ivory Coast, and Kati in Soudan. In August of 1951 a fourth school was opened at Ouagadougou, the capital of Upper Volta.[49] Each school had between 70 and 120 pupils, who were chosen among sons of active and retired career soldiers, with a priority given to sons of veterans of the First World War. Upon completion of the curriculum of primary instruction (the E.P.S., or *Enseignement Primaire Supérieur*) at age eighteen, or at age nineteen whether finished or not, graduates were inducted directly into the ATA with the rank of corporal after six months of training, and with the promise of a career as non-commissioned officer or better, if promotion warranted this. Parents were required to sign a statement of awareness of a clause which enabled the government of FWA to recoup half the cost of education should a boy quit school or refuse the commitment to enlist for a five-year term upon graduation.[50] After 1945 when their names were changed to *Ecoles Militaires Préparatoires Africaines*, or EMPAs, the number of places was increased and the curriculum up-graded to reflect the wider aspirations of the African petty bourgeoisie. Indeed, African intellectuals were anxious to see more African officers trained, and urged the transformation of these schools into modern academic *collèges*, with four years of secondary preparation leading to the *Brévet Elémentaire*. The French High Command refused, however, arguing that the goal of the schools was to accelerate to NCO rank the sons of soldiers, not to create an African elite.[51] Nevertheless, pressure from Africans persisted, and by 1955 the *Brévet* was being offered at two of the four EMPAs.

Men from the interior colonies came to see the military as a means of maintaining or acquiring status for their sons. Demand for entry to the EMPAs was high. In 1953, for example, only 17 percent or 213 of 1255 candidates were admitted to the schools; a similar rate obtained the following year. As was the pattern in the ATA generally, a proportionately higher volume of applicants came from the interior colonies of Upper Volta and Soudan.[52]

Curriculum at these schools, in addition to the fundamental subjects such as French, Mathematics, Physical and Natural Science, English, History, Geography, Art, and Music, also included Military Instruction as well as what was termed "Instruction Civique et Morale." The military subjects covered discipline, garrison duty, infantry manoeuvres, marching drill, and sports. So-called "Moral Education" contained a good deal of the Jacobin military ideology. As General Nyo put it, its purpose was to:

> developper chez les élèves des sentiments de loyauté, de franchise, de solidarité, de sens de l'honneur et des devoirs militaires, la fierté professionelle. L'Ecole doit constituer une grande famille militaire . . . où l'on évite toute sévèrité excessive et surtout brutalité de nature à créer de fâcheux complexes.[53]

The army had reason to be satisfied with the results achieved by the EMPAs. With its careful selection procedures carried out by means of entrance exams, there was little attrition. Only nine of over two hundred cadets were dropped from the program in 1952-53, six for not working sufficiently, one for lack of discipline, one for intellectual ineptitude, and one for physical ineptitude.[54] More significantly, in 1955 results of the military academy in Saint Louis outstripped those of the civilian school there by a good margin. Whereas only 25 of 88 or 28.4 percent of the civilian students passed the Brevet Elémentaire that year, no less than 18 of 21, or 85.7 percent of the young cadets at the EMPA of Saint-Louis were successful.

Thus, over the thirty-five years from their creation in 1923 to the eve of independence in 1958, the EETs and EMPAs served the French well. The special privilege of access to these schools not only rewarded a caste of petty bourgeois soldiers, it also committed the next generation to serve the ATA and the State as well. As if to enshrine the process and consolidate the ideology, the colonial state even encouraged the creation of a formal "old boys' network" through the formation of an *Amicale des Anciens Enfants de Troupe de l'A.O.F.* or AAETA. Its president in 1953 was a serving African officer, Lieutenant Sekou Traoré.[55] Distinguished members of the *Amicale* would have included the Malians Yaro Diakité and Colonel Moussa Traoré.[56]

One of the best ways to observe the process of social differentiation of the African military is by examining the history of veterans' affairs in French West Africa following the Second World War. Unlike their fathers and uncles who had returned in 1918 to a FWA which allowed no non-violent means of political expression, the veterans of

1945 faced a new political situation. African politicians from the *Rassemblement Démocratique Africaine* (RDA) to the Gaullists coveted the veterans' political support.[57] In the first post-war elections, veterans constituted the majority of the greatly extended franchise to select African deputies to the Constituent Assembly.[58] Even if the franchise rolls grew more extensive thereafter, it remained true that veterans constituted a core group of militants in virtually every new African political party after 1945.

The Colonial State also recognized the importance of veterans. An *Office Nationale des Anciens Combattants* was created to control veterans but also as a vehicle for distributing financial benefits, which were much more substantial than they had been after 1918.[59]

Veterans for their part developed a strong consciousness. They shared with African soldiers of the ATA a reconstructed Jacobin ideology. It held that Africans had fought more bravely than any other single constituency in the French Union in an unsuccessful effort to defend France from the enemy in 1940, that Africans had rallied most rapidly and effectively to de Gaulle, that they were the bulwark of the Free French Forces and responsible for the victories in North Africa and southern Europe, and that those Frenchmen who refused to acknowledge this colossal sacrifice were unrepentant racists.[60] Finally, because of such brutal errors as the Thiaroye massacres, and also because it no longer could be said that African *Tirailleurs* were essentially slaves, there was now sympathy for veterans among the general West African population.[61]

As a group, the Second World War veterans were not so easily reabsorbed into peasant agriculture, even if many in the end reluctantly returned to the land. Those with some means congregated in the rapidly burgeoning towns of FWA and became recognizably petty bourgeois in lifestyle and occupation. Of course, significant regional variations occurred. In Western Upper Volta and Ivory Coast, the political militancy of the veterans within the RDA brought them in conflict with the Colonial State.[62] Elsewhere, the vets supported parties that collaborated with the State. The veterans chose their parties based on where power lay, rather than on ideology. In Ivory Coast and Guinée the majority of veterans backed the RDA, in Senegal the Indépendants d'Outre-Mer (IOM), and so on.

So long as the African deputies in Paris competed with each other in support of veterans' interests, there were no major conflicts among veterans across FWA regardless of their differing regional political affiliations. The period from 1946 to 1951 constituted this militant phase when veterans sought equal compensation with French veterans from the State for their losses under the slogan, *"mêmes sacrifices, mêmes droits."*[63] This mirrors what railway workers were seeking, for example, in the major strike of 1947-48. After 1951, when the French State finally passed legislation dramatically increasing pensions for veterans and for career soldiers, the veterans' militancy ended.[64] Like Houphouet-Boigny himself, the veterans became everywhere the conservative force their interests dictated. As talk of independence mounted in the late 1950s the veterans identified still more closely with the Colonial State, fearing (correctly, as it happened) that their pensions and benefits would be at risk once independence from France was established and they ceased to count in French domestic politics.

Of course, it is unfair to generalize about veterans' behaviour for all the French West African Federation. In Sénégal there was more disunity than elsewhere, with veterans grouped within a dazzling variety of different organizations.[65] In Mauritania, since the veterans were black Africans and the political notables Moors, veterans had very little impact.[66] In the similarly sparsely settled sahel colony of Niger, veterans had hoped to win chiefships and were disappointed not to receive many. Those few Niger "vets" who were qualified had no difficulty finding reserved jobs in the police and other State niches.[67] Often the Niger vets were joined by ex-servicemen from Dahomey where there were more qualified veterans than reserved jobs to go round.[68]

Soudan and Guinée offered contrasting situations. While the veterans of Soudan were well-organized and militant supporters of the RDA, the dominant political voice in that colony, their counterparts in Guinée were the slowest to organize, for reasons not obvious from archival records.[69]

The highest level of political consciousness among veterans occurred in Ivory Coast and Upper Volta, still one colony administratively in the years immediately following the war. In the south, veterans uniformly supported the RDA but were rewarded with a significant number of jobs by the French Colonial State since the economy expanded dramatically after 1945. In the north, a schism developed between the veterans in the Bobo-Dioulasso area on the one hand, who were solidly for the RDA, and the more conservative Mossi veterans of Ouagadougou who backed parties loyal to the Colonial State.[70]

Senegalese personalities dominated the federal veterans' associations but the important political figures emerged in the individual colonies, where the real power resided. In Ivory Coast in particular the two dominant figures in veterans' politics were Olivier Reinach, the French Socialist who was the bane of the French administration there, and Philippe Yacé, whose political career in the RDA was launched as Houphouet-Boigny's main lieutenant for veterans' affairs.[71]

The leading French official assigned to veterans' affairs was Commandant Henri Ligier. In the late 1940s and early 1950s he travelled the length and breadth of FWA and opened no less than 250,000 dossiers, registering the claims of widows, orphans, and ex-soldiers alike for back pay and various other forms of compensation.[72] By the mid 1950s, while thousands of veterans may have died off, saving the French exchequer millions, it can be said that veterans no longer had a feeling of glaring injustice, even if they were not quite on a basis of equality with French veterans.

EVEN IF RELATIVELY few soldiers qualified for the perquisites of army service, these benefits had ideological as much as economic significance. They marked the beginning of a process of social differentiation that characterized government service during the colonial period. Of course, the common conscript who entered the army, served his three years, and returned to his village can hardly be said to have changed his class or social relations. He remained a peasant temporarily conscripted into a sort of forced labour. But for the married, westernized veteran of fifteen years' service, clear changes occurred. He could install himself and his family in a quarter of one of the new colonial towns springing up all over FWA and live comfortably on his pension, augmented perhaps by some government employment reserved for veterans alone.[73] Such an individual was a far cry from the slave soldier who watered gardens and tended goats in the old French forts of the coast and river. In the colonial town of Bamako, the administrative capital of the French Sudan, there was even a term, *quinzandougou*, for the section of town where veterans of fifteen years settled.[74]

A focus on the social origins of soldiers begs the question of what these soldiers had become. Those ATs who made the army a career were becoming part of the biggest class transformation of the French colonial era, the creation of a salaried petty bourgeoisie. This transformation, moreover, was one that the French authorities applauded. They saw the advantage in differentiating an African military from its peasant origins by extending to this class fraction inexpensive but effective symbolic rewards of status and privilege: uniforms and military discipline, exemptions from head taxes, medical care for themselves and their children, proportional pensions and low-level reserved employment in the colonial bureaucracy. Such rewards helped French authorities maintain social control by raising their loyal troops above the mass of West African society, even as this exacerbated already existing social contradictions within these same African societies.

Not everybody saw the army as an attractive vehicle for upward mobility. Soldiering continued to attract men from the bottom, and a few from the top, of African society. Those who were consistently under-represented were the emerging middle sectors, educated Africans who looked to the professions and the civil service for their careers. Nevertheless, for men who stayed on in military service, the Army had a levelling effect. Men transcended ethnic loyalties and even social differences while acquiring new bonds. Many began to express a new federal French West African identity in the 1950s in place of ethnic or regional ones. This incipient ideology was to prove important in the years following Independence, as the francophone African military, like its counterparts elsewhere in Africa and Latin America, came to view the State not only as its most precious ally, but as an objective well worth capturing.

Notes

1. Louis XIV's perhaps apocryphal remarks are cited without attribution in an unsigned article, "La France et les cadres africains et malgaches: 1. les cadres avant l'indépendance," *Frères d'Armes*, 10 (1964), 15-23.
2. For a general history of the *Tirailleur Sénégalais* regiments, see Shelby C. Davis, *Reservoirs of Men: A History of the Black Troops of French West Africa* (Westport, Conn., 1970), reprint of the 1934 original edition.
3. For a general overview of the various units making up the French Colonial Army, see Anthony Clayton, *France, Soldiers and Africa* (London, 1988).
4. Jacques Hymans, *Léopold S. Senghor: An Intellectual Biography* (Edinburgh, 1971).
5. Myron Echenberg, "Slaves into Soldiers: Social Origins of the *Tirailleurs Sénégalais*," in *Africans in Bondage: Studies in Slavery and the Slave Trade*, ed. Paul E. Lovejoy (Madison, 1986), pp. 311-33.
6. Marc Michel, *L'Appel à l'Afrique: Contributions et réactions à l'effort de guerre en A.O.F., 1914-1919* (Paris, 1982).
7. Maurice Abadie, *La défense des colonies* (Paris, 1937), pp. 210-16.
8. Michel, *L'Appel*, pp. 405-08.
9. Myron Echenberg, "Paying the Blood Tax: Military Conscription in French West Africa, 1914-1929," *Canadian Journal of African Studies*, 9 (1975), 171-192.
10. Myron Echenberg, " 'Morts pour la France': The African Soldier in France during the Second World War," *Journal of African History*, 26 (1985), 364-65.
11. Ibid., pp. 364-65.
12. General Magnan, Général Commandant Supérieur, to Governor-General of A.O.F., Dakar, 27 October 1946 in Archives de l'Afrique occidentale française (hereaftrer AAOF), Dakar, 4D 90/81; and Report of Lt. Col. Villard, Chef de Cabinet Militaire, Dakar, 1 October 1954, AAOF, Dakar, 4D 175/143.
13. Report of Lt. Col. Villard, Chef de Cabinet Militaire, Dakar, 15 October 1954, AAOF, Dakar, 4D 175/143.
14. For more on this notion of warlike peoples, especially with regard to the Brit-

ish Empire, see Anthony Kirk-Greene, " 'Damnosa Hereditas': Ethnic Ranking and the Martial Races Imperative in Africa," *Ethnic and Racial Studies*, 3 (October 1980), 393-414.

15. Mangin called the book in which he first advocated a professional standing army of black Africans, *La Force Noire*. It was published in Paris in 1910.

16. Marc Michel, "Un mythe: la 'Force Noire' avant 1914," *Relations internationales* (1974, no. 2), 86.

17. Mangin, *La Force Noire*, p. 277.

18. Gilbert de Boisseson, *Le recrutement en AOF et AEF* (Paris, 1956), p. 5.

19. See, for example, Stephen Baier and Paul E. Lovejoy, "The Tuareg of the Central Sudan: Gradations in Servility at the Desert Edge (Niger and Nigeria)," in *Slavery in Africa: Historical and Anthropological Perspectives*, ed. Suzanne Miers and Igor Kopytoff (Madison, 1977), pp. 391-444; Dennis D. Cordell, *Dar Al-Kuti and the Last Years of the Trans-Saharan Slave Trade* (Madison, 1985); and Anne McDougall, "A Topsy-Turvy World: Clients and *Captifs* in Colonial Mauritania," in *The End of Slavery in Africa*, ed. Suzanne Miers and Richard Roberts (Madison, 1987).

20. Commandant Chailley, *Les Grandes Missions Françaises en Afrique Occidentale* (Dakar, 1953), p. 78.

21. There were some fifteen recorded incidents, mostly occurring in the south of France, but one in Versailles, one in Monshire Camp at Huyton, near Liverpool in the U.K., and one at the Thiaroye barracks on the outskirts of Dakar, Senegal. The Thiaroye uprising was by far the most famous and significant of these soldiers' protests. See Echenberg, " 'Morts pour la France,' " 375-76; and "Tragedy at Thiaroye: The Senegalese Soldiers' Uprising of 1944," in *African Labor History*, ed. Peter C.W. Gutkind, Robin Cohen, and Jean Copans (Beverly Hills, 1978), pp. 109-28.

22. See the opening statement of this essay.

23. Quoted in "La France et les cadres africains," 16.

24. Virginia Thompson and Richard Adloff, *French West Africa* (Stanford, 1957), pp. 227-29.

25. Fall was promoted to General of the Senegalese national army in December, 1960. *Paris-Dakar*, 2 December 1960.

26. *Souvenir et Devenir*, 8e année, 1971, 15.

27. Hippolyte-Victor Marceau, *Le Tirailleur Soudanais* (Paris, 1911), p. 3.

28. Ibid., pp. 2-3.

29. Ibid.

30. Ibid.

31. See for example Boisseson, *Le recrutement en AOF et AEF*, p. 5.

32. Charles Mangin, *La mission des Troupes Noires, compte-rendu fait devant le Comité de l'Afrique française* (Paris, 1911), pp. 1-37.

33. Myron Echenberg, "Les Migrations militaires en Afrique occidentale française, 1900-1945," *Canadian Journal of African Studies*, 14 (1980), 430-32.

34. "Etudes sur le recrutement en A.O.F. Répartition du contingent, résultats des sondages effectués dans les colonies du Groupe en 1922" (hereafter "Sondages-1922"), Cabinet militaire, Dakar, 5 July 1923, in AAOF, Dakar, 4D 72/81.

35. G. Wesley Johnson, Jr., *The Emergence of Black Politics in Senegal* (Stanford, 1971), p. 190.

36. General Doré, "Rapport sur le recrutement des troupes indigènes en A.O.F." (Paris), 6 May 1931, AAOF, 4D 42/28.
37. Governor-General's circular letter to all Lieutenants-Governor, Dakar, 17 September 1931, AAOF, 4D 143/100.
38. Echenberg, "Les migrations militaires," 14 (1980), 435-37.
39. Ibid., p. 437.
40. Jean Suret-Canale, *French Colonialism in Tropical Africa, 1900-1945* (London, 1971), pp. 443-45.
41. General Benoit, 1/7/29, AAOF, Dakar, 4D 42/28.
42. Ibid.
43. For more on military labour see Myron Echenberg and Jean Filipovich, "African Military Labour and the Building of the *Office du Niger* Installations, 1925-1950," *Journal of African History*, 27 (1986), 533-51.
44. In 1911, for example, the base pay for soldiers was 60 centimes a day, or 250 francs *per annum*, one half the pay of day labourers. Marceau, *Le Tirailleur Soudanais*, p. 37.
45. R. Lassalle-Séré, *Le Recrutement de l'armée noire* (Paris, 1929).
46. *Historique du 1er Régiment de Tirailleurs Sénégalais* (Saint-Louis, Senegal, n.d.).
47. Général Commandant Superieur Caudrelier to Lieutenant-Colonel Mangin, Dakar, 6 July 1910, Dakar, AAOF, 149/AP4.
48. Chef de Bataillon Chailley, "L'Africanisation des cadres de l'Armée," 1er trimestre, 1957, AAOF, Dakar, 4D 175/143.
49. Report of Lt. Col. Villard, Chef de Cabinet Militaire, to M. le Directeur-Général des Finances, Dakar, 12 September 1953, AAOF, Dakar, 4D 170/143.
50. Instruction of 10 September 1948, G.C.S. Magnan to all Governors, AAOF, Dakar, 4D 170/143.
51. Général Commandant Supérieur Borgnis Desbordes to Ministre de la France Outre-Mer, Dakar, 25 May 1949, in AAOF, Dakar, 4D 170/143, commenting on a request he had received from Mamadou Dia, then a Senator from Senegal in the French Parliament.
52. AAOF, Dakar, 4D 174/143 for statistics on EMPAs for both years.
53. General Nyo to Governor-General FWA, Dakar, 10 July 1952, in AAOF, Dakar, 4D 170/143.
54. AAOF, Dakar, 4D 170/143.
55. AAOF, Dakar, 4D 174/143.
56. Diakité studied at the Kati EET until 1951 when he became an NCO at the age of nineteen. He later underwent officers' training at Saint-Maixent. Colonel Traoré studied as a boy at the Kati EET, became an NCO and underwent officers' training at Fréjus in the 1950s. See *Souvenir et Devenir*, 8e année, n.s., no.15 (1971).
57. Thompson and Adloff, *French West Africa*, pp. 227f.
58. Ruth S. Morganthau, *Political Parties in French-Speaking West Africa* (Oxford, 1964), pp. 27f.
59. Thompson and Adloff, *French West Africa*, p. 228.
60. For a fuller treatment of this military ideology, see Echenberg, "'Morts pour la France,'" 371-78.
61. Echenberg, "Tragedy at Thiaroye," 109-28.
62. "Renseignements," Abidjan, 5 March 1947, in AAOF, Dakar, 2D 23/14.
63. Thompson and Adloff, *French West Africa*, p. 229.

64. Secretaire-Géneral de l'Office National to Chef de Cabinet Militaire, Dakar, 19 December 1952, AAOF, Dakar, 4D 172/143.

65. "Renseignements," Dakar, 30 May 1947, in AAOF, Dakar, 2D 23/14.

66. Report, Saint-Louis, July, 1946, in AAOF, Dakar, 2D 21/14.

67. Report, Niamey, February, 1946, in AAOF, Dakar, 2D 21/14.

68. Governor of Dahomey to Governor-General of FWA, Cotonou, 31 July 1946, in AAOF, Dakar, 2D 23/14.

69. "Renseignements," Bamako, 31 May 1947, in AAOF, Dakar, 2D 23/14; "Renseignements," Conakry, 10 April 1947, AAOF, Dakar, 2D 23/14.

70. "Renseignements," Abidjan, 5 March 1947, in AAOF, Dakar, 2D 23/14.

71. "Renseignements," Dakar, 23 September 1948, AAOF, Dakar, 4D 178/144.

72. Thompson and Adloff, *French West Africa*, p. 229.

73. Echenberg, "Les Migrations Militaires," 445-46.

74. The term literally means "fifteen years city" since "*dougou*" is the Mande suffix for city or town.

THE AMERICAN ARMY AND
THE INDIAN

BRUCE WHITE

On a rainy day in the early 1750s, according to a nineteenth-century New Hampshire historian, three young frontiersmen went hunting along the Asquamchumauke River near Moosilauke Mountain. Robert Rogers and John Stark of Dunbarton and Samuel Orr of nearby Goffstown spent the day conversing with three Indian visitors. Shortly before nightfall the Indians departed. Stark and Orr subsequently noticed that Rogers was missing, and their apprehensions mounted as the hour neared midnight. In the middle of the night, however, Rogers returned, and nonchalantly tossed the bloody scalps of three Indians into a corner of the cabin. Upon being reproved by Stark for murdering Indians in peacetime, Rogers replied: "Oh! Damn it! There'll be war before another year."[1]

Apocryphal or not, it was believable to nineteenth-century New Hampshire residents and, to many historians, at least illustrative of the attitudes of white frontiersmen and the transformation of the limited, formalized warfare of early modern Europe into one of total war in the wilderness of the New World. In *A Wilderness of Miseries: War and Warriors in Early America*, John Ferling concludes that the Indian wars were "total, a savage struggle for the survival not just of individuals but of entire cultures."[2] It was in such an environment, Alden Vaughan has written, that the transition from ethnocentric to racist attitudes took place in the minds of whites, and "the image of the Indian as vicious savage made deep inroads on the Anglo-American psyche."[3] Vaughan has also argued that much of the blame for the bloody conflict with the Indians in Virginia may be attributed to the fact that Virginia's leaders in the Company period were mainly "professional militarists," "hardened veterans" who had lived by the sword; "they were not reluctant to wield it against recalcitrant natives." New England's more peaceable early relations, he argues, can be explained in part by the fact that few of the early magistrates had had military experience. In later years, he concludes, New England was progressively militarized; he finds it significant for the outbreak of King Philip's War in 1675 that the governors of both

Massachusetts Bay and Plymouth were veterans of the English civil wars.[4]

The reality of the formation of racist attitudes and of an American military tradition was somewhat different. As the leader of ranger units composed of men of varying backgrounds and abilities but commonly engaged in harrowing adventures and bloody acts, Robert Rogers would not seem a candidate for harbouring any tender sentiments toward Indians. Yet, in both his *Concise Account of North America*, published in London in 1765, and in his tragedy *Ponteach*, which appeared anonymously the following year, he discussed Native Americans in a sympathetic manner. He wrote approvingly of many Indian qualities, such as personal dignity, patience, "natural good sense and ingenuity," imagination, unselfishness, and courage. His discussion of the role of religion, child-rearing, burial customs, dreams, and other aspects of Indian society were well-informed and show Rogers to have been an astute observer of the tribes with which he came into contact. Obviously, the impact of the frontier on Rogers was something other than progressive brutalization.[5]

John Smith, Miles Standish, and the other veterans of European wars hardly compiled an enviable record, but the least attractive of the military men, in my estimation, were those who became most integrated into the social, political, and economic structure of their colony. In Virginia, Sir George Yeardley's preoccupation with his tobacco interests, to the detriment of the colony's defences, contributed to the Indians' decision to attack in 1622. Following the uprising, Yeardley commanded expeditions to seize Indian corn, then sold it to starving colonists and pocketed the money.[6] In Massachusetts Bay, John Mason, a politically ambitious Puritan, was the most relentlessly hostile; he is perhaps best known for giving the order to set fire to Indian dwellings during the assault on the Pequot stronghold near the Mystic River in 1637, and to encircle the burning fort and kill anyone trying to escape. "We had formerly concluded," he wrote, "to destroy them by the Sword and save the Plunder." It was God's will that the Indians be burned and shot. "God was above them," and He "laughed his Enemies and the Enemies of his People to Scorn, making them as a fiery Oven . . . burning them up in the fire of his Wrath, and dunging the Ground with their Flesh: It was the Lord's Doings, and it is marvellous in our Eyes!"[7]

Frederick Fausz has persuasively argued that the two periods of full-scale warfare in early Virginia history were precipitated by the reaction of the Powhatan confederacy to the policy of forced acculturation following the reorganization of the Virginia Company in 1609. In Massachusetts Bay, King Philip's War was precipitated more by cultural than by land pressures. Philip was especially enraged by assimilation attempts and the cultural change reservation life was producing, as well as by Puritan attempts to impose a legal code requiring capital punishment for blasphemy and forced observation of the Puritan sabbath. In both wars, the depths of racial hatred were not reached until after the end of the conflicts when Indian military resistance was shattered. In Virginia, the shrillest calls for genocide came from officers of the Virginia Company in England. Virginia colonists still viewed Indians as formidable foes, and their subsequent actions showed their main concerns were security and adequate food supplies; they expediently cultivated some tribes as friends.[8] The ingredients of contempt and ridicule which convinced Virginians that Native Americans were a distinct and inferior race more properly belong to the aftermath of the 1644-46 uprising when the power of the Virginia confederacy was recognized as broken forever. In New England, supremacy over the Native tribes evoked the same feelings, and subsequent writing about Indians was more oriented toward discussing the Indian's "inherent nature."[9]

Although some American colonists had been professional soldiers, and though others became semi-professionals, especially in South Carolina because of the lack of an effective militia and the consequent necessity for economic inducements for military service, the citizen soldier was the norm. Those attracted to the military life, while they might have had militia training, received their real experience in the crucible of combat. The most successful, in my estimation, both in innovative, flexible leadership and in relating to Native Americans on their own terms and developing close relationships, were those whose ties with white society had been diminished by their identification with a frontier environment but whose continuing associations with white colonial society allowed them to escape the near-genocidal attitudes of many frontiersmen.

The pre-eminent figure in the seventeenth century was Benjamin Church. Often living on the New England frontier, Church grew more critical of Puritan Indian policies and, among his contemporaries, was uniquely able to relate to Indians on equal terms as human beings. He became the most effective military leader in King Philip's War, and his flexible and innovative employment of friendly Indians both reflected and deepened his insights. Few relationships during wartime have the poignancy of Church's account of his pursuit and capture of Annawon. After being assured by Church that he would attempt to ensure his safety, Annawon ritualistically presented tokens of submission; Church accepted in the prescribed Native manner, and the two warriors spent the night conversing about other battles. Church turned over his captives to the Plymouth authorities; later he saw Annawon's head displayed there on a pole.[10]

Despite the attachment of historians to the idea of "total war" during the colonial era and of the buckskin-clad, forest-wise Indian-fighting colonist, this was a short-lived era. As the frontier receded and France and Spain superseded the Indian as the main threat, expeditionary forces made up increasingly of those on the fringes of society became the norm, while the militia became increasingly a social organization. In addition, the militia tended to "unlearn" its seventeenth-century lessons, basing its training not on frontier experience, but on military manuals and on the formalized warfare of the European professional soldier. The continuing horrors of frontier conflict were very real, but localized. By the end of the seventeenth century most colonies and the majority of colonists were no longer fearful of massacre by Indians, and the frontier war was to become the American norm.

Although the militias surprised the British by their effectiveness in defending hearth and home, the trend toward a professional force would be institutionalized during the 1790s, when Federalists and Republicans debated the necessity for and wisdom of a standing army. The creation of a national military establishment has often been seen as a Federalist victory over those Jeffersonians who feared a standing army and were emotionally attached to the militia as the proper bulwark of the nation's defence. But the Jeffersonians agreed with the Federalists that a "frontier constabulary" was needed as an Indian-fighting force; the result was the creation of the nineteenth-century frontier army. Because of the experience of the preceding century, Republican leaders knew the militia could not provide the military arm to support their expansionist aims; the roots of this belief lay not in a colonial period of "total war," but one when fears for survival were transformed into a "frontier problem."

The army that was charged with making the west safe for the white emigrant was an increasingly professional one, and this is the key, it seems to me, to understanding Indian-white military relations during the nineteenth century. As William Skelton has observed, it was one of the first American institutions to organize along functional, bureaucratic lines, adumbrating developments in other professions. The emergence of the long-term military career, with West Point as the central institution, and the development of an intellectual tradition in which European professionalism became the model, conditioned military responses to frontier problems.[11] At West Point cadets learned how to fight wars with European powers, with little thought or instruction devoted to conflict with Indians on the frontier.

As professionals with careers to further, who accepted their subordination to civil authority and identified with the basic values and goals of their society, military men did not question the desirability of white hegemony in the west. Although many nineteenth-century Americans charged that the army was planning to exterminate the Indian by killing as many as possible and confining the remainder on reservations under military control until the race died out, the army acted mainly as an understaffed police force, and military comments on the capabilities and future of the Indian were actually quite conventional. When some officers, such as John Gibbon, spoke of the Indian's impending extinction, they meant, as did civilians, that his race was dying out by natural processes.[12] But, after making such statements, many officers went on to outline ways and means to civilize and assimilate the Indian; the word "extinction" really meant assimilation or amalgamation.

In the heat of the unconventional warfare with which they were faced, some military men called for the physical destruction of as many Indian opponents as possible, and some soldiers were progressively brutalized by the experience. "Exasperated," wrote Lieutenant Britton Davis, "our senses blunted by Indian atrocities, we hunted them and killed them as we hunted and killed wolves."[13] A kind of collective brutalization sometimes occurred when the military, frustrated by the failure of traditional tactics, deviated from its accustomed methods of operation. In the Florida wars against the Seminole, when the army turned to systematic destruction of Indian villages and food supplies, some officers talked bitterly about utter destruction of the tribe. In the Trans-Mississippi West, the strategy of winter warfare against Indian villages hardened military attitudes toward Native bands and families.

Skirmishes against Indians, however, were brief and intermittent; the majority of military men complained more about the boredom of frontier service than anything else. In addition, the military was involved in a large number of Indian activities other than combat, which reinforced the sense of being the agent of governmental policy in the west, as did the army's role in western exploration and economic development. Although it has become fashionable in recent years for historians to emphasize the humanitarianism of army officers, fostered by frontier experience, this was circumscribed by the army's roles. Most officers concluded that tribalism and communal living stood in the way of the desired acculturation of Native to white values of individualism, materialism, and the work ethic. A few officers, such as John Gregory Bourke, Washington Matthews, Garrick Mallery, and William Philo Clark were serious students of Indian culture, but this was a civilian trend as well, motivated most often by the desire to record Native culture before it was gone. Most military men who studied Indian ways were motivated also by the practical goal of finding and subduing Native war parties.

The overwhelming sentiment of army officers was that the Indian must be confined on reservations and eventually be given land in severalty. Aware of Indian resistance to this idea and also aware of the difficulties of farming arid or semi-arid land, some officers advocated stock raising, sheep herding, fishing, and other options, but to no greater extent than knowledgeable civilians, and military men were no more likely to call for the more reasonable alternative of tribal corporations on the reservation with decision-making powers.

Lacking formal doctrine which would precondition their responses, military men did learn from their cooperative as well as antagonistic experiences with Indians and from the operations of civilian agencies in the west, which they found wanting. The reports of officers throughout the century are filled with denunciations of fraud, graft, and corruption inside the Office of Indian Affairs as well as by western frontiersmen. The same arguments, however, as well as the same solutions could be found in the writings of eastern reformers such as Helen Hunt Jackson, although she would hardly have been comfortable had a contemporary pointed out the similarities. Neither would the army.

What did distinguish military men from eastern reformers, of course, was the conviction that force was an inevitable and probably desirable component in human relations, and that the Indian must be defeated militarily before he would respect whites and appreciate kindness and generosity. In addition, while most army officers believed that Indians should be Christianized and educated as a concomitant of their civilization, they were less inclined to press the issue for pragmatic reasons – churches and educators could and did cause problems for the army. Most officers argued against compulsory education and the removal of Indian children to eastern boarding schools to avoid involvement rather than for ideological reasons, although officers serving as Indian agents increasingly advocated compulsory education, but in reservation day schools. In advocating such schools they were often ahead of eastern reformers.

It was obvious to military men that in bringing white civilization to the west and in subduing and confining the Indian to reservations or on small allotments they were suppressing the martial qualities many officers admired. In their critique of the impact of reservation life, they could be quite insightful about the apathy and self-destructive qualities reservation life would induce. Even George Armstrong Custer, not noted for his intellect, subtlety, or prudence, concluded in his autobiography that the Indian would be "only a pale reflection of his former self" on the reservation.[14] Providing a legitimate outlet for the Indian's aggressive drives was a motivation for the formation of Indian troops and companies in the 1890s, although more powerful ones were facilitating the conquest of intractable tribes by exploiting differences and grievances, heading off possible restlessness and discontent on the reservations, and furthering assimilation and acculturation by diminishing tribal ties and encouraging individual initiative and action.

Differences from civilians in the appreciation of martial qualities was a matter of timing, however. Following the end of the Indian wars, Americans in general were quick to glamorize and romanticize Indian military leaders as freedom fighters for their way of life. Like other Americans, army officers rated Indian tribes on an ethnocentric scale, with those tribes with the most complex economies and society and the greatest degree of assimilation and acculturation at the top. Warlike Plains and Southwest tribes produced a mixed reaction, with their martial traits being admired but their motives and trustworthiness questioned. Lowest on the scale were the most primitive hunting and gathering bands of the Great Basin and California.

In the postbellum years, military men argued for the transfer of Indian affairs back to the War Department, and Congress came near to doing so on several occasions. A reasonable guess as to the consequences of transfer can be made by examining instances where the army controlled areas or tribes. The best aspects of military control were greater honesty, an increase in the quantity and quality of supplies, which actually reached their intended destination, and less wrenching pressures for assimilation and acculturation. The ending of divided authority might also have diminished the number of violent encounters resulting from rivalries, cross-purposes, and missed signals. The worst aspects were occasional brutalities and harsh regimentation, on the one hand, and a paternalism which did little or nothing to prepare Indians to live in a white world on the other, as was the case in the quarter-century of military control of Geronimo and his band of Chiricahua Apaches. Neglect was also a tragedy.

IF THE MILITARY experience for whites was a short period where settlers struggled for survival in a hostile environment, followed by the creation of a small, increasingly professional army fighting on a receding frontier, the experience for Native Americans was the reverse. What had been, before the "invasion of America" by Europeans, small-scale raids — to capture prisoners for "mourning war" purposes, to augment the power of the tribe, to acquire status and prestige, to chastise aggressive neighbours, to establish dominance over a weaker tribe, or as clashes over hunting or agricultural grounds — now became increasingly devastating. When whites first appeared, they were often viewed in terms of usefulness, as allies against other Indians or as a means of furthering the careers of individuals within the band or tribe.

The ultimate result, however, was a situation of "total war," in which Indians struggled for physical and cultural survival. Already weakened by the white man's diseases, Indians became increasingly dependent on white trading goods, and the scale of intertribal conflict intensified as Indians competed to supply furs, control hunting grounds and access to trade centres, conquer nearby tribes as buffers, and capture slaves to sell to the English. Increasing pressures from the colonizing powers for assimilation and acculturation and for land stimulated increasingly desperate military responses or flight, and pressures from retreating eastern tribes pushed more westerly ones onto the plains, exacerbating conflict there.

At the same time, despite initial attempts to exclude them, Indians were drawn into military service by whites, in mixed raiding parties, as auxiliaries in expeditions, as screens of friendly Indians, and as allied tribes in the wars among European powers. The use of Indians as scouts and auxiliaries was regularized following the intensification of Indian-white conflict during the Civil War, when the Army authorized the enlistment of up to 1,000 Indian scouts who were to receive the same pay and allowances as white soldiers. The culmination of this trend toward absorption of Indians into the army occurred in March 1891 when a general order was issued by the War Department authorizing one troop of Indians in each cavalry regiment and one company in each infantry regiment in units stationed west of the Mississippi River, with the exception of the black regiments.

To some extent, Indians' motivations for enlistment resembled those of whites; pay, bounties, rations, adventure, opportunities for travel, support of dependents and, in some cases, conscription all played their part. For Indians, military service facilitated self-defence and revenge on enemies, the acquisition of plunder, the attaining of status and prestige through military exploits, escape from the boredom of reservation life and farming activities, accommodation to white power, and improving relationships with dominant whites. Few historians have as yet analyzed the impact of military service on individual Indians or that of scouting or soldiering on bands and tribes. In an article on the military use of Indians in colonial New England, Richard Johnson reaches negative conclusions. Enlistment, Johnson finds, was a measure of increasing dependency on whites and of rootlessness and marginality. Indians who enlisted were doing so as a "personal strategy of survival," but the result, despite resulting personal ties and loyalties, deepened the gulf between the races. White fears increased, for "In seeking Indian aid," Johnson concludes, "the whites were requiring the Indian to be precisely what they most detested in him — savage, bloodthirsty, relentless, skulking, terrorizing and tearing the scalp from his opponents."[15]

In his monograph *Wolves for the Blue Soldiers*, Thomas Dunlay strikes a more positive note; military service, he argues, facilitated a necessary adjustment to living with whites, at least during the latter half of the nineteenth century. "The army," he concludes,

> gave many Indian men their first real introduction to the culture that would soon dominate their lives. By providing them with a mode of assimilation congenial to their inclinations, their talents, and their self-respect, scouting may have made that introduction a good deal less painful than any planned by either humanitarians or exterminationists.[16]

Neither Johnson nor Dunlay try to trace the subsequent lives of former scouts and soldiers upon their return or assess their impact on their bands and tribes, although the effects were considerable and lasting. While conducting interviews with Indian veterans in South Dakota, I found that conflict still exists between families whose ancestors served as scouts and those whose forebears fought them. There has also been little systematic investigation of Indian attitudes toward the military. Genuine friendships were formed, as well as bitterness and hatred forged in the heat of battle. In general, Indians were more negative when expressing contempt for military inefficiency and indecision than in resentment at military brutalities; they found honesty, trustworthiness, and the clarity of military expectations and demands to be the most praiseworthy traits of white military men, as well as leadership qualities, courage, and endurance. Commenting about Lieutenant John Bullis, one of his former Seminole scouts concluded:

> Lieutenant Bullis was the only officer ever did stay the longest with us. That fella suffer jest like we all did out in de woods. He was a good man. He was a Injun fighter. He was tuff. He didn't care how big a bunch dey was, he went into 'em everytime, but he look after his men. His men was on equality, too. He didn't stan' back and say, "Go yonder"; he would say, "Come on, Boys, let's go get 'em."[17]

One Apache concluded about a military agent that "When Major Randall was here we were all happy; when he promised a thing he did it; when he said a word he meant it; but all that he did was for our own good and we believed in him and we think of him yet." Another told George Crook: "When you were here, whenever you said a thing we knew that it was true, and we kept it in our minds."[18] Indians hardly considered the army their best friend, but, faced with unpalatable alternatives, they sometimes found soldiers less unpalatable than

eastern reformers, governmental representatives, and western frontiersmen.

The early 1890s were a watershed in the relationship between
the Indian and the army. For the former, military resistance was no
longer an option in dealing with the white presence. For the latter,
the failure of the experiment with Indian troops and companies as
integral parts of the regular army convinced the army that Indians
should be assimilated as individuals as thoroughly as possible into
white units. Although the military had permitted considerable flexibil-
ity when using Indians as scouts, its rigidity when the Indian was one
of its own, especially in peacetime, produced cultural shock and
alienation on the part of Indians and disillusionment for the military.
By 1894 Indian soldiers were seizing on any pretext for an early discharge; one group requested discharge because they were not receiv-
ing as many pies and cakes as the other companies, and in another
instance an Indian bugler claimed that blowing his bugle made him
chronically ill.[19]

Proposals for Indian units during the Spanish-American War
were rejected, and on the eve of World War I the Chief of the War
College Division of the General Staff stated that anything that
"inclines them to think in Indian terms only and to hold themselves
as a class apart with interests distinct from those of other citizens is
undesirable and contrary to the object of the institution and to the
best interests of the United States."[20] This policy, which became a
permanent one, contrasted sharply with the military policy of strict
segregation of blacks. This segregation not only continued, but racial
antipathies toward blacks intensified, and previous attempts at equal
military justice deteriorated as the climate of opinion within the army
reflected the heightened racism of the civilian world.

THE CENTURIES OF Indian warfare had left an enduring impact on
the military mind, however. In the Philippine Islands, attitudes
toward the insurgents and methods of fighting were conditioned by
the army's experiences with Indians. In the navy, submarine service
was sometimes promoted as a chance to adopt Indian methods of
warfare.[21] Although ultimately rejecting concepts of guerrilla warfare, the army continued to think of its Indian soldiers as possessing
the same skills as their plains ancestors. A questionnaire drawn up
during World War I and distributed by the Historical Section of the
General Staff to over 1,500 units of the American Expeditionary
Forces elicited what it sought — that Indian soldiers displayed courage, endurance, keenness of sense, dexterity at crawling, crouching,
and running, stealth of movement, stoicism, a good sense of direction
and orientation (especially at night in the woods), good use of cover

and camouflage, and a native ability to draw sketches and to recognize natural landmarks. In addition, it was argued, Indians liked the excitement of patrols and raids, and their skin did not reflect moonlight or the glare of flares at night. Captured documents indicate the Germans had their own stereotypes; they worried about the savagery and barbarism of the wild Indian.[22] In both world wars Indians were often placed in inordinately dangerous positions because of supposed abilities, sometimes with fatal consequences.

The War Department policy of avoiding separate Indian units continued during World War II, although the army's main concern was now efficiency. The officers who remembered the experiment of the 1890s were gone from the service, and new commanders were more concerned about finding qualified specialists for the more mechanized, complex modern army. Also, the army worried that additional resources and special training would be needed, as it was apparent that many of the requests for separate units were motivated by the special difficulties Indians would have in regular units because of language difficulties and cultural shock. In World War I almost one-fourth of all draftees had initially been classified as illiterate or non-English-speaking, and the army was anxious to avoid the development battalions established during 1917 and 1918, as well as the difficulties of integrating separately trained units into larger organizations.

Ultimately, the army's manpower needs were too great to maintain its standard of rejecting inductees who lacked the equivalent of a fourth grade education, as determined by army tests, and, in August 1942, units were authorized at reception centres to teach illiterates and the poorly educated the minimum reading ability and vocabulary needed for military training. The army was mainly concerned about the problems of black soldiers, but several memoranda show that Indian soldiers were recruited as instructors to train non-English-speaking Indians, particularly Navajos. Many were sent home, but language difficulties continued to plague other Indians who were inducted. In one instance the story had an unusual ending. Andrew Begay, who had been seriously wounded in the Pacific, assumed that when he was discharged from an army hospital he was free to return home. Apprehended by the military for being AWOL, Begay was finally discharged. After the war, he received an invitation to appear on Ralph Edwards' CBS program, "This Is Your Life." Confronted by a stream of former friends and acquaintances, and given a saddle blanket and ten lambs, Begay must have been more confused by "This Is Your Life" than by the military.[23]

Problems encountered by Indian soldiers were usually lessened if service was in a largely Indian unit, which existed in both wars in a *de facto* manner in the southwest and in some northern plains areas. While merely tolerating such units, the army showed considerable enthusiasm about using Indians as communications specialists, particularly as telephone operators speaking in Native languages. In World War I the Germans apparently failed to decipher Choctaw, and in the Second World War army use of Indians as Native-speaking communications specialists was actually greater than the more widely publicized Marine use of Navajos as "code talkers" in the South Pacific. Despite the concerns of Army Intelligence that German students of anthropology in the United States during the interwar years might have been spies learning Indian languages, as might Japanese-Americans employed by the Office of Indian Affairs, and about the security of such transmissions, the military used Native speakers on the Air Operational Voice Circuit in the South Pacific, as well as in North Africa, Italy, and France. Among the first paratroopers to be dropped into France on June 6, 1944, were thirteen Yaqui and Cherokee members of an engineer demolition unit, known in training as "the Filthy Thirteen," who jumped in full war paint.[24]

When Indians were used as communications specialists, the lack of military terms in Indian languages presented a problem, which was partially solved by improvisation; in the 32nd Division, for example, a tank became a turtle and airplanes became various kinds of insects. On one occasion the Navajo language proved too difficult for the army itself. Army censors were unable to read four letters from Private William Peshlakai, mailed from Australia, so they were sent to the Smithsonian Institution for translation. Surprisingly, no one at the Smithsonian could read Navajo, so they were forwarded to Window Rock, Arizona, where William Morgan of the Navajo Service translated them and returned them to Washington. The Peshlakai family later received the letters in English translation, which they were unable to read.[25]

The most negative aspect of War Department influence on Indian tribes and reservations was military appropriation of Indian land for airports, bombing and aerial gunnery ranges, shore batteries and other defence installations on the west coast, and cantonments and rights of way in various parts of the country. In all, more than 875,000 acres were used for war purposes, and some of it was never returned. In any event, the dislocations of families were often permanent, far outweighing the employment given Navajos and other Indians in wartime ordnance depots. The most drastic changes were wrought in Alaska, where military activities brought about abrupt changes of life for Aleuts, Inuit, and Athabascan Indians. The army provided temporary employment on construction projects, but the old hunting and trapping occupations were given up. In many of the villages war workers and servicemen demoralized the Natives by introducing liquor, stealing or destroying Native property, slaughtering game, and seducing or raping Native women. One incident, however, was partial atonement. In Nome, a white army sergeant invited a mixed-blood Inuit woman to the movies; they were forced by the police to leave, however, for they were sitting on the side of the theatre for whites only. The sergeant publicized the incident in the army paper at the Nome base, resulting in strong support for the woman for the annual Queen of Nome. She was elected.[26]

THE FEW STUDIES which have thus far appeared on Indian reactions to service in the two world wars have overemphasized Native enthusiasm, probably because they have taken self-serving contemporary accounts too literally. In both wars confusion about eligibility for the draft was greater than actual resistance, although in World War I there was resistance among the Gosiute, Shoshone, Ute, Navajo, and Mission Indians, and in World War II among the Papago, Hopi, Zuni, Ute, and Seminole. In most cases resisting bands were those most isolated from tribal and white influences, or reacting to ongoing factional disputes.

In World War I, there were difficulties of communication regarding the technicalities of draft procedures, and in determining which Indians were citizens and thus subject to the draft; anyone who has tried to explain the citizenship status of Indians in 1917 to students can sympathize with this problem. There were also assertions, however, of the separate status of Indian nations and of the desirability of participating in a "white man's war." The Senecas and Onondagas declared war on Germany separately, and many Indian parents questioned the desirability of military service. Shortly before American entry into World War II, several cases came before the courts in which the defendant argued that the Selective Service Act of 1940 violated treaties between the tribe and the United States government. In *Ex Parte Green* in New York and in *Totus, et al., v. the United States* in the state of Washington, however, courts ruled that this act of Congress superseded previous Indian treaties.[27] Some individual Indians and a few bands argued that military service should be voluntary and continental; others charged that Selective Service was an insult to their patriotism, or that the country should atone for its manifestly unfair treatment of their race by giving them special consideration now.

To some extent there was a generational difference, with older Indians, a number of them veterans of the First World War and a few of the Spanish-American War, more likely to assume that the voluntary principle should apply; they were also more likely to argue that only the homeland should be defended. On the other hand, in the Yakima case it was the younger, draft-age Indians who pressed the lawsuit; as the minutes of the tribal council show, older tribal members strongly opposed it.[28] This was also true in some instances in New York, where younger Indians assumed tribal leadership and led the resistance.

The Japanese attack on Pearl Harbor unified red as well as white America. Even before American entry into the war, the Navajo Tribal Council had passed a resolution reaffirming their loyalty and patriotism. Their nicknames for Hitler (mustache smeller) and for Mussolini (gourd-chin) were widely publicized, as were the patriotism and enthusiasm of Indian soldiers; wartime reservation efforts and activities, such as increased food production, scrap collections, civil defense activities, patriotic rallies, clubs and associations; and the rifle brigade formed by forty Chippewa women to capture invading enemy parachutists. During the war more than $17,000,000 in tribal funds was spent on war bonds, a figure that Commissioner of Indian Affairs John Collier helped to achieve, however, by refusing approval of per capita distributions of tribal funds when requested "because of the lack of adequate justification and the greater service which such moneys can be to the Government."[29]

In both wars, but particularly in World War II, warrior societies were revitalized, as were tribal ceremonials and rituals, especially protective ceremonials performed before departure, war dances and the dedication of other dances to those in service, and reintegrating ceremonies upon the return of a soldier, such as the Navajo Blessing Way and the Enemy Way. In 1942, at Standing Rock Reservation, the Sioux performed their first pre-battle sun dance of the twentieth century to pray for the defeat of the Axis and for the safe return of more than 2,000 Sioux servicemen. Although the government prohibited the passing of rawhide thongs through the flesh, the memories were still there. Henry One-Bull, now 97 years old, still bore the scars from the ceremonial dance before the Battle of the Little Big Horn.[30] Such ceremonies, particularly in their integration of the American flag and other patriotic and military symbols, stimulated a deeply felt sense of patriotism to the nation; the celebration of warrior traditions was a bridge for Indians from fighting a government to supporting it.

The experiences and reactions of the approximately 25,000 Indian men and 350 Indian women who served in the army from July 1940 to December 1945 varied widely. For some it was an exhilarating experience. "The army life is great," wrote one Indian from Montana in 1942, "both wholesome and clean. . . . I am proud to be a member of the greatest army on God's earth and I'll gladly die in the service. I am proud of my reservation for the representation it has in the United States Army. We'll show those Japs where to head in, and that goes for Hitler, too."[31] Others found their military service produced only frustrations and resentments. Many who wanted to volunteer were never inducted, having been rejected for illiteracy, physical health or psychiatric reasons. Rejection rates in all categories were high for Native Americans, although psychiatric rejections resulted more from the cultural shock of the tests than indicative of mental disorders.

During the nineteenth century such factors as the short military haircut, inoculations, and contact with dead bodies or being in a building where a death had taken place had violated Native American mores and produced discontent. During World War II these only occasionally surfaced. Many Indians carried sacred meal or amulets into combat, but the general tendency was toward accepting military practices while in the army, even if the old ways persisted and were blended with the new upon return home. Some Indians complained of discrimination by their fellow soldiers or commanders, although the paternalism of being called "chief" or being asked to "give us a war whoop" was a more common problem. Some Indians complained of being refused service in public establishments, particularly alcohol in southwestern bars. Denying liquor to an Indian who was in any way a ward of the government was required by federal law, but since the army did not discriminate against Indians at post exchanges and the bartenders in the middle west and east paid little attention to the law, liquor was widely available to Indian soldiers. Following the war, under pressure from Indian veterans, Congress repealed the federal Indian liquor laws over the protests of many tribal leaders, leaving the question up to individual states for off-reservation communities and to tribal councils for reservation lands.

Other experiences frequently commented on included the homogenizing experience of wearing army clothing, the unbelievable abundance of food, clothing and equipment, the shock of discovery that many whites were crude and illiterate, and the desirability of disassociating oneself from blacks and Mexican-Americans. On the east coast, where there were many mixed-blood Indians, they rebelled at being classified as black by local boards, despite the military position that all inductees other than blacks should be classified as white. The single most important experience, other than the traumatizing shock of combat, was travel — exposure to new attitudes and ways of life which differed widely from the reservation experience.

In the postwar period veterans were a force for change, despite the manifold problems many faced upon return — combat fatigue, alcoholism, readjustment to reservation life, difficult relationships with tribal and clan leaders, difficulties in obtaining loans because banks and other lending institutions would not accept the risk on tribal lands and trust allotments, broken homes and marriages, and massive unemployment. On a few reservations, such as the Zuni, which had had a long history of resisting white influences and among whom warfare had never been an important feature of life, the veterans were forced to conform to pre-existing patterns or leave. In one instance a Zuni mother would not even touch her returning son until he had been through purification ceremonies.[32] In most tribes, however, veterans pushed for modernization, emerged as tribal leaders, and participated in emerging Native American activist organizations. In both Arizona and New Mexico, the plaintiffs in the 1948 cases which gave Indians the vote were veterans.

In some instances veterans represented a third force, challenging both the authority of traditional tribal leaders and the progressives who cooperated with and depended on the Bureau of Indian Affairs. In many cases there is a pattern of individual upward mobility following the war, particularly for veterans of the Women's Army Corps, many of whom were already acquainted with Anglo culture before the war as teachers or employees of the Bureau of Indian Affairs, and whose military service enhanced their prospects. Wilma Victor, a Choctaw, was a teacher on the Navajo reservation before she enlisted in the Women's Army Corps, became an officer, served in military intelligence and army administration, and in 1971 became special assistant to Secretary of the Interior Rogers Morton.[33]

The war accelerated the movement of veterans into urban areas, as it did for other Indians, whether through dissatisfaction with reservation life and conditions or acquaintance with urban areas through wartime experience. The returning veterans themselves, of course, created economic problems and strained reservation resources, which encouraged individual migration or acceptance of the government's relocation program. Having had wartime experience outside the reservation, veterans had a better chance of succeeding in urban areas than other Indians. There is fragmentary evidence that veterans of the Korean War and the war in Vietnam were more likely than Second World War veterans to return to the reservation, sometimes after spending time in the city. A study of the return of relocatees to the Navajo reservation also found that some Navajos already living in urban areas returned to the reservation because military service had dislocated them from urban life.[34] Veterans now travel frequently between the reservation and the city, as do other Indians.

Although few studies of the Korean and Vietnam eras have yet appeared, there is obviously a continuing strain of patriotism in many Indian communities, stemming from the influence of ceremonies honouring veterans and the prestige which personal bravery and courage displayed in military service still commands. Tom Holm has argued that these factors eased the readjustment of many Indian veterans of Vietnam and purged them of post-traumatic stress disorder, which was heightened in all veterans because of rejection by the nation upon their return.[35] In addition, Harold Barse of the Oklahoma City veterans' centre and others have promoted annual Veterans' Day intertribal powwows, revitalized traditional warriors' dances such as the Kiowa Gourd Dance, and organized veterans' associations.

Such cathartic activities have been important in the reintegration of Vietnam veterans, although reintegrating ceremonialism takes place mainly on the larger and more traditional reservations. In South Dakota the Missouri River is almost a dividing line; veterans living east of the river, where there are few reservation areas and Indians are more assimilated into white society, are both more critical of the war and less likely to have volunteered for service in it. Indian veterans, however, often see no contradiction between their criticism of the war and their continued high regard for military service, an attitude shared by many Indians. Where ceremonies take place, surviving veterans of all wars are honoured, which creates a bond between the generations.

Some veterans, however, were quite frustrated because their parents, particularly their fathers, did not view the war as immoral and unjust. By the late 1960s strain was evident in Indian as well as white America, as some young Indians participated in anti-war activities, a few tribes and bands condemned the war, and those at home grieved as the toll of killed and maimed mounted. "I hate your Uncle Sam," one Chippewa/Flathead woman asserted. "He can take his dollar and shove it down his throat . . . they take my grandchildren, they'll always take the grandchildren, they'll take all the finest, the best, the nicest of the young men off the reservation."[36] A Kiowa/Apache woman was embittered when all agencies refused a loan to install an indoor bathroom so that her son, a Vietnam amputee, would not have to be carried to the outhouse.[37] "Well, being Indian," remarked an Oglala Sioux veteran, "there's no connection in fighting for the Army over in another country. Let alone they are the same army that almost wiped out most of the Indians at Wounded Knee. . . . When I look at it, being an Indian, I shouldn't even have gone in the Army. And I don't even respect the guy that would honor fighting for the white man's problems."[38]

As the bitter feelings of a difficult era fade, the relationship between the Indian and the military will continue. For both sides

there has been continuity – for the army, the continuity of assimilationist attitudes and practices, first as a solution to the "Indian problem," in the days of mutual violence, then as a policy of military
recruitment in the twentieth century. In this, as in most matters, the
military has reflected the sentiments and goals of American society.
For Native Americans, there has been the continuous struggle to protect their way of life from the encroachment of whites, first physically
and then culturally. There are ironies here, however. In its struggle
with Indians, the army had to rely on their cultural traits and to some
extent reinforce them, utilizing the military skills of scouts, auxiliaries and soldiers. For Indians, the symbols of the nation they fought
have been important in preserving Native culture and society in the
face of assimilationist and acculturationist pressures.

The cultural distinctiveness of Indian America is still apparent.
At a Native meeting in South Dakota in 1968, the chairman told of a
letter from an Indian, on his third tour in Vietnam, whose unit had
been ordered to occupy a hill. On the way to the objective he
dreamed that he had climbed the hill and that he had noticed that one
section of the jungle was a different shade of green. On the following
day, when they reached the objective, the mismatched patch of
jungle was exactly as he had dreamed. When they arrived at the spot
he had reached in his dream, he persuaded his commander to have
the unit open fire. All the Viet Cong snipers waiting in ambush were
killed.[39]

Notes

1. William Little, *The History of Weare, New Hampshire, 1735-1888* (Lowell, Mass., 1888), p. 59.
2. John E. Ferling, *A Wilderness of Miseries: War and Warriors in Early America* (Westport, Conn., 1980), pp. 53-54.
3. Alden T. Vaughan, "From White Man to Redskin: Changing Anglo-American Perceptions of the American Indian," *American Historical Review* 87 (1982), 941.
4. Alden T. Vaughan, *New England Frontier: Puritans and Indians, 1620-1675*, rev. ed. (New York and London, 1979), p. xl.
5. The standard biography of Rogers is John R. Cuneo, *Robert Rogers of the Rangers* (New York, 1959). See also the long introductory essay by Allan Nevins in *Ponteach: Or the Savages of America* (New York, 1971). The dis-cussion of Indians in *A Concise Account of North America* (London, 1765) is on pp. 205-53.
6. J. Frederick Fausz, "The Powhatan Uprising of 1622: A Historical Study of Ethnocentrism and Cultural Conflict" (Ph.D. diss., College of William and Mary, 1977), pp. 318-19, 476-78.
7. John Mason, "A Brief History of the Pequot War," in *History of the Pequot War: the Contemporary Accounts of Mason, Underhill, Vincent and Gar-dener*, ed. Charles Orr (Cleveland, 1987), pp. 28, 30, and 35.
8. Susan Myra Kingsbury, ed., *The Records of the Virginia Company of Lon-

don, III, pp. 614, 671-72; Karen Ordahl Kupperman, *Settling with the Indians: The Meeting of English and Indian Cultures in America, 1580-1640* (Totowa, New Jersey, 1980), pp. 176-82; Fausz, "The Powhatan Uprising of 1622," pp. 446-60.

9. William John Burton, "Hellish Fiends and Brutish Men: Amerindian-Euroamerican Interaction in Southern New England, an Interdisciplinary Analysis, 1600-1750" (Ph.D. diss., Kent State University, 1976), pp. 296-302.

10. Benjamin Church, "Entertaining Passages Relating to Philip's War," in *So Dreadful a Judgment: Puritan Responses to King Philip's War, 1676-1677,* ed. Richard Slotkin and James K. Folsom (Middletown, Conn., 1978), pp. 453-62.

11. William B. Skelton, "Professionalization in the U.S. Army Officer Corps During the Age of Jackson," *Armed Forces and Society* 1 (1975), 465-66.

12. John Gibbon, "Our Indian Question," *Journal of the Military Service Institution* 2 (1881), 101-20.

13. Britton Davis, *The Truth About Geronimo,* ed. Milo Milton Quaife (Chicago, 1951), p. 77.

14. George Armstrong Custer, *My Life on the Plains; or, Personal Experiences with Indians,* new ed. (Norman, Oklahoma, 1962), pp. 13-21.

15. Richard R. Johnson, "The Search for a Usable Indian: An Aspect of the Defense of Colonial New England," *Journal of American History* 64 (1977), 649-50.

16. Thomas W. Dunlay, *Wolves for the Blue Soldiers: Indian Scouts and Auxiliaries with the United States Army, 1860-90* (Lincoln, Nebraska, 1982), p. 198.

17. Grady E. McCright, "John Bullis," *True West* 28 (October 1981), 13.

18. John G. Bourke, *On the Border With Crook* (Lincoln and London, 1971), p. 436.

19. "Report of an Inspection of Fort Apache, Arizona . . . ," 27 April 1893, Record Group 159, Records of the Inspector General's Office, 23 I 1893; "Report of an Inspection . . . of the Post of Fort Keogh, Montana . . . ," 28 Sept. 1892, ibid., 26 K 1892, National Archives of the United States (hereafter N.A.U.S.).

20. M.M. Macomb, "Memorandum for the Chief of Staff," 30 July 1915, Record Group 94, Records of the Adjutant General's Office, 1865-1917, 2250014, N.A.U.S.

21. Thomas C. Leonard, *Above the Battle: War-Making in America From Appomattox to Versailles* (New York, 1978), p. 103.

22. The original directive and replies are in the Record Group 120, Records of the American Expeditionary Forces, 1917-1923, General Headquarters, Historical Section, Boxes 3471-3473, N.A.U.S.

23. *Arizona Republic,* 24 May 1950, p. 29.

24. *Talks,* July 1944, p. 2, discussed in A. Marjorie Taylor, comp., *The Language of World War II* (New York, 1948), pp. 80-81.

25. J.M. Stewart to the Office of Indian Affairs, 13 October 1943, Box 477, Navajo Agency File, National Defense Program — Military Service Reports, WWII (hereinafter cited as NDP-MSR, WWII), Record Group 75, Records of the Bureau of Indian Affairs, N.A.U.S.

26. Muktuk Marston, *Men of the Tundra: Eskimos at War* (New York, 1969), pp. 134-37.

27. *Ex Parte Green*, 123F 2d 862 (1941); *Totus, et al., v. United States*, 39 Fed. Supp 7 (E.D. Wash., 1941).
28. "Meeting of the Yakima Tribal Council," 28 January 1941, Box 478, Yakima Agency File, NDP-MSR, WWI, Record Group 75, Records of the Bureau of Indian Affairs, N.A.U.S.
29. John Collier, "The Indian and the War," Box 475, Department Orders File, NDP-MSR, WWII, Record Group 75, N.A.U.S.
30. *Indians At Work*, 10 (July-September 1942), p. 18.
31. *Community News*, Fort Belknap Agency III (March 1942), p. 8.
32. John Adair and Evon Vogt, "Navajo and Zuni Veterans: A Study of Contrasting Modes of Culture Change," *American Anthropologist* 51 (1949), 550. See also John Joseph Adair, "A Study of Culture Resistance: The Veterans of World War II at Zuni Pueblo" (Ph.D. diss., University of New Mexico, 1948).
33. Marion E. Gridley, *American Indian Women* (New York, 1974), pp. 154-61.
34. Navajo Agency, *Navajo Yearbook*, Report No. 7 (Window Rock, Arizona, 1957), p. 321.
35. Tom Holm, "Culture, Ceremonialism, and Stress: American Indian Veterans and the Vietnam War," *Armed Forces & Society* 12 (1986), 237-51.
36. Doris Duke Oral History Collection, University of South Dakota, Vermillion, South Dakota.
37. Interview with Irene Poolaw, T-605-A, Doris Duke Oral History Collection, Western History Collections, University of Oklahoma, Norman, Oklahoma.
38. Interview with Russell Adams, 7 May 1972, Interview # 821, Doris Duke Oral History Collection, University of South Dakota.
39. Tape 082, Doris Duke Oral History Collection, University of South Dakota.

RACE AND THE AMERICAN MILITARY: PAST AND PRESENT

EDWIN DORN*

THIS PAPER HAS three purposes. The first is to summarize the history of black involvement in the United States armed forces. Blacks have gone through periods of total rejection, periods of grudging and limited acceptance, and recently a period of extensive participation. Generally speaking, their experiences with the armed forces have reflected their experiences in the larger society.

The second purpose is to describe statistically the role black Americans play in the contemporary armed forces. Like other English-speaking industrialized nations, the United States now uses economic incentives rather than conscription to meet its military personnel needs. In the period since the all-volunteer force was established in 1973, the racial composition of the American military has changed dramatically. Today, blacks make up about 20 percent of all active duty military personnel, which means that they are overrepresented in comparison to their 12 percent representation in the overall population. About 400,000 blacks are on active duty, making the military a major provider of employment, training, and career opportunities. On the other hand, blacks would comprise a large percentage of American casualties in a major conventional conflict.

My third purpose is to explore some of the controversies that have been raised by the changing racial composition of the military. We hear suggestions that a heavily black force does not "represent" the society it is supposed to defend. We hear speculation that black soldiers may prove to be unreliable in certain military situations. We hear complaints that young black men and women actually are being "forced" by economic necessity to join the armed forces.

Underlying the specific points of controversy is a larger question about race. We all know that race is an important feature of American life. But _how_ it matters has changed significantly during the past

* The Joint Center for Political and Economic Studies' clearinghouse on military affairs is funded by a grant from the Ford Foundation, whose support is gratefully acknowledged. The views expressed here are solely those of the author.

two or three decades. As a society, the United States is in a curious position, somewhere between an overtly racist past and a future that many people hope will be colour-blind.

Many of our arguments about politics and public policy reflect different perceptions of where we are along that continuum. Thus, figuring out when and how race matters is not merely an academic exercise. It has important ramifications for behaviour, including the behaviour of the people who shape American military policy. As several studies in this volume suggest, racial and ethnic considerations also affect the armed forces of a number of other nations.

Historical Overview

THE UNITED STATES has wrestled with a profound dilemma throughout its 200-year history. The nation was founded on the conviction, expressed in the Declaration of Independence of 1776, "that all Men are created equal, that they are endowed by their Creator with certain unalienable Rights, that among these are Life, Liberty, and the Pursuit of Happiness." The nation's basic political document, the Constitution, established an elaborate system of structures and procedures designed to ensure that no group, region or economic interest would be able to dictate public affairs.

For most of its history, however, the United States has been racist in both law and custom. I mean "racist" in the strict sense of the term: people were assigned by birth to membership in one or another racial group, and members of one group enjoyed rights and privileges that members of the other group were denied. In the Supreme Court's famous 1857 *Dred Scott* decision, Chief Justice Taney succinctly described the situation that existed prior to the Civil War. He wrote that blacks "had for more than a century before been regarded as beings of an inferior race, and altogether unfit to associate with the white race, either in social or political relations, and so far inferior that they had no rights which the white man was bound to respect. . . . [T]he Negro might justly and lawfully be reduced to slavery for his benefit."[1]

The nation's founders recognized the contradiction between their stated ideals and the racist regime they created. Indeed, reconciling that contradiction occupied a great deal of time when representatives of the original 13 colonies gathered in Philadelphia in 1787 to draft the Constitution. One point of dispute was the amount of power — voting strength — each state would have in the Congress. The framers agreed to establish a bicameral legislature. Each state would have equal representation in the Senate, while seats in the House of Representatives would be apportioned according to the population of each state.

This set off a conflict between the states that had large numbers of slaves and those that did not — essentially a conflict between North and South. The northeastern states and the southern states were roughly equal in total population, about 1.9 million people in each region. But the northeastern states had only about 67,000 blacks, while more than a third of the South's population (690,000) was black.[2] Obviously, the South wanted to count the blacks for purposes of apportioning seats in the House. Northern delegates responded that slaves should be considered property for purposes of allocating taxes among the states. A compromise was struck: a black would count as three-fifths of a person.

James Madison, who represented Virginia at the Constitutional Convention and later served as the nation's fourth President, explained the compromise this way: it is not true, he argued, that slaves are regarded solely as property. Rather, the slaves were "considered by our laws, in some respects, as persons, and in other respects as property."[3] Madison wrote that in one of a series of articles that he, Alexander Hamilton, and John Jay published to generate support for the Constitution, which needed ratifying. If one reads the explanation carefully, one begins to sense that Madison's collaborators, who were from New York, did not go along. All 86 of their articles, which originally appeared in the newspapers of New York between the fall of 1787 and the spring of 1788 and later were published as *The Federalist Papers*, bear the pen name Publius. However, Madison did not put his explanation of the three-fifths compromise in Publius's voice. Rather, he put quotation marks around much of the article and attributed it to "one of our southern brethren."

The Constitution that Madison helped to write and ratify established the nation's basic political structure. But it also codified the nation's racial policy. During the colonial period the status of blacks, slave and free, varied greatly from colony to colony as the settlers sought to adapt British common law to circumstances in the New World. There were huge arguments over the very existence of slavery and extensive legal disputes over the status of blacks *vis-à-vis* white indentured servants.[4] With the Constitution, the new nation began to establish a strict and consistent division between blacks and whites, one that would endure for many decades.

The political tensions, competing economic interests, and moral contradictions that the founders sought to reconcile during the Constitutional Convention finally came to a head in 1861, when the southern states seceded from the Union and brought on the Civil War. In its aftermath the triumphant North enacted the Thirteenth, Fourteenth, and Fifteenth Amendments to the Constitution. These outlawed slavery, established in principle that blacks were citizens, and guaranteed all citizens "equal protection of the laws."

During the period of Reconstruction, which lasted from the end of the Civil War to the late 1870s, a number of steps were taken to improve the status of blacks. A Freedman's Bureau was established to resettle the recently liberated slaves; schools were established for blacks in the South; and blacks teamed up with settlers from the North (the "carpetbaggers") to dominate politics in parts of the South. Several blacks were elected to Congress; one served briefly as governor of Louisiana.

Unfortunately, the measures needed to turn the former slaves into whole, free, economically viable citizens were not taken. A proposal to confiscate former slaveowners' land and give it to the freemen in the form of reparations — the "forty acres and a mule" scheme — was vetoed by President Abraham Lincoln's successor, Andrew Johnson.

The beginning of the end of Reconstruction occurred in 1876. In exchange for southern support, presidential candidate Rutherford B. Hayes essentially promised not to enforce the laws intended to protect blacks' rights. Over the next few years state after state in the South enacted laws to re-establish the pattern of racial dominance that had existed prior to the Civil War. "Jim Crow" laws ensured strict segregation; "grandfather clauses" disenfranchised blacks and re-enfranchised their former masters; some states forbade blacks' entering certain professions and businesses.

The federal government accepted and sometimes encouraged these retrenchments. Evidence of the changing mood is provided by two Supreme Court cases. In the *Slaughter-House* cases of 1873, Justice Miller wrote eloquently of the nation's concern for "the freedom of the slave race, the security and firm establishment of that freedom, and the protection of the newly-made freeman and citizen from the oppressions of those who had formerly exercised unlimited dominion over him."[5] Just two decades later, the Supreme Court would approve resurgent racism by writing that "If one race be superior to the other socially, the Constitution of the United States cannot put them on the same plane. . . ."[6]

The legal retrenchments were buttressed by a virulent racist ideology and by raw physical intimidation. During the first decade of the twentieth century, blacks were being lynched in the South at a rate of about one hundred a year.[7] Until well into the twentieth century, blacks in the South lived under what could best be described as a regime of racial tyranny. Unless one can grasp the nature of that situation, unless one can understand the degree to which blacks continued to have few rights that whites were bound to respect, one has trouble appreciating the profound significance of what has happened during the past two or three decades.

Incidentally, the conditions under which blacks lived in the South were different only in degree from the practices that prevailed elsewhere in the nation. Discrimination and segregation were common throughout the United States. What distinguished the South were the rigidity of the practices and the violence used to enforce them. Nor are blacks the only group that has experienced discrimination in the United States. American Indians, Orientals, and white ethnics all have been subjected to one or another form of prejudice, and each group developed distinctive patterns of coping with the experience. What distinguishes blacks from most other groups are the pervasive nature of the discrimination, its grounding in law and ideology, its longevity, and its persisting effects.

Black Americans' experiences with the armed forces tended to reflect their experiences in the larger society. During the colonial period, there was ambivalence about the use of blacks in local militia units: "Although general policy in early America was to exclude Negroes from militia service, manpower shortages often outweighed the reluctance to give the Negro a gun; hence official attitudes did not always mirror actual practice. . . ."[8]

The southern colonies generally opposed enlisting blacks, while some of the northern colonies did not. General George Washington thus confronted a confusing situation when he was charged with establishing the Continental Army. The result was a series of conflicting decisions regarding blacks. In October 1775 the Council of War of the Continental Army unanimously approved a resolution "to reject all slaves," and a majority of the Council agreed "to reject Negroes altogether."[9] But only a few weeks later Washington wrote to the Continental Congress "advising that he would begin recruiting free blacks and re-enlisting those discarded as a result of the recent ban on accepting Negroes."[10] Washington's turnaround may have been a reaction to Lord Dunmore, the crown's representative in Virginia, who in November 1775 promised freedom to blacks who were "willing to bear arms" in support of "his Majesty's crown and dignity."[11]

Confusion and disagreement over the use of blacks in the military persisted for several years. South Carolina and Georgia declined to enlist slaves, while Virginia accepted slaves as substitutes for their masters. A 1783 Act of the Virginia Legislature promised freedom for those who "have faithfully served agreeable to the terms of their enlistment. . . ."[12] In 1781 the New York legislature approved the enlistment of slaves "without firearms, but with all the shovels, spades, pickaxes, and hoes they can provide themselves with" to help defend the northern frontier.[13]

During the Revolutionary War and the War of 1812, blacks may have comprised up to one-quarter of the Navy's seamen, partly because whites would desert rather than tolerate the harsh conditions aboard ship.[14] But the Marine Corps, in 1798, adopted a policy expressly forbidding the enlistment of blacks — that policy would remain in effect until World War II.[15]

Within a few decades after the founding of the Republic, the nation's leaders had settled on a consistent set of policies and practices regarding the use of blacks in the military; many of them were to remain in effect until the middle of the twentieth century:

1. Blacks were to be enlisted only when a shortage of whites rendered it a necessity of last resort, and they were to be demobilized as soon as military exigencies permitted. General Andrew Jackson, desperate to fortify New Orleans during the War of 1812, issued a call "to the free colored inhabitants of Louisiana" which stated: "Through a mistaken policy you have heretofore been deprived of participation in the glorious struggle for national rights in which your country is engaged. This [policy] shall no longer exist."[16] Once the emergency had passed, however, blacks were told they were no longer needed. In 1820, the War Department determined that "No Negro or mulatto will be received as a recruit of the army."[17]

2. The number of blacks in the military was to be restricted. In 1839 the Navy expressed concern about "the number of blacks and other colored persons entered at some of the recruiting stations, and the consequent underproportion of white persons . . . ," and established a 5 percent quota on black enlistments.[18] The Army followed suit, although wartime emergencies sometimes caused the policy to be altered. In 1862, for example, Congress authorized President Lincoln "to employ as many persons of African descent as he may deem necessary and proper for the suppression of this rebellion."[19] Martin Delaney became the nation's first black field officer when he was given the rank of major and sent to the South to help recruit blacks into the Union Army.[20] More than 180,000 blacks served in the Union Army and some 29,000 served in the Union Navy during the Civil War.[21] Between the end of the Civil War and 1950, however, the quota on black enlistments remained around 10 percent.

3. Blacks were to serve in segregated units. To the extent practicable, these units were to be garrisoned separately from white units and away from large concentrations of white civilians. Shortly after the Civil War, a debate ensued over the garrisoning of the black 24th Infantry Regiment, which for several years had been stationed along the Rio Grande River, the border between Texas and Mexico. Both

President Hayes and General Sherman preferred that the unit be kept on duty in the South, perhaps in New Orleans or Little Rock. In the end, however, concern about white reactions carried the day, and the regiment was sent to the sparsely populated Dakota Territory. One southern commander wrote:

> [T]here is no doubt of the fact that a strong prejudice exists in the South against colored troops . . . [T]here is the danger that some reckless or drunken person may abuse one or a party of these soldiers in the streets . . . I had two very serious disturbances in Texas among the colored troops growing out of these questions and they are liable to occur at any time in the South.[22]

Two of the most notorious incidents involving black soldiers and white townspeople occurred in Brownsville, Texas in 1906 and in Houston in 1917. In both instances, there was considerable evidence that white townspeople had provoked or, in Brownsville, fabricated an incident. But in both cases the black soldiers were held responsible and were severely punished. The Brownsville incident, which involved shots being fired from the direction of the garrison into the town, resulted in the dishonorable discharge of 167 black soldiers. The beating of two black soldiers in Houston led to a riot in which 16 whites and four black soldiers died. Ultimately, 80 black soldiers were tried for the incident. All but five were convicted, and 29 were sentenced to death.[23]

4. The black units were to be commanded by white officers, and under no circumstances were blacks to command white soldiers. The first black to graduate from the U.S. Military Academy was Henry Flipper who was commissioned in 1877 and assigned to the black Tenth Cavalry on the western frontier.[24] But between the end of the Civil War and World War I, only a handful of blacks served in the officer corps. In 1917 the War Department established a program to train black officers in Des Moines, Iowa; but the inability of blacks to command white troops continued to restrict black officers' advancement. The highest ranking black officer at the eve of World War I was Colonel Charles Young, who commanded the Tenth Cavalry at Fort Huachuca, Arizona. Young was forcibly retired under the guise of ill health, apparently in order to prevent his appointment to brigadier general.[25] Because of the restricted opportunities available to black officers, the regular Army had only five black commissioned officers at the eve of World War II; and three of them were chaplains.

5. Blacks were to serve in support capacities – as cooks, stewards, and labourers – but not as combat troops. More than 350,000 blacks served in the Army during World War I. They made up 9 percent of the Army and approximately 8 percent of the American Expe-

ditionary Force; but they were less than 3 percent of the Army's combat strength.[26] General Pershing, commander of the AEF, was reluctant to put blacks into combat. But he agreed to assign four regiments of the Negro 92d Division "to be used as combat units with French divisions."[27] When Pershing asked that the units be returned to his control, he encountered opposition from the commander of the allied forces, Marshal Foch, who believed that the black soldiers had performed well in combat under French control, and thought it silly to reassign them to digging trenches.[28]

One reason for the practices described above is obvious: Whites were very fearful of giving blacks the military training and arms that could be used in slave revolts. Since racial domination persisted long after the end of slavery, so did the reluctance to arm black Americans. Further, slaves were property and as such had considerable economic value. Slaveowners demanded compensation for losing their property; so in many instances it was cheaper to rely on whites, especially on recent immigrants in whom no investment had been made.[29]

Perhaps more fundamentally, sending blacks into battle to fight alongside white Americans would have placed in sharp relief some nagging questions about the position of blacks in America. This was obvious very early on. When the Massachusetts legislature debated the enlistment of blacks in February 1778, for example, it had to consider the "inconsistency . . . in assigning slaves to defend the liberties of America. . . ."[30]

Indeed, it appears that many blacks saw military service as a means of establishing, even purchasing, their citizenship. As the nation entered World War I, the situation of blacks in the United States was deteriorating. Woodrow Wilson had secured black support during the 1912 presidential election by promising a sympathetic hearing for blacks' grievances. But Wilson actually imposed even more stringent rules against the employment of blacks in the federal government, the one major American institution that had not already been resegregated.

Nevertheless, W.E.B. DuBois, who was a leader of the National Association for the Advancement of Colored People (NAACP), urged blacks to enlist in the war against the Central Powers. In the July 1918 issue of the NAACP's *Crisis* magazine, he wrote:

> We of the colored race have no ordinary interest in the outcome. That which the German power represents today spells death to the aspirations of Negroes and all darker races for equality, freedom and democracy. Let us not hesitate. Let us, while this war lasts, forget our special grievances and close ranks shoulder to shoulder with our own white fellow citizens and the allied nations that are fighting for democracy.

We make no ordinary sacrifice, but we make it gladly and willingly with our eyes lifted to the hills.[31]

The following month, DuBois wrote that "the American Negro . . . is more than willing to do his full share in helping to win this war for democracy and he expects his full share of the fruits thereof. . . ."[32]

He must have been disillusioned by what actually happened. At the same time that DuBois was urging blacks to join the fight for democracy, the leaders of the American Expeditionary Force were cautioning their French allies to avoid "any pronounced degree of intimacy between French officers and black officers," to avoid commending "too highly the black American troops," and generally to avoid "spoiling the Negroes."[33]

The disillusionment turned to bitterness and defiance when several returning black members of the AEF were lynched still wearing the uniform of their country.[34] An editorial that DuBois wrote for the May 1919 issue of *Crisis* indicates the change of attitude:

> We return from the slavery of uniform which the world's madness demanded us to don to the freedom of civilian garb. We stand again to look America squarely in the face and call a spade a spade. . . . This country of ours . . . is yet a shameful land. It lynches. . . . It disfranchises its own citizens. . . . It encourages ignorance. . . . It steals from us. . . . It insults us. . . . We return from fighting. We return fighting. Make way for Democracy. We saved it in France, and by the Great Jehova, we will save it in the USA, or know the reason why.[35]

The aftermath of the Second World War, in contrast, carried a sea of change in race relations. It began in 1946 when President Truman established a committee to investigate the state of civil rights, and it culminated in the 1960s with the passage of several important civil rights bills.

Three factors help to explain the change. First, the war against Nazism exposed the calamitous consequences of unbridled bigotry, and caused white Americans to see their nation's racism in a new light. One suspects that it was not the images of mass murders and mass graves that produced reflection, although those images were shocking. Rather, for many Americans the holocaust became a story of individual victims and individual tormentors, of Anne Frank and Adolph Eichmann. Similarly, one suspects that racial oppression in the South began to take on a human face. The dry statistics produced by scholars such as Gunnar Myrdal in *An American Dilemma* probably had greatest impact when they could be vivified by flesh-and-blood human beings. There, on America's television screens, was Rosa Parks, the dignified black woman who became a *cause célèbre* when she was arrested for refusing to yield her seat to a white man on a crowded bus in Montgomery, Alabama. And there was "southern justice" — Sheriff "Bull" Connor using police dogs and electrified cattle prods to disperse peaceful civil rights demonstrators.

Second, the United States entered the Cold War only a few years after the defeat of Germany and Japan. In the political rhetoric of the time, this became a contest between the "free world" and the "communist bloc," and much of it was being played out in the newly emerging nations of Africa and Asia. This gave the nation's civil rights leaders a great opportunity: vivid evidence of racial oppression in the United States gave the "free world" a major propaganda problem.

Third, the nation's black leaders united behind a single strategy. Since the 1890s, black Americans had been divided over civil rights. The principal antagonists were Booker T. Washington and W.E.B. DuBois. Without great distortion, their conflict can be characterized as follows: Washington urged blacks to accept the racial status quo that existed around the turn of the century and cautioned against advocating racial equality. DuBois, one of the founders of the NAACP, is generally portrayed as a proponent of racial equality.

Not surprisingly, whites tended to support Washington. He was feted at the White House; white newspapers described him as *the* leader of black people; and the college he headed, Tuskegee Institute, benefited from a great deal of white philanthropy. Washington died in 1915. By the 1940s, people such as DuBois, Walter White, A. Philip Randolph, Charles Houston, and William Hastie were beginning to gain support for a strategy that was far less accommodationist than Washington's.

The period from the late 1940s through the 1960s is often described as America's Second Reconstruction. In 1948, President Truman helped convince the Democratic Party to include a civil rights plank in its platform. (To protest, Strom Thurmond led his southern "Dixiecrat" colleagues out of the convention. Thurmond later converted to the Republican Party and, in the early 1980s, chaired the Senate committee that oversees civil rights.)

In 1954, the Supreme Court's *Brown* decision essentially overturned the "separate but equal" doctrine that had been the Constitutional mainstay of segregation since the *Plessy* decision of 1896. A year later Martin Luther King, Jr. began the Montgomery bus boycott. A decade of racial upheaval followed. President Eisenhower used federal troops to desegregate Little Rock's Central High School; "freedom riders" were arrested, beaten, and murdered; black homes and churches were bombed; several civil rights activists were assassinated. All of this culminated with the passage of the 1964 Civil Rights Act and the 1965 Voting Rights Act. The assassination of Dr.

Martin Luther King, Jr. in the spring of 1968 is often cited as the end of that dramatic period of change.

Interestingly, the military was not following the larger society during this period but, rather, leading it. In 1948 Truman issued Executive Order 9981, which required that "[T]here shall be equality of treatment and opportunity for all persons in the armed services without regard to race, color, religion or national origin."[36]

Of itself, EO 9981 did not eliminate segregation in the military or abolish the quota on black enlistments. In fact, Truman established a commission to determine precisely how it should be implemented. There then ensued a two-year debate involving the White House, the War Department, and the commission chaired by Charles Fahy. In the end, the Fahy committee recommended the phasing out of all-black units and the end of quotas.

The committee's recommendations encountered a great deal of bureaucratic resistance. The Army, in particular, was worried that ending quotas would result in an over-representation of blacks. Those concerns were allayed by an agreement which permitted "the substitution of an achievement quota for the present racial quota."[37] David Niles, a member of the White House staff, explained to Truman how this would work:

> Judging by World War II figures, only 16.6 percent of all Negro men of military age will score 90 or better on the GCT test. Hence, with a cut-off score of 90, this percentage would be the maximum of Negroes enlisting in the army. . . . The true number, of course, would be much smaller than this. . . .[38]

Niles went on to note that the "navy and air force have already discovered this fact, have substituted a GCT quota for a racial quota, and are very pleased with the results." Army Secretary Gray agreed with this approach and clarified its implications in a memorandum to Truman:

> If, as a result of a fair trial of this new system, there ensues a disproportionate balance of racial strengths in the army, it is my understanding that I have your authority to return to a system which will, in effect, control enlistments by race.[39]

Truman scribbled "Approved, Harry S Truman" on Gray's memorandum, and with that, the Army Staff issued an order dated 27 March 1950 which opened enlistments "to all qualified applicants without regard to race or color." The modern tools of psychometrics, which had been used to control the quality of people enlisting in the military, could in future be used to control opportunities for black Americans.

The degree to which test scores actually have been used purposefully to restrict black enlistments is not clear. What is clear is that the armed services, like other institutions in American society, have been suspected of using them in that way. In 1971, for example, the NAACP suggested that the military was using the Armed Forces Qualification Test to restrict opportunities for blacks, and called for "a thorough re-examination" to ensure that it could be validated in terms of job performance.[40]

Under any circumstances, the representation of blacks in the enlisted ranks remained roughly at general population proportions during the 1950s and 1960s, and the representation of blacks in the officer corps remained below 3 percent. That situation began to change as draft-era inductees were replaced by All-Volunteer Force (AVF) volunteers in the 1970s.

Blacks in the AVF

RICHARD NIXON ENDORSED the all-volunteer force during his 1968 presidential campaign against Hubert Humphrey.[41] Although Nixon changed his mind in the years following his departure from the Oval Office,[42] the AVF continues to enjoy the support of the nation's citizens and leaders. The Reagan administration admitted no serious reservations about it.[43] And of the eight contenders for the Democratic Party's presidential nomination in 1984, only one – Senator Ernest Hollings of South Carolina – publicly supported a return to conscription. Nevertheless, as House Armed Services Committee Chairman Les Aspin (D-Wisconsin) has pointed out, critics of the AVF are "lurking in the weeds," waiting for an opportune moment to strike.[44]

One sticking point about the AVF has always been its racial composition. Members of Congress raised the matter when Nixon's proposal was being considered in 1972. Thomas Gates, who chaired the commission Nixon appointed to develop the AVF proposal, considered the possibility that the force would become disproportionately black, but dismissed it. Then-Defense Secretary Melvin Laird stated that "[W]e do not foresee any significant difference between the racial composition of the all-volunteer force and the racial composition of the nation."[45]

Gates, Laird, and other supporters of Nixon's proposal clearly were wrong, as will be demonstrated below. Later, we will consider the arguments that have developed over the significance of their errors for military policy and for the nation as a whole.

A few cautionary notes are in order before we examine the statistical trends. First, terms such as "under-representation" and "over-representation" assume a standard of comparison. Different standards should be kept in mind for different sets of data. Blacks comprise 11.8 percent of the total population of the United States, but they are approximately 13 percent of the population aged 18 to 21, which is the age range of most first-term enlistees.[46] Blacks comprise about 9 percent of the population that has completed four years or more of college; this figure should be kept in mind in assessing the degree to which blacks are under-represented in the officer corps, because a college education is a virtual prerequisite for commissioning.[47]

Second, the data are on the active duty forces and do not reflect the reserve components. As of September 1984, 2,123,428 men and women were on active duty, 403,079 or 19 percent of whom were black.[48] Of the men and women in the reserve and National Guard units, 259,465 or 18 percent were black.[49] Since the reserve and National Guard units are not used in precisely the same ways that active duty forces are used, some of the benefits and burdens of active service do not apply to the reserve components.

Third, the statistics cover the years 1972 to 1984, a period that included one relatively mild recession (1974-75) and one very deep recession (1981-83). The slack labour market associated with the Reagan recession made the military more attractive to white youth and caused a slight reduction in black accessions. This effect probably will be temporary. Absent major changes in military manpower policy or continuing problems in the economy, the representation of blacks in the military is likely to remain high for the foreseeable future. Indeed, it may increase, because the cohort that will reach enlistment age in the next few years contains a higher percentage of blacks (and Hispanics and Asian-Americans) than does the current enlistment age cohort.

Trends in Representation

CHANGES IN THE representation of blacks in the active forces from 1972 (the last year of conscription) through the end of fiscal year 1984 can be traced from available statistics. Overall, black representation has nearly doubled, from 11.1 to 19.0 percent, with a high of 19.8 percent in 1981.[50] The trends vary from service to service. The Army had the highest percentage of blacks in the early 1970s, and the Army's trend line increased sharply throughout that decade. By contrast, black representation in the Navy has been relatively low; at no time has the percentage of blacks in that service exceeded the percentage of blacks in the service-age population.

Black "over-representation" is confined to the enlisted ranks. This is probably related to the fact that the unemployment rate of black youth has been around 40 percent for much of the past decade, more than twice the rate of white youth. According to one estimate, 42 percent of black youth who are eligible for military service actually enlist, compared with 14 percent of white youth.[51]

Black representation among enlisted personnel increased steadily for most of the 1970s, then leveled off toward the end of the decade. Statistics also reveal different trends for different ranks. Declines in black enlistment correspond roughly with the brief recession of the mid-1970s and with increases in youth unemployment that preceded the 1981-83 recession. This trend suggests that economic downturns cause the military to become more attractive to white youth. Whites tend to score higher than blacks on the military's standardized entry examination (the Armed Forces Qualification Test, AFQT), so an increase in white interest tends to reduce black representation (when enlistment standards and accession needs are held constant).

The modest downturn in black representation at the E-4 level (the re-entering rank) may be the result of changes in *re*-enlistment standards. During the mid-1970s an error in grading the AFQT caused the services to admit a number of people who normally would have been rejected. It is possible that blacks were disproportionately affected when the services began to stiffen re-enlistment requirements in order to correct the effects of the error. Statistics also indicate that black representation at the senior non-commissioned officer levels continues to grow.

High black representation in the enlisted ranks reflects the combined effects of high black enlistment and re-enlistment rates. In 1984, 54.6 percent of black Army personnel re-enlisted, compared to only 35.8 percent of white soldiers.[52]

In 1984 blacks made up 6.2 percent of active duty commissioned officers, a dramatic increase from the 2.2 percent level that existed in 1972.[53] If the size of the "recruitment pool" is taken into consideration — blacks are 8.8 percent of the college-educated population — then blacks are not greatly under-represented in the officer corps. As with enlisted personnel, black officers are most prominent in the Army and least prominent in the Navy.

Since it takes time to "make rank" in the military, it is not surprising that blacks are more heavily represented in the lower officer grades than higher up in the rank structure. It takes about ten years for an officer to move from O-1 (lieutenant or Navy ensign) to O-4 (major or Navy lieutenant commander), and more than twenty years to move from O-1 to O-6 (colonel or Navy captain). The officers who had attained the rank of colonel by 1984 came from the pool of officers who were commissioned in the early 1960s, and that cohort contained very few blacks. The relatively large percentage of blacks who received commissions during the late 1970s and early 1980s may help to increase black representation in the senior officer grades in the 1990s. There is a countervailing trend, however: in recent years, the attrition trends of black junior officers have tended to be higher than those of white cohorts.[54]

Black Women in the Military

THE ROLE OF women in the armed services began to change shortly after the AVF was established. All-female units such as the Women's Army Corps were abolished and the services began to integrate women into traditionally all-male units and career fields. Today fewer than 100 of the services' more than 300 major occupational groups are closed to women, and those fields contain only about 10 percent of all enlisted personnel.[55] Overall, the representation of women in the active forces grew from 4.0 percent in 1972 to 9.5 percent in 1984.

As former Assistant Secretary of Defense for Manpower Lawrence Korb has pointed out, the combat exclusion policy — or the ways in which the services have interpreted the policy — is the major impediment to increased female participation.[56] But other factors also come into play. For one thing, the services have had little difficulty finding male recruits in recent years, so there is less internal pressure to increase the use of women. Further, after a brief exposure to non-traditional fields during the 1970s, many female personnel may themselves have chosen to build their careers around more traditional jobs — not because women are unable or reluctant to compete with men, but because some of the jobs that enlisted men perform are very unpleasant. Whatever the reasons, women continue to be concentrated in fields such as administration, medical services, and certain technical specialties.

Generally, the military services have defended their restrictions on the use of women by arguing that the American public simply will not support putting women in hazardous jobs. There is some evidence, however, that the services have been more conservative than public opinion would justify. A survey conducted by the National Opinion Research Center in 1982 indicates, for example, that 62.4 percent of the public believes women should be permitted to serve as jet fighter pilots, and 57.4 percent believes women should be permitted to serve as crew members on combat ships. On the other hand, very few survey respondents said that women should be placed in units where they might become involved in hand-to-hand combat.[57]

Black women have been an important part of the changes that have occurred during the past decade. Overall, the representation of black women has grown from 11.7 percent of all women in 1972 to

26.5 percent in 1984. The change has been particularly dramatic in the Army, where black women are now 42 percent of all enlisted women and 12.1 percent of female officers.[58] Black women are even more heavily represented in the services than are black men. This is true of both the officer and the enlisted ranks. Indeed, when we examine changes in black representation in the officer corps, it is important to keep in mind that a significant portion of the improvement is traceable to increased numbers of black female officers.[59]

Like black men, black women are more likely than their white counterparts to enlist in the military and to re-enlist. Further, black women are more likely than white women to complete their first tour of duty. In short, black women have been one of the success stories of the AVF. But as is the case with black men, the success of black women in the military may be traceable in part to a lack of viable alternatives in the civilian economy.

Distribution of Blacks Across Units and Specialties

TWO QUESTIONS ARE prominent in discussions of the benefits and burdens of military service: are blacks in the kinds of units and jobs that would cause them to experience heavy casualties in time of war; and, are young black soldiers, sailors, and airmen obtaining the skills and experiences that will enhance their post-service employment opportunities?

Blacks are more heavily represented in the Army and the Marine Corps than in the Air Force and Navy. The former two services tend to experience the highest casualty rates during conventional conflicts. Some analysts have projected that blacks would comprise one-third or more of American casualties if hostilities broke out in Europe or Korea.[60]

But the real effects would depend upon the specifics of the conflict — where it occurred, how large it became, how long it lasted, and which units were engaged. In 1984 blacks made up 28 percent of all Army personnel. Of the Army's 16 combat divisions, black representation was above that percentage in ten divisions, and under that percentage in six. Black representation was highest (38 percent) in the 24th Infantry Division, which is stationed at Fort Stewart, Georgia and would be used to reinforce V Corps or VII Corps in the event of hostilities in Europe. On the other hand, blacks were noticeably under-represented in the 82d Airborne Division, which is the kind of unit that might be deployed rapidly to fight limited conflicts in areas such as the Persian Gulf or Central America.[61] (In 1984 Hispanics constituted 3.8 percent of Army personnel, slightly below their estimated 5 percent representation in the general population. Among combat divisions, they were concentrated most heavily in the 82d

Airborne. Other minority groups, mostly Asian-Americans, made up another 4 percent of the Army. Among combat divisions, Asian-Americans were concentrated most heavily in the 2nd Division in Korea, the 25th Infantry in Hawaii, and the 7th Infantry Division at Fort Ord, California.)

An answer to the question about skills development and post-career possibilities can be gleaned from available statistics. Blacks are heavily concentrated in routine support, administrative, service, and supply jobs, the military equivalent of traditional, low-skilled blue collar jobs. By contrast, blacks are not prominent in highly technical or craft jobs.

One reason for this distribution is that black educational achievement continues to lag behind that of whites. The military services use scores on the Armed Services Qualification Test to determine "trainability" and ultimately to assign personnel to occupational specialties. On average, the AFQT scores of blacks and Hispanics are considerably lower than those of whites, which means that blacks and Hispanics are more likely than whites to wind up in "soft" skill jobs.[62]

This does not necessarily mean that blacks gain little from serving in the military. The increasing number of black NCOs and officers suggests that many blacks are finding meaningful career opportunities in the armed services. And the fact that blacks are heavily represented in low-skill military specialties should be weighed against the fact that thousands of young black men and women are obtaining technical skills and experience that will serve them well when they return to the civilian economy. Further, military service may help to instill a number of other traits that are crucial to success, such as discipline, teamwork, and leadership.

One must hasten to point out, however, that questions about post-service experiences have not been studied carefully, partly because the issue falls between bureaucratic cracks. The Defense Department recruits people and is fully responsible for them while they are in the service. Once they leave the service they become the responsibility of the Veterans Administration if they are entitled to benefits, and the Department of Labor begins to include them in the data and programs covering civilian members of the labour force. As this shift in responsibility occurs, a number of important issues appear to get overlooked. Thus, we lack the knowledge needed to make definitive statements about the relationship between military service and subsequent civilian employment.

Closing Observations

SEVERAL FACTORS COMBINE to influence the representation of blacks in the AVF: the size and racial/ethnic mix of the enlistment age population, the services' needs for a force of a certain size and quality, policies affecting the role of women, and the state of the civilian labour market. The size of the enlistment age population is declining, from 2.1 million 18-year-old males in 1980 to about 1.6 million in the early 1990s.[63] Blacks and other minorities will comprise a larger proportion of that shrinking cohort, so their representation in the armed forces is likely to increase during the next decade.

Some analysts are predicting that the next decade will be a difficult one for the AVF.[64] The Defense Department is trying to maintain a force of more than two million active duty personnel in the face of a shrinking pool of potential male enlistees, and it is trying to upgrade the quality of personnel because military technology and tactics are growing more sophisticated. If the civilian economy remains healthy, the AVF's existing enlistment incentives will be put to a severe test. At some point, the services may find themselves in the situation that existed in the mid-1970s, when they increased opportunities for women in order to compensate for a shortage of qualified men.[65]

In assessing the potential burdens of military service, one must keep in mind the prognosis offered by former national security advisor McGeorge Bundy and other strategic analysts: A major war in Europe or the Far East is not likely to occur.[66] A more likely scenario, according to William J. Taylor, Jr., director of the Center for Strategic and International Studies, is American involvement in "low intensity conflicts in the third world."[67] These are the kinds of situations that would call for the rapid deployment of airborne units to contain a conflict or protect specific targets, or the long-term insertion of small Special Forces-type units. A potential always exists, of course, for such limited missions to escalate.

It is likely that young black men and women are joining the military in large numbers because of the lack of opportunities in the civilian economy. But this does not mean that the military is serving as an employer of last resort. Quite the contrary: According to one estimate, fewer than half of the nation's young black men are qualified to join today's armed forces.[68]

Controversies over Racial Representation

ARGUMENTS OVER THE high level of black representation in the armed forces can be categorized most memorably through alliteration: readiness, reliability, respect, repercussions of conflict, *realpolitik*, and representativeness. The arguments are as follows:

Readiness. – As was stated earlier, the educational achievement levels of black Americans tend to be lower than those of their white cohorts. From this, some commentators have leaped to the speculation that a heavily black force will be less skilled, less well-trained, and therefore less tactically ready than a force that has fewer blacks.

Reliability. – At the extreme, commentators present a scenario in which the United States decides to intervene to help protect the current government of South Africa, and we are asked whether black soldiers would eagerly sacrifice their lives to defend apartheid.

Respect. – According to one version of this argument, a heavily black force will lose the support of the American people because whites will not be able to shake the notion that their military has become an employer of last resort for blacks. Another line of thinking posits a "tipping" effect: at some point, young white men and women will become reluctant to join the armed forces because they do not want to be surrounded by blacks.

Repercussions of Conflict. – There is no escaping the fact that blacks would comprise about one-third of initial American casualties in the event of a major conventional conflict. This would have significant repercussions for American politics; large numbers of black and white Americans would protest that blacks were bearing an egregiously unfair burden.

Realpolitik. – This argument is that, regardless of whether we have a war, the way we man the force is cynical and inherently unfair. The complaint was put most eloquently by a former member of the U.S. Congress, John Cavanaugh:

> . . . the fatal defect of the All-Volunteer Force is that . . . it is not a volunteer system at all. The AVF has proven an unjust and inequitable system of economic and racial conscription. A system in which those who have the least in our society are offered the opportunity to be trained to risk all in exchange for the very thing they have been denied by the society they are asked to defend, a job.[69]

Representativeness. – Finally, there is the broadest, most encompassing, and in many ways the vaguest charge: regardless of the truth or falsity of all the other complaints, the problem simply is that these black soldiers "do not represent the nation."[70]

Before these points of controversy are addressed, two preliminary observations are in order. One of them has to do with the identities of the major participants; the other with the state of black America.

Although blacks are the subject of the controversies, very few blacks have participated actively in the public arguments. In 1984, for example, the U.S. Naval Academy sponsored a major conference on the AVF, and much of the discussion had to do with the racial composition of the force. Of the 25 policy makers and scholars who spoke at that conference, none was black. A similar pattern emerged at a 1985 conference on military manpower sponsored by the Center for Strategic and International Studies. The exceptions, which include former Army Secretary Clifford Alexander, House Armed Services Committee member Ronald Dellums, and scholars John Butler and Alvin Schexnider, serve to prove the rule: very few black scholars or political leaders have made their presence felt on an issue that clearly is pertinent to black Americans.

For the benefit of those who do not live in the United States or who do not follow racial issues closely, I also want to make some observations about the current *civilian* situation. This may provide us a context for assessing the several "R-rated" controversies listed above.

On average, the socioeconomic status of blacks continues to lag behind that of whites. Median black family income is about 56 percent of median white family income; the black unemployment rate is about 15 percent, more than twice the white rate. And more than 40 percent of black families are headed by single parents, mostly women. (The relationship between the deterioration of black families and the socioeconomic status of black families is gaining increasing attention in the United States. It is possible that the high percentage of female-headed families is related to the labour-force status of black men: unemployed men do not make very good marriage partners, but the laws of economics do not arrest the laws of biology.)

Overt racism has subsided markedly in the United States over the past two decades, partly because of the civil rights legislation that was passed in the 1960s. At the most rudimentary level, this means that a black American can drive cross-country and not worry about whether he will be able to find a restaurant that will serve him or a hotel that will let him spend the night. This was not true 25 or 30 years ago. On the other hand, it would be a grave mistake to presume that discrimination and segregation are things of the past. We still see ample evidence of discrimination in employment, housing, and so on. Many neighbourhoods remain segregated. A few months ago, for example, a young couple caused a near-riot when they became the first black family to move into a Philadelphia neighbourhood. Some of their new neighbours taunted and threatened them; their house was ransacked. Out of fear, they moved out.

So racist incidents still occur, but they occur far less frequently than several decades ago. On a day-to-day basis, blacks and whites tend to mingle comfortably at the office and on the factory floor. Places of work tend to be far better integrated than schools, neighbourhoods, and churches. Put it this way: if one were to visit a restaurant in downtown Washington, D.C. at lunchtime, one would see black office workers dining comfortably with their white colleagues. If one were to visit that same restaurant on a Saturday evening, one would not see nearly the same degree of interracial camaraderie. And, while most religious denominations preach racial tolerance, most American churches remain highly segregated.

To a large extent, blacks and whites still live in two different Americas. This became clear from a survey that my organization conducted in 1984:

> ... America is a society in which blacks and whites have different needs and expectations. The two races apparently view neither the past, nor the present, nor the future in the same terms, and American society seems to be dominated by complacent and indifferent whites who, for the most part, neither comprehend nor share the concerns of most blacks.[71]

For example, 38 percent of blacks listed civil rights as one of the three most important issues in the 1984 presidential campaign, while only 6 percent of whites did so; a plurality (43 percent) of black respondents said their families were financially worse off in 1984 than in 1980, while a plurality (46 percent) of white respondents said their families were better off; 82 percent of blacks disapproved of President Reagan's performance in office, while a majority of whites (57 percent) approved of Reagan's job performance.[72] Incidentally, our survey revealed that on most issues black opinion was fairly uniform across income, education, and even party. Eighty-six percent of black Democrats disapproved of Reagan's job performance, for example, but 73 percent of black Republicans also disapproved of their party's leader.

Obviously, the people who serve in the armed forces reflect many of the attitudes and perspectives they developed in the civilian world. Thus, one finds that the armed services are very well integrated during working hours, much less so after hours: "[T]he more military the setting, the more favorable are race relations. Racial harmony is more evident in the field than in garrison, on duty than off duty, and on-post than off-post."[73] As in the civilian world, when the quitting whistle sounds, blacks tend to go one direction, whites another.

Still, there is one significant difference. The military, and particularly the Army, remains one of the few institutions in American society where whites at some point or other almost assuredly will be supervised, trained, commanded, and ultimately judged by blacks. This has a salutary effect: racial prejudices will decline as more whites (and blacks) begin to see blacks in positions of authority.

These brief notes on the state of black America and on the state of race relations may provide us some perspective from which to view specific controversies about blacks in the military.

What do we know about the six "R" word controversies? What facts or insights can we bring to bear in an effort to discern which of them should be considered seriously?

Readiness

PARTLY IN RESPONSE to questions about the capability of people in the AVF, the Pentagon conducted a major study designed to compare enlistees with the total enlistment-age pool.[74] Generally, the Pentagon claimed to have been pleased with what it found: the AVF is not attracting "dummies." Even though black enlistees, on average, scored below white enlistees on the military's standardized tests, this trend is mitigated by two other factors. A higher percentage of black than white enlistees has completed high school, which is an important indicator of persistence. Further, a higher percentage of blacks than whites completes the first enlistment and remains in the service beyond the first enlistment; this reduces the services' recruiting and training needs, and providing it with a valuable cadre of NCOs. Thus, the racial composition of the force, *per se*, does not appear to have affected readiness.[75]

However, there is a larger set of questions, having nothing to do with race, that has not been addressed satisfactorily. These have to do with the match between the skills that our soldiers possess, and the skills that actually are needed to perform in the complex technological and tactical situations a fighting force is likely to encounter in future conflicts. We know what skills are needed to perform discrete tasks — read a map, operate a piece of hardware, lead an infantry squad — and we are satisfied that our soldiers can do those things. What we do not know, and perhaps cannot know, is how all those discrete skills will fit together to produce effective soldiers and effective units in time of war. We do not know, in other words, how the friction of battle that Clausewitz wrote about will affect soldiers on some future battlefield.

One bothersome indicator may be the services' increasing reliance on rear-echelon support and private contractors to perform a large range of maintenance and even everyday operational functions.

Civilian contractors, for example, are stationed aboard ships to make sure that the Navy's fancy hardware and software operate properly. Further, there may be a growing disharmony between tactics and technology. Many military strategists and tacticians are thinking of future wars that have few fixed boundaries and of situations in which relatively small units may have to operate independently for sustained periods of time, cut off from rear support echelons. But much of our military technology appears to make combat units increasingly dependent on immediate and continual support from rear-echelon supply and maintenance units.

These problems have virtually nothing to do with race. Indeed, these are instances in which a preoccupation with race may divert attention from more fundamental questions such as the proper relationship between men and materiel. Military policy makers appear to have emphasized hardware, under the assumption that we can obtain or train the people needed to operate it. Regardless of the racial composition of the force, we may need to consider whether military policy makers spend too much time worrying about hardware and too little time worrying about whether and how people can actually use it.[76]

Reliability

DURING A RECENT conference on military manpower, one speaker wondered aloud how Hispanic soldiers would perform if asked to fire on other Hispanics in the event U.S. forces became actively engaged in Central America. Another speaker asked about how reliable black soldiers would be if they were part of an American effort to help defend the government of South Africa. Interestingly, none of the speakers mentioned a very real experience: President Kennedy's agonizing over whether he could rely on the all-white Mississippi National Guard to protect James Meredith when he sought to become the first black to enroll at the University of Mississippi.

To my knowledge, nothing in American military experience justifies questioning the loyalty/reliability of black or Hispanic soldiers. One must ask, therefore, why such questions are raised. It is likely that they reveal something about persisting patterns of racial dominance, exclusion, and alienation in American society. Very few blacks, Hispanics, or women have ever occupied senior policy-making positions in the State Department or the Defense Department. The first black to occupy a cabinet-level position at Defense was Clifford Alexander who served as Secretary of the Army during the Carter Administration.

The tendency toward chauvinism and exclusivity may be particularly pronounced among members of the national security establishment. After all, these are people who work closely together in an effort to determine what is best for the nation. They handle matters that may involve a great deal of secrecy, and their decisions may have global ramifications. For all their internal bickering, they become members of a very exclusive "club." Opening things up to "outsiders" therefore becomes very difficult.

Further, given the patterns of dominance in the United States, the white males who control crucial institutions feel comfortable making decisions that affect blacks and women without bothering to consult those who are affected. When members of the affected groups charge that the decisions are misguided, the decision makers are psychologically predisposed toward charging the protesters with putting their "special interests" above the "national interest."

Breaking down these tendencies can be very difficult, as former UN Ambassador Jeane Kirkpatrick learned. She claims to have been excluded from a number of important decisions, largely because the men surrounding President Reagan did not give much weight to women's views. When she complained, the President's men simply responded that she was engaging in typical female whining.

The idea that American blacks may take a special interest in certain foreign and defence policy issues – and that their views should be taken seriously – has not yet penetrated through some arenas. That is why some defence analysts can imagine scenarios that would bring blacks' loyalties into question, and why they appear to have trouble imagining scenarios in which the patriotism of whites would be brought into question.

Unless these patterns are broken, national security policy will continue to have a kind of we/they dynamic – "we" being the exclusive circle of people who make policy, "they" being those who disagree. The tensions and suspicions become particularly pronounced when the "we" represent a different socioeconomic stratum or race than the "they." In such a situation, it becomes much easier to question the patriotism of the excluded groups than to reconsider the decisions or to widen the circle of decision makers.

Respect

THERE HAS BEEN much speculation that a heavily black force would, for that very reason, begin to lose the support of the American people. Not until 1982 did we have the data needed to test the speculation. A survey conducted by the National Opinion Research Center yielded two pertinent findings. First, neither blacks nor whites appear to be particularly bothered by the relatively high percentage of blacks in the armed forces. When told the percentages and asked whether there were "too many blacks," whether there "should be

more blacks" or whether the numbers were "about right," 67.4 percent of the sample population responded that the numbers were
about right; 70.8 percent of whites and 47.5 percent of blacks
appeared to be satisfied. Indeed, respondents were more likely to say
that there "should be more blacks" than that there were "too many."
Second, there was no evidence that the high percentage of blacks
affected public confidence in the armed forces.[77] What this appears
to suggest is that some of those who focus on military affairs are
more race-conscious than is the general public.

Repercussions of conflict

THE ATTITUDES DESCRIBED above could change markedly if U.S.
forces were actually fighting and dying. "In the event of future hostilities," writes Charles Moskos, "it is naive, if not duplicitous, to state
that disproportionately high black casualties will have no or only
minor consequences on the domestic political scene."[78]

It is difficult to contest Moskos' point, although a qualifying
observation is in order. Ultimately, the way the American people will
respond to military conflict depends upon what the fighting is all
about. Military engagements that are undertaken for clearly compelling reasons greatly enhance the likelihood of public support and also
raise the threshold at which resistance to the war begins to take hold.
If policy makers send people to fight and die simply so that the
United States can help determine which competing group of political
thugs will dominate some distant banana republic, they should not
expect the support of the American public. One suspects that black
Americans are as willing to fight, and to see their loved ones fight, as
any other group – as long as there is a good reason for doing so.

Realpolitik

WHETHER OR NOT our soldiers are sent into battle, and whether
nor not they are adequately prepared to fight, we must confront a
basic moral issue. Serving in the military is not just another job. The
relatively comfortable, "9-to-5" work routine of the peacetime AVF
masks a nasty reality: military service is the only "job" in which
people can be compelled to make the ultimate sacrifice. By their
presence, black Americans are saying that they are willing to make
that sacrifice. But have we structured their options in such a way that
their only real choices are the military or the unemployment line? By
this line of thinking, blacks in the military are victims of a kind of
double-whammy: the nation refused to provide them fair opportunities to secure decent education and civilian employment, then cyni-
cally enticed them into the military where they can serve as cannon
fodder for our next military adventure.

But that line of reasoning appears to beg a question: are the young black men and women who are joining the armed services the same people who otherwise would wind up on the unemployment lines? It would appear safe to assume that they are; indeed, that assumption guided earlier portions of this paper. However, one must also note something else. More than 90 percent of black enlistees are high school graduates, while only 64 percent of all black youth have finished high school. Indeed, a much higher percentage of black enlistees than white enlistees have completed high school.[79]

Those facts have led some observers to suggest that the blacks who are enlisting in the AVF are not in fact those who have no other options. That speculation is buttressed by something else mentioned earlier: a very high percentage of young black men — by one estimate, more than half — are not qualified to enlist. Recall also that a very high percentage of young blacks who are qualified to enlist — the estimate was 42 percent — actually do so. In fact, the socio-economic background of black enlistees is more similar to that of blacks enrolled in two-year colleges than to drop-outs and the chronically unemployed.[80]

If all these things are true, then the AVF presents us with a very curious situation. It is taking a very high number of the "best and brightest" of black American youth, but leaving those who are least capable, least employable, least likely to become productive citizens and fathers.

These observations do not resolve the moral question. Rather, they suggest that the moral issue may be a bit different than has been posed previously. It is not just a question of whether blacks are being forced by circumstances to bear an unfair burden; it also is a question of whether the blacks who are bearing the burden are those that the society most needs to preserve. What kind of society is it, Charles Moskos asks, that "excuses its privileged from serving in the ranks of its military?"[81] Here, Moskos is thinking in terms of class rather than in terms of race.

Here again, however, a focus on the military may divert us from the real issue. The American economy is undergoing a great deal of structural change, one manifestation of which is growing unemployment. For reasons discussed earlier, blacks are more adversely affected than whites. But the real issue is not composition of the military; it is the nature of the economy. To worry about the high percentage of blacks (or poor whites) in the armed forces is to worry about symptoms, not causes.

Representativeness

EARLIER IN THIS paper I discussed the degree to which blacks are "over-represented" – statistically speaking – in the armed services, and identified some of the implications of the statistical trends, e.g., that blacks would make up a high percentage of combat casualties. But the issue of representativeness has broader connotations than that. There appears to be a consensus in the United States that the armed forces should be a reflection of the society. From very early on in our history the idea of a "citizen army" has been part of our civic culture. The lore promulgated in novels and Hollywood movies captures this spirit of the military as a melting pot where poor farm boys can rub elbows with Harvard men, where bigoted white kids learn to respect their black comrades-in-arms, and so on.

But we also have the image of the military as a predominantly white institution, just as we have the image of America as predominantly a white society. When Americans think of military heroism, they think of Teddy Roosevelt charging up San Juan Hill to liberate Cuba, of Audie Murphy single-handedly overwhelming a company of enemy soldiers, of General MacArthur announcing "I have returned" to a throng of grateful Filipinos. They remember war movies starring John Wayne and Ronald Reagan. When Americans think of military exploits, they do not think of the black soldiers who actually did the fighting and dying for Roosevelt; and they do not think of Dorie Miller, the black mess steward who manned a gun aboard his sinking ship and was credited with shooting down several Japanese planes during the Pearl Harbor attack. (A few years ago, the black actor Lou Gossett, Jr., played a tough marine drill sergeant in the movie, *An Officer and a Gentleman*. Gossett had to fight very hard to get that part. Why? Because it was not a "black" role, and it had never occurred to the movie's producer and director that a black could be considered for it. Gossett's casting was thus something of a breakthrough – one of the few times a black had been cast in a motion picture role that had nothing to do with race.)

Thus, when James Fallows complains that the nation's black soldiers "may well be first-class fighting men; but they do not represent the nation," he is revealing something about our national psyche – our deeply ingrained sense of how blacks fit in. Of course, blacks should serve in the armed forces, and of course, they should be given every opportunity to attain the highest ranks. But those who focus on the representativeness issue appear to be saying that when we have too many blacks, the reality of the military stands in too sharp contrast to our image of the military. This is yet another example of the way in which our preoccupation with race can pervert judgement.

When we see a group of blacks in uniform what we think of first is their colour, not their character.

With all due respect to Fallows (who generally is a thoughtful and perceptive writer), what his charge appears to reflect is a failure to think seriously. Specifically, we have not stated carefully what we mean when we say that the military should reflect the society, and we have failed to re-examine the meaning of race in contemporary American society.

When we say that the military should reflect the society, we clearly have in mind that it should in some way reflect the nation's diversity; it should not be manned disproportionately by people from one region, economic stratum, racial or ethnic group. (Of course, we have never really had a representative military in this statistical sense. Even when the draft was in effect, the enlisted ranks — especially of the Army — consisted largely of young men from the lower socioeconomic strata, and the South was more heavily represented than other regions.)

More importantly, however, we want the military to reflect — or represent — the nation's basic values. We do not want the armed forces to consist essentially of "mercenaries" who are more interested in how much they are being paid than in the values they are being paid to protect. In this sense, as Robert Fullinwider argues, we can say that a heavily black military is "unrepresentative" only if we believe that black soldiers' values and commitments are fundamentally different from the values of other Americans — so different that blacks are essentially "aliens."[82] One suspects that Fallows, if he were to reflect on the matter, would not wish to make so extreme a charge.

On the other hand, some of the survey data alluded to earlier in this paper indicated that modal black opinion does diverge from modal white opinion on a wide range of issues. Can those findings be used to support the implicit assumption that black Americans are indeed alien to, or alienated from, the rest of American society? I think not. In survey data, we tend to get at opinions toward specific issues such as support for certain political leaders or policies. Surveys do not tend to get at questions about fundamental values or commitments. One suspects that blacks and whites agree on the basics — democratic political processes, the free enterprise system, equal opportunity for all, and so on. The racial disagreements have to do largely with how those values can be attained, and more specifically, over how black Americans can best take advantage of them. The disagreements are significant — they produce huge controversies and clearly have ramifications for politics — but they are not sufficient to merit judging blacks to be aliens in their own country.

One other point needs to be made. Most of the people who have been arguing over blacks in the armed forces know only one side of the issue, the armed forces. Few of them have thought deeply about blacks, per se. Roger Wilkins has described this problem eloquently:

> Those who care little about gross inequalities in opportunity in this society seem capable of real concern only when the inequalities have an impact on the institutions established to defend that society. They then seek to attend to the problems of the institutions rather than to the problems of the American citizens who – in their view – are weakening the institution. Dealt with in that fashion, few of the problems will be solved. . . .[83]

Conclusion

FOR MORE THAN 200 years we have been debating how blacks fit into American society. At various points we have offered answers that were, in turns, morally objectionable, incomplete, and grudging. After the Civil War we determined that blacks could not be regarded as property, not even partly. But the steps needed to convert former property into whole, free citizens were not taken. Roughly a century after the Civil War we offered another answer – that blacks were entitled to all the rights and opportunities that whites enjoyed. But again, the steps needed "to fulfill these rights" (to quote the title of President Lyndon Johnson's memorable 1965 commencement speech at Howard University) were not taken. Thus, the nation continues to wrestle with the dilemma of racial inequality.

At various points, circumstances conspired to force us to confront that dilemma. George Washington had to confront it when he was trying to assemble a rag-tag group of soldiers to fight the War of Independence. And the armed forces are confronting it again as its critics charge that there is something fundamentally wrong with its racial composition.

But as Roger Wilkins pointed out in the passage quoted above, the military's problem cannot be resolved as long as it is perceived solely as the military's problem. That is what has been wrong with arguments to date over blacks in the military: it has been carried out by a group of people, "experts," who see only one side of the issue. They may be clever enough to devise some stratagem that will reduce the numbers of blacks in the armed forces and thus get the critics off their backs temporarily. But they are not clever enough to dispose of the problem altogether because their frame of reference is far too narrow.

We cannot fault military affairs specialists for failing to solve a problem that has eluded solution for two centuries. In the end, we can solve their problem only when we solve society's, and solving that larger problem requires us to confront some questions that we have not yet answered in compelling fashion: how do black Americans fit in? Do we really want racial equality? And, how much are we willing to pay to attain it?

This paper has been about race and the American armed forces. Exploring that topic required a survey – a dredging up – of one of my country's most pervasive, divisive, and morally embarrassing issues. Although I have sought to note that a tremendous amount of progress has been made in recent decades, there is always the danger that the negative has been given more attention than the positive. I want to close therefore on a more positive note and on an observation that is in keeping with the theme of this volume.

In many ways the United States has been very fortunate, even with respect to the matter of race. I was in England for several months during 1967 and 1968 when that country was confronting an influx of non-whites from its former colonies. One of the most outspoken Members of Parliament at the time was Enoch Powell, who warned that the Thames, like the River Tiber, would run red with blood if England did not keep the coloureds out. Powell made frequent references to the United States, especially to the race riots that had occurred in many American cities in the mid-1960s. Following Martin Luther King's assassination in 1968, President Lyndon Johnson could peer out of his White House windows and watch portions of Washington burning just a few blocks away.

As I was preparing to leave England in June of 1968 another firebrand, the Reverend Ian Paisley, was gaining notoriety. The recurring pattern of violence that the English politely call "the troubles" was starting up again.

With a few exceptions, such as Miami a few years ago, the streets of America's cities have been relatively free of racial violence since 1968. During that same period, more than 2,000 people have died on the streets of Belfast. If we consider what has been going on for decades or even centuries in Belfast, in Beirut, in the Basque region of Spain, then we may be able to see the American experience in a different light. We can marvel at the progress that has occurred in the United States in recent decades. Even as we argue over the distance we have yet to travel, we can take great pride in how far we have come.

Similarly, the United States military has been fortunate. Blacks and whites share a common language, have basically the same set of religious beliefs, mores, aspirations and political values. The United States does not have the huge cultural rifts that fragment other nations and undermine their capacity for self-protection.[84] Nor are there fundamental disagreements over the identity of major U.S. allies and adversaries, although considerable argument persists over specific uses of American military force.

Still, race remains a highly visible dividing line. As in other multi-racial or multi-ethnic societies, the salient issue is not the existence of the line, but its location, the precise manner in which it slices across the political landscape. When it separates the powerful from the powerless, isolates those who make decisions from those who are most directly affected by them, then the viability of basic state institutions will be weakened.

Ultimately, resolving these problems is a test of statesmanship. True statesmanship lies in developing decision-making processes that are inclusive rather than exclusive. It lies in resisting ethnic chauvinism and in aggressively combating racial privilege. These are formidable tasks, and they become even more forbidding when cleavages based on race, religion, language and region reinforce one another. In some societies, for example, what we observe is not one military force but several competing forces that manifest many of the characteristics of classic warlordism.

Nevertheless, the problem in so many countries, including the United States to some extent, may not be that some of the soldiers are lacking in quality or loyalty; it may be that many of the leaders are lacking in statesmanship.

Notes

1. *Dred Scott v. Sanford*, 19 How. (U.S.) 393 (1857).
2. Bureau of The Census, *Historical Statistics of the United States*, Part 1 (Washington, 1975), p. 22.
3. *The Federalist Papers*, Number 54.
4. See A. Leon Higginbothan, Jr., *In the Matter of Color* (New York, 1978), esp. pp. 26-27 and 154-55.
5. 21 L. Ed. 394 (1873).
6. *Plessy v. Ferguson*, 163 U.S. 537 (1896).
7. John Hope Franklin, *From Slavery to Freedom: A History of Negro Americans*, 5th edition (New York, 1980), p. 313.
8. Benjamin Quarles, *The Negro in the American Revolution* (Chapel Hill, 1961), p. 8.
9. Bernard C. Nalty and Morris J. MacGregor, eds., *Blacks in the Military: Essential Documents* (Wilmington, Delaware, 1981), p. 7. This is a valuable resource. For convenience, references to documents contained in that volume will refer to the volume's page number rather than to the full title of the original document.
10. Ibid., p. 8.
11. Quarles, p. 10.
12. Nalty and MacGregor, p. 10.
13. Ibid., p. 8.
14. Robert W. Mullen, *Blacks in America's Wars* (New York, 1973), p. 31.

15. Nalty and MacGregor, p. 14.
16. Ibid., p. 16.
17. Ibid., p. 17.
18. Ibid., p. 18.
19. Ibid., p. 24.
20. Benjamin Quarles, *The Negro in the Civil War* (Boston, 1969), p. 328.
21. Ibid., p. xii.
22. Nalty and MacGregor, pp. 50-51.
23. See Mary Frances Berry and John W. Blassingame, *Long Memory: The Black Experience in America* (New York, 1982), pp. 310-12 and 315-16. In 1972 the Army cleared the records of the Brownsville soldiers.
24. Department of Defense, *Black Americans in Defense of Our Nation* (Washington, 1985), p. 27. In 1881 Flipper was discharged from the Army for embezzling public funds. In 1976 the Army "reviewed the circumstances surrounding Flipper's discharge and issued an Honorable discharge in his name."
25. Ibid., p. 30.
26. Nalty and MacGregor, p. 89.
27. Ibid., p. 81.
28. Ibid., p. 83.
29. See Quarles, *The Negro in the American Revolution*, pp. 13 and 55. Recent immigrants from Ireland provided much of the North's manpower during the Civil War. An 1863 draft riot in New York City claimed a thousand lives. See Thomas Sowell, *Ethnic America* (New York, 1981), p. 26.
30. Ibid., p. 55.
31. Julius Lester, ed., *The Seventh Son: The Thought and Writings of W.E.B. DuBois*, vol. 2 (New York, 1971), p. 73.
32. Nalty and MacGregor, pp. 88-89.
33. Ibid.
34. Franklin, p. 346.
35. Quoted ibid., p. 345.
36. Nalty and MacGregor, p. 239.
37. Ibid., p. 263.
38. Ibid.
39. Ibid.
40. *The Search for Military Justice: Report of an NAACP Inquiry into the Problems of the Negro Serviceman in West Germany* (New York, 1971), p. 20.
41. Robert K. Griffith, Jr., "About Face? The U.S. Army and the Draft," *Armed Forces & Society*, vol. 12, no. 1 (fall 1985), pp. 108-33.
42. Richard Nixon, *The Real War* (New York, 1980), cited in John G. Kesler, "The Reasons to Draft," in *The All-Volunteer Force After a Decade*, ed. William Bowman, Roger Little, and G. Thomas Sicilia (Washington, 1986).
43. Military Manpower Task Force, *A Report to the President on the Status and Prospects of the All Volunteer Force*, Revised Edition (Washington, 1982).
44. Les Aspin, "The AVF: A View From Capitol Hill," in *Who Defends America? Race, Sex and Class in the Armed Forces*, ed. Edwin Dorn (Washington, 1989).
45. Quoted in Martin Binkin, Mark J. Eitelberg, Alvin Schexnider and Marvin M. Smith, *Blacks and the Military* (Washington, 1982), p. 3.
46. Bureau of the Census, "General Population Characteristics," PC 80-1-B1, *U.S. Summary, 1980 Census of Population* (Washington, 1980), p. 31.

47. U.S. Department of Commerce, "Years of School Completed, by Race, Sex, and Age, 1982," *Statistical Abstract of the United States* (Washington, 1984), p. 225.
48. Department of Defense, Defense Manpower Data Center.
49. Department of Defense, *Reserve Component Common Personnel Data System (RCCPD)* (Washington: Office of the Assistant Secretary of Defense, Guards/Reserves, Manpower, and Personnel, September 1984).
50. Defense Manpower Data Center.
51. Mark J. Eitelberg and Brian K. Waters, "Relatively Bright and Ready to Fight: A Qualitative Comparison of Military Recruits and American Youth," prepared for the Office of the Assistant Secretary of Defense (Manpower, Reserve Affairs and Logistics) by Human Resources Research Organization, April 1982, p. 21.
52. Department of Defense, DCSPER 597 Report, from Enlisted Soldiers Master File (Washington: Office of Military Personnel Management, Enlisted Programs Branch, 1984).
53. Defense Manpower Data Center.
54. Edwin Dorn, "Officer Attrition," *Focus*, vol. 12, no. 1 (January 1984), pp. 1a-2a.
55. Defense Manpower Data Center.
56. Lawrence J. Korb, "Defense Policy Personnel Needs and the All-Volunteer Force," in Dorn, ed., *Who Defends America?*
57. James A. Davis, Jennifer Lauby and Paul B. Sheatsley, "Americans View the Military," Report No. 131 (Chicago: National Opinion Research Center, University of Chicago, April 1983). See also A. Wade Smith, "Public Attitudes Toward the Military," *Focus*, vol. 11, no. 3 (March 1983), p. 5.
58. Defense Manpower Data Center.
59. See James R. Daugherty, "Black Women in the Military," *Focus*, vol. 13, no. 7 (July 1985), p. 3.
60. Binkin *et al.*, p. 68.
61. Revision of DA Pamphlet 600-26, "Department of Army Affirmative Action Plan," Memorandum dated December 17, 1984.
62. Department of Defense, *Profile of American Youth: 1980 Nationwide Administration of the Armed Services Vocational Aptitude Battery*, Office of the Assistant Secretary of Defense (Manpower, Reserve Affairs and Logistics), March 1982.
63. Richard V.L. Cooper, "Military Manpower Procurement Policy in the 1980s," in *Military Service in the United States*, ed. General Brent Scowcroft (Englewood Cliffs, NJ, 1982).
64. See for example Martin Binkin, *America's Volunteer Military: Progress and Prospects* (Washington, 1984); also Charles C. Moskos, Jr., "The Marketplace All-Volunteer Force: A critique," in Bowman, Little, and Sicilia, eds., *The All-Volunteer Force.*
65. James R. Daugherty, "Minorities and Military Recruitment," *Focus*, vol. 13, no. 1 (January 1985), pp. 3-4.
66. McGeorge Bundy, "Continuity and Change in National Security Policy," in Dorn, ed., *Who Defends America?*
67. Introductory comments at a conference on The Strategic Dimensions of Military Manpower, sponsored by the Center for Strategic and International Studies, May 21-22, 1985.
68. Binkin *et al.*, *Blacks in the Military*, p. 98.

69. Quoted in Robert K. Fullinwider, "Race and The All-Volunteer Force," in Dorn, ed., *Who Defends America?*

70. James Fallows, "The Draft: Why the Country Needs It," *Atlantic*, 245, April 1980, quoted in Robert K. Fullinwider, "Racial Representation and the AVF: Policies and Principles," in Dorn, ed., *Who Defends America?*

71. Thomas E. Cavanagh, *Inside Black America: The Message of the Black Vote in the 1984 Elections* (Washington, 1985), p. 6.

72. Ibid.; and Joint Center for Political Studies press release, August 30, 1984.

73. Charles C. Moskos, "The American Enlisted Man in the All-Volunteer Army," in David R. Segal and H. Wallace Sinaiko, eds., *Life in the Rank and File* (Washington, 1986).

74. Department of Defense, *Profile of American Youth*.

75. Not everyone agrees with the Pentagon's assessment. Charles Moskos, for example, has pointed out that the AVF contains far fewer college-educated enlistees. See "The Marketplace All-Volunteer Force: A Critique," in Bowman, Little and Sicilia, eds., *The All-Volunteer Force*. Other critics have argued that the services have lowered their enlistment standards in order to obtain sufficient numbers of recruits. See Kester.

76. For some examples of the ways weapons systems get built with little attention to the human component, see James Fallows, *National Defense* (New York, 1981), especially chapters three and four.

77. Wade Smith, "Public Attitudes Toward the Military," *Focus*, vol. 11, no. 3 (March 1983), pp. 4-5.

78. Charles C. Moskos, "Race, Class and the AVF: Issues for Society," in Dorn, ed., *Who Defends America?* See also Moskos, "Social Considerations of the All-Volunteer Force," in Scowcroft, ed., *Military Service in the United States*.

79. Department of Defense, *Profile of American Youth*, p. 26.

80. Sue E. Berryman, "Images and Realities; The Social Composition of Nineteenth and Twentieth Century Enlisted Forces," in Segal and Sinaiko, eds., *Life in the Rank and File*.

81. "Social Considerations of the All-Volunteer Force," in Scowcroft, ed., *Military Service in the United States*.

82. Fullinwider, "Racial Representation and the AVF."

83. Roger Wilkins, "Who Defends America? Some Concluding Observations," in Dorn, ed., *Who Defends America?*

84. Cynthia Enloe, *Ethnic Soldiers: State Security in a Divided Society* (Athens, 1980).

"BROTHERHOOD IN ARMS": THE ETHNIC FACTOR IN THE SOVIET ARMED FORCES

TERESA RAKOWSKA-HARMSTONE*

THE POPULAR WESTERN image of the Soviet Armed Forces (SAF) is that they are "Russian." But in fact the forces are composed of many national groups, and military service is seen as an important educational experience which integrates young men of varying culture and ethnic origin into a common "Soviet" mould. The Soviet Armed Forces are seen as the "school of the nation." The conscripts are inculcated with a set of common Soviet values and behavioural patterns that maximize the forces' cohesion and combat readiness, while also endowing each soldier with a capability to transcend the parochial confines of his native environment and to lead socially useful civilian life following the service. In this task the management in the forces of the ethnic factor has been of major significance. It has been at the centre of concern of the SAF's organization and manpower distribution, and in the forefront of political-military training.

The ethnic mix of each conscript cohort reflects that of the country at large, but their distribution in the ranks fits an "ethnic security map" that favours the Russian element. In the 1980s the

* This paper is a much abbreviated and revised version of my chapter on the Soviet Armed Forces in the report: Teresa Rakowska-Harmstone, Christopher D. Jones, John Jaworsky, Ivan Sylvain, and Zoltan Barany, "Warsaw Pact: The Question of Cohesion, Phase II — Volume 3, Union of Soviet Socialist Republics, Bulgaria, Czechoslovakia and Hungary; Bibliography," ORAE Extramural Paper No. 39 (Ottawa, Department of National Defence, March 1986). It was prepared for publication in 1987 and updated in mid-1989. For the analysis of the ethnic factor in the military in the historical perspective I am indebted to C.D. Jones. Information for the statistical tables in this chapter has been obtained from the following sources: *Narodnoe khoziaistvo SSSR v 1970 g.* (Moscow, 1971), pp. 10-11 and 18-21; *Naselenie SSSR po dannym perepisi naseleniia 1979 goda* (Moscow, 1980), pp. 23-30; and Murray Feshbach, "The Soviet Union: Population Trends and Dilemmas," *Population Bulletin* 37 (Aug. 1982), Table 15 (p. 37); and for Table 2, the 1979 USSR census data: *Chislennost' i sostav naseleniia SSSR, po dannym Vsesoiuznoi Perepisi Naseleniia 1979 goda* (Moscow, 1984), pp. 71-73. The early results of the 1989 census were not adequate for the purpose of analysis in this paper.

123

Russians comprised approximately half of the Soviet population. The
other half was made up of more than one hundred national groups,
among whom the other Slavs (Ukrainians and Belorussians) and the
rapidly expanding Moslem group were the most numerous (see
Table 1). Differences in size, levels of development, culture and attitudes of Soviet national groups have made the ethnic factor an
important variable in military policy since the Red Army's birth, the
importance of which has in fact grown in the decades since World
War II.

An image of a "Russian" army is nevertheless well justified. The
forces are Russian in the language of command and daily usage, in
traditions, character and practices. Soviet military historians explicitly trace Soviet military lineage to the Imperial Russian Army. Soviet
minority spokesmen have always considered the Soviet Armed
Forces to be an instrument of Russification. Their concern was
expressed overtly in the early 1920s and covertly since. A model
Soviet soldier is in fact a Russian soldier, an image that has been
increasingly at odds with the self-perception of the more nationally
conscious non-Russians, whose share of military manpower has been
growing. Some form of ethnic military formations would seem to be
an obvious solution to this dilemma, a solution that would fit both the
"internationalist" rhetoric of the system and its federal state structure. Yet, after a period of experimentation with territorial units in
the 1920s, and their brief revival in World War II, the chosen model
of the organization of the SAF has been that of an integrated national
(*de facto* Russian) army.

Since 1938 all citizens are subject to universal military service
on the principle of individual recruitment, and serve in ethnically
mixed units. The language of the forces is exclusively Russian and
ethnic Russians predominate in the professional cadre. In comparison with the old Imperial Army, which was predominantly Slav, the
ethnic composition of the rank and file of the SAF more closely
reflects that of the population. Forty-five national groups were
exempt from the draft before 1917, while every male Soviet citizen is
now subject to it. The professional cadre, on the other hand, appears
to have become more Russian in ethnic colouration, at least among
the general officers.[1]

As in the Imperial Army, the Soviet Armed Forces are the focus
of Russian patriotism – now under the label of "Soviet patriotism."
The traditions of the Imperial Army also survive in the approach to
doctrine and technology, in the in-service training methods (the
emphasis on discipline, drill and habit-forming tactical exercises),
and in the training of officers.[2] The imperial military characteristics
now appear in an "internationalist" packaging, but the heritage is

TABLE 1

USSR MAJOR NATIONAL GROUPS: SIZE, URBANIZATION AND RESIDENCE INDICATORS

| National Groups | Numbers in Thousands | | % Change | % of USSR Population | | Settlement Pattern (% of total) | | | | | |
| | | | | | | Reside in Own Republic | | Reside in Contiguous Region | | Reside in Other Parts of USSR | |
	1970	1979	1970-79	1970	1979	1970	1979	1970	1979	1970	1979
Russians	129,015	137,397	6.5	53.37	52.42	82.5	82.6	—	—	16.5	17.4
Ukrainians	40,753	42,347	3.9	16.86	16.16	86.6	86.2	1.3	2.2	11.5	11.6
Uzbeks	9,195	12,456	35.5	3.80	4.75	84.1	84.9	15.0	14.4	0.9	0.8
Belorussians	9,052	9,463	4.5	3.74	3.61	80.5	79.9	6.0	6.5	13.5	13.6
Kazakhs	5,299	6,556	23.7	2.19	2.50	78.5	80.7	12.2	11.0	9.3	8.3
Tatars	5,931	6,317	6.5	2.45	2.41	NA	NA	NA	NA	NA	NA
Azerbaidzhani	4,380	5,477	25.0	1.81	2.09	86.2	85.9	8.3	9.4	5.7	4.7
Armenians	3,559	4,151	16.6	1.47	1.58	62.0	65.6	26.3	22.2	11.7	12.2
Georgians	3,245	3,571	9.7	1.34	1.36	96.5	96.1	—	—	3.5	3.9
Moldavians	2,698	2,968	10.0	1.12	1.13	85.4	85.1	9.8	9.9	4.8	5.0
Tadzhiks	2,136	2,898	35.7	0.88	1.10	76.3	77.2	22.4	21.3	1.3	1.5
Lithuanians	2,665	2,851	7.0	1.10	1.09	94.1	95.1	1.5	1.3	4.4	3.6
Turkmen	1,525	2,028	33.0	0.63	0.77	92.9	93.2	4.6	5.2	2.5	1.6
Germans	1,846	1,936	4.9	0.77	0.74	NA	NA	NA	NA	NA	NA
Kirgiz	1,452	1,906	31.3	0.60	0.73	88.5	88.5	10.0	10.0	1.5	1.5
Jews	2,151	1,811	-15.8	0.89	0.69	NA	NA	NA	NA	NA	NA
Chuvashi	1,694	1,751	3.4	0.70	0.67	NA	NA	NA	NA	NA	NA
Latvians	1,430	1,419	0.6	0.59	0.55	93.2	93.4	—	—	6.8	6.6
Bashkirs	1,240	1,371	10.6	0.51	0.52	NA	NA	NA	NA	NA	NA
Mordvinians	1,263	1,192	-5.6	0.52	0.45	NA	NA	NA	NA	NA	NA
Poles	1,167	1,151	-1.4	0.48	0.44	NA	NA	NA	NA	NA	NA
Estonians	1,007	1,020	1.3	0.42	0.39	91.8	92.9	—	—	8.2	7.1
Others	9,017	10,028	—	3.73	3.82	—	—	—	—	—	—
USSR Total	241,720	262,085	8.4	99.97	100.01						

unmistakable. Not surprisingly, perhaps, the continuity appears to have been functional in contributing to the effectiveness of the forces, except for a highly dissonant new factor, that of a growing national self-assertion among the minorities.

The history of Soviet ethnic relations in society at large and in the armed forces fits well Cynthia Enloe's perceptive concept of an "ethnic security map,"[3] the need for which forges another link between the imperial past and the Soviet present. The Revolution did not change the Russians' quantitative and qualitative hegemony in society. Neither did it change their distrust of minorities. Both have been reflected in the unwritten rules that underlie Russian determination to maintain the hegemony which, they feel, is theirs by natural right. This determination is more pronounced in the armed forces than it is in any other part of society, with the possible exception of the KGB.

Loyalty of the non-Russians has historically been an important concern in the management of the Imperial/Soviet army. Only "loyal" minorities were conscripted in the Imperial period; the native peoples of the Caucasus, Siberia and Turkestan were exempt from military service, although ethnic units formed on a voluntary basis were allowed. In the Soviet period certain groups were also initially excluded from the draft, but gradually conscription was extended to all. The last to be included in the draft (in 1931), were the the natives of Central Asia.[4]

The Evolution of the Red Army: 1917-41

THE REVOLUTIONARY AND separatist potential of national minorities was well understood by V.I. Lenin and was used by him to excellent advantage in facilitating the breakup of the Empire through Bolshevik advocacy of the right of the rebellious minorities to national self-determination. Revolutionary ferment among the minority soldiers of the Imperial Army significantly contributed to its disintegration and to the loss of its combat effectiveness at the front. But, unfortunately from the Bolshevik point of view, as the time came to build a new Soviet state and to consolidate Soviet power the minorities invariably opted either for independence or for broad autonomy. To counter this trend both Lenin and Stalin modified the principle of national self-determination by subordinating it to the principle of class unity. Lenin is on record insisting that "the interests of socialism are higher than the interests of the right of nations to self-determination";[5] Stalin also argued that the right of the working class to consolidate its power was a "higher" right than the right to national self-determination.[6]

The potential disloyalty of the minorities in the newly formed

Red Army was the focus of early concern, and has remained so to this day. Despite his attention to national rights in other areas, Lenin never deviated from a conviction that in military matters central control was essential. Consequently he resisted all proposals for minorities' autonomy in the Red Army.[7] The history of national-territorial formations in the SAF illustrates both the desire of the minorities to organize autonomous military units, and the determination of the leadership to maintain an integrated army under a central leadership.

The RKKA (Workers'-Peasants' Red Army) was established on 28 January 1918 by a decree of the newly formed Council of People's Commissars of the Russian Soviet Federated Socialist Republic (RSFSR). Soviet republics were established in the western borderlands (Ukrainian, Belorussian-Lithuanian, Latvian and Estonian), in competition with non-Soviet rivals and each with its own army. National republics with their own national forces were also established in Transcaucasia by the non-Bolshevik elements: Mensheviks in Georgia, Dashnak in Armenia, and Musavat in Azerbaijan. In Tataria and Bashkiria pro-Soviet Moslem military units were formed in Kazan in 1918 under Moslem officers.[8]

The Red Army started as a voluntary proletarian army, but compulsory service was introduced on 19 July 1918, and by the end of that year military professionalism and discipline were firmly established with the help of ex-tsarist officers recruited by Leon Trotsky, then the Commissar of War. The new institution of political commissars was created to assure political reliability.

The Soviet armies of the western borderlands were willing to cooperate with the Red Army, but they were unwilling to give up their national autonomy and national interests for the sake of this cooperation. Soviet sources explicitly admit that separatism was rampant in Soviet western armies, and that the Bolsheviks had to move quickly to subordinate them to Red Army command. All military units were placed under the command of the RSFSR's Revolutionary Military Council (*Revvoensovet*) 19 May 1919, and a unified command system was established the following June,[9] although it took some time for the western units to be actually incorporated into the Red Army.

A similar fate met the national military formations of the Transcaucasian republics after the RKKA reconquered the region in 1920-1921. Moslem military formations, which contributed significantly to the Reds' victory in the Civil War, were dissolved as separate entities in 1920. In Kazakhstan, the *Alash Orda* political movement for autonomy was eventually destroyed, as was the armed conservative Moslem opposition (*Basmachi*) in Central Asia. Pro-Soviet Moslem volunteers there were recruited into Moslem formations, but these formations were part of the Red Army and were usually commanded by Russian officers. Thus by the end of the Civil War all national autonomous military formations were dissolved. Information available for 1921 indicates that the Red Army was then predominantly Slav in national composition, with a Russian majority.[10]

The issue of military service as the instrument of Russification for the non-Russians, as well as all other issues bearing on national autonomy, came to a head at the 12th Congress of the Russian Communist Party (bolsheviks) (RKPb) in 1923. Ukrainian communists, supported by other non-Russians, advocated a system of national territorial militia formations in preference to an integrated army. Eventually a compromise was worked out which was an extension of a policy of *korenizatsiia* (rooting in) designed earlier by Lenin to bring autonomous cadres into state and party *apparati* in minority areas. The compromise resulted in a coexistence, under a unified command, of a cadre army with territorial national minority formations.

The military reorganization of 1924 created four types of formations in the RKKA. The core of the forces was made up of a relatively small regular cadre army composed predominantly of Slavs, mostly Russians. Most minority recruits served in one of three types of national formations. These were, first, the national military divisions recruited in union republics and larger autonomous republics and, second, "ethnic units," (regiments and smaller units) recruited from among smaller ethnic groups — both parts of the regular standing army — and third, minority formations constituted in minority areas as a reserve force of territorial divisions of militia.[11]

Between 1924 and 1935 national divisions and units and a reserve militia force were formed in all republics and major autonomous entities. But the concessions to the national principle proved to be illusory. Except in their name and the ethnic origins of their soldiers, the units did not differ from regular (cadre) forces in any other respect. Most were small infantry or cavalry units, and all were part of larger regular formations. Russian officers constituted the hard command core, even though an effort was made in the 1920s to train non-Russian officers. By the late 1920s and early 1930s nevertheless, national formations were already de-emphasized, in view of the centralization policies pursued by Stalin, the purges of "bourgeois nationalists" among the leading communist cadres of the republics, and a revival in the USSR of Russian national ethos.

The national formations were abolished in the military reform of 7 March 1938 on the pretext that they had become superfluous in view of the high level of "internationalization" achieved by the Soviet people. But the real reason, engendered by an increasingly tense international situation, was their doubtful combat value and reliability. Instead, the reform introduced a new system of individual conscription into multinational units, which still remains the principle of recruitment in the SAF.

The Great Patriotic War

THE NAZI ATTACK on the Soviet Union in June 1941 caught Soviet forces unprepared, and in the chaos of retreat and hasty mobilization it was found expedient selectively to restore national formations. In retrospect the reasons for the temporary concession to the national principle seem fairly clear. As a result of the Germans' fast advance, the one manpower pool still available to the SAF in the fall of 1941 was in Central Asia, the Caucasus, and non-Russian areas of the RSFSR, i.e., the areas where the people were still largely unassimilated, and only a few spoke Russian. Moreover, wartime mobilization of reserves resulted in units which closely reflected the ethnic colouration of the manpower resident in a given locality. The official recognition of the units' specific ethnic character served to enhance morale, facilitate command and socialization tasks (which were conducted primarily in local languages), and mobilize the support of the soldiers' home communities. The explanation for the revival of national formations given in Soviet sources is that the State Defence Council agreed to form national units in November 1941, "responding to requests" from party leaders of the union and autonomous republics.[12] Translated, this indicates that a campaign was launched there to mobilize the non-Russians for the defence of the "Motherland." The revival of national patriotic feelings among the Russians as well as the non-Russians was to prove essential in the defence of the country and in turning the tide of the war.

The new units differed from the pre-1938 formations. Organized as units of a cadre army they were "filled mostly by representatives of the local population of the union and autonomous republics who spoke Russian poorly or not at all. Other representatives of the local population were called up to serve in the usual cadre army."[13]

"Volunteers" apparently constituted a substantial part of the personnel of the new units.[14] The non-Russian speakers were presumably encouraged to volunteer, while Russian speakers were not, except in the case of politically reliable ethnic cadre needed as political personnel and translators. Local party and Soviet organizations are said to have helped in mobilizing the national formations and in the "selection" of "their command staff."[15] In view of the shortage of trained ethnic officers and undoubtedly also for security reasons, the regular Slav officers remained as the crucial element of the command structure, but were assisted by Russian-speaking ethnic personnel.

National formations of the new type were formed in Kazakhstan, the republics of Central Asia and Transcaucasus, and from among the personnel of Baltic ethnic origins, after the newly conquered Baltic republics were lost to the invading German armies. There is no record of Ukrainian and Belorussian national formations. Understandably, none were formed in November 1941 because at that time their national areas were overrun by the enemy; but none were formed when the areas were recovered. Instead, there was massive conscription of Ukrainians and Belorussians into regular integrated units after 1943.

At the time of their formation in 1941, the titular groups constituted either a plurality or a majority (apparently up to 90 percent) of total personnel in "their" national units. But, as the war progressed, their share dwindled. By the end of the war, titular ethnic personnel constituted at best 10 to 15 percent of the units' total, in most cases only 1 or 2 percent.[16] Clearly, all ethnic formations underwent a rapid process of "internationalization," reverting to the standard preferred multi-ethnic pattern, and retaining their national character in name only. The decline in the share of ethnic manpower in "their" units was the result of several factors. First, there was a magnitude of defections and the ever-present problem of reliability.[17] Second, units withdrawn from combat zone were reinforced by manpower locally available and, by 1943, as German-occupied parts of the USSR were recovered, the Slavs became available again. The final and very important reason was the high rate of casualties.

No exact figures for Central Asian and Caucasian participation in the war effort are available, but the numbers were substantial and the losses were high. Scattered information in Soviet sources indicates that their numbers in May 1942 came to 1.2 million soldiers; thus their share of Soviet military manpower at that point amounted to one-fifth of the total and was about three times greater than their 1939 weight in the Soviet population. On the crucial Caucasus and Stalingrad fronts in the fall of 1942 the Moslems and the Caucasians may have constituted nearly one-half of the troops.[18] The war effort by all Soviet national groups is always carefully (albeit proportionately) acknowledged in Soviet propaganda. But the major role played by the Moslems and the Georgians and the Armenians in the two crucial battles of the war has yet to be highlighted.

The Baltic formations were the one exception to the rule of ethnic attrition. Formed in the RSFSR in late 1941 from pro-Soviet Baltic refugees and expatriates, their ethnic character was carefully preserved as the war progressed.[19] The Baltic command and political cadre, which was loyal to Moscow, was carefully preserved in order to take over the leadership of their republics at war's end. Their task, as in the case of Polish and Czechoslovak communist cadre serving in Soviet-sponsored national military units in World War II, was to lend legitimacy to the pacification campaign conducted by Soviet forces against anti-Soviet national resistance in their native countries after the "liberation."

The revival of national formations in wartime was clearly a temporary expedient that provided for most effective utilization of manpower. Most of the formations, by then ethnic in name only, survived until the mid-fifties. The concept of a territorial militia was seemingly revived by N.S. Khrushchev. In 1958 he was quoted saying that eventually the standing army should be replaced by a territorial militia system, and that it was only the pressure from capitalists that forced the Soviet Union to maintain a powerful standing army.[20] But there was no follow-up. It may be remembered that the Thaw of 1957-58 was also a period of concessions to national republics, as well as a period of confrontation with and the demotion of the hero of the Great Patriotic War and the then Minister of Defence, Marshal Georgi Zhukov.

Social Setting

Ethnic Composition and Demographic Trends

THE CONSCRIPT ARMY'S make-up is supposed to reflect that of the population, although the Slav elements have been favoured (as shall be seen below), and the soldiers' attitudes mirror the views and perceptions prevalent in their original social setting. As noted earlier, the Soviet population mix consists of over one hundred various nations and nationalities, but the proportions are uneven. According to the 1979 population census ethnic Russians constituted 52.42 percent of the 262 million total. Twenty-one other groups numbered over one million people each, while the remainder of the 70 enumerated groups accounted for only 5 percent of the population. In 1979 fifteen of the largest groups (including the Russians) had the status of union republic nations under the Soviet federal system; four had autonomous republic status, while three were geographically dispersed and had no autonomous rights whatsoever. Next to the Russians, the Ukrainians were the most numerous with more than 40 million people. The Moslem Uzbeks were in third place with 12.5 million people, and the Belorussians were fourth with 9.5 million people (see Table 1).

In ethnocultural terms the Soviet nations fall into two major clusters and several subgroups. The Slavs (Russians, Ukrainians, Belorussians and the dispersed Poles remaining in the western borderlands and in their places of exile) constituted 72.8 percent — almost three-fourths — of the USSR population in 1979. The second cluster consisted of the Moslems with 44 million, or 17 percent of the population. The Moslems included the Kazakhs, the Central Asians (Uzbeks, Tadzhiks, Turkmen and Kirgiz), the Azerbaidzhani (Azeri Turks) of Transcaucasia, the two major Moslem groups in the RSFSR (Tatars and Bashkirs), and various smaller Moslem groups of Central Asia, the Caucasus, the RSFSR, and other republics. The subgroups were Transcaucasian Christians (Georgians and Armenians), with 3 percent of the Soviet population; the Balts (Lithuanians, Latvians and Estonians) with 2 percent; the Jews and the Germans, with 1.5 percent each; and the Moldavians with about 1 percent. The mixed "others" totalled an approximate 5 percent of the population.

Soviet national groups differ widely in their historical and economic development, and represent a variety of divergent cultures. Thus Soviet conscripts range from sophisticated urbanites of Riga, Leningrad, Kiev or Moscow to traditional villagers of Central Asian *kishlaks*, and from Siberian industrial workers or woodsmen to mountain shepherds of the Pamirs and reindeer herders of the Far North. They speak a variety of languages and possess different cultural norms and perceptions, levels of skill and education. Many still come from a non-urban environment. All are now basically literate in their native tongues. But many still do not know, or have only the barest rudiments of, the Russian language, the country's common *lingua franca* and the language of the SAF.

After World War II losses, the Soviet population showed an annual rate of growth of 1.8 percent through the 1950s. But the rate began to decline in the 1960s, and in the 1970s it amounted to only 0.8 percent. The reasons were a decline in fertility rates, accompanied by an increase in death rates especially among infants and young males. Alcoholism was apparently a major contributing cause to both phenomena.[21]

Differentials in the decline of the rates of growth of major national groups reflected the differentials in their modernization and cultural backgrounds. Reproduction rates of most of the western and northwestern economically more advanced groups fell steeply, while those of the still largely rural southeastern groups were reduced slowly or increased. Demographic dynamism of the Russians suffered a marked decline, while Moslems underwent a population explosion. In consequence the population of the Slavic and Baltic republics grew by one-quarter to one-third only between 1950 and 1981, while the population of Central Asia and the Transcaucasian republics (except Georgia) increased by one to one and a half times. Thus, if current growth rates continue, the Moslems can double their population in less than thirty years (a feat that the Uzbeks and some others have already accomplished in the 1959-79 intercensal period), while the Slavs would need a century and a half to do the same.[22]

The immediate result of differential growth rates was a shift in the relative weight in the population of the two major clusters. Between 1959 and 1979 the share of the Slavic group dropped from 76 to 72 percent of the total, while that of the Moslems increased from 12 to 17 percent. Assuming no major changes in current trends, projections indicated that in the year 2000 the share of the Slavs would decline to 65 percent, while that of the Moslems would rise to between 20 and 25 percent of the total. Some analysts project that both clusters would become approximately equal in size in the next one hundred years and, by 2080, will account for 40 percent of the population each.[23]

The new population census was conducted in the Soviet Union in early 1989. Advance information that had sporadically become available indicated that the rates of decline (in the case of the European populations) and the growth rates (of the Moslem groups) have been actually steeper than had been anticipated.

National Attitudes vs. Integration

CREATING A "NEW Soviet man" out of the divergent elements which comprise the Soviet population has not been easy. The one "Soviet people" was proclaimed to have become a reality by the late Secretary General of the CPSU, L.I. Brezhnev in 1971. As officially interpreted, the "Soviet People" encompass and stand above the constituent Soviet nations and nationalities; their loyalty to the Soviet Motherland overrides all lesser national loyalties. Nevertheless, conflicts in ethnic relations are recognized to have survived in the Soviet population, and are expected to remain for a considerable period, because of the dynamics of interaction between two major trends which are said to have affected these relations since 1917.

These dialectically inter-related trends are toward the consolidation by major Soviet nations of their national identity, characterized as their "national flowering" (*rastsvet*), and toward their "ever growing closer together" or rapprochement (*sblizhenie*). In the official view it is the on-going rapprochement that is the trend of the future, and it is this trend that has been instrumental in the emergence of the "Soviet People." Manifestations of ethnic nationalism have reached an unprecedented level of openness and intensity under the impact of Gorbachev's policy of *glasnost*, but the official emphasis on the rapprochement as the trend of the future has not been changed.[24]

A process of assimilation, which has been a feature of Soviet ethnic dynamism, has contributed to both *rastsvet* and *sblizhenie*. An assimilation of the culturally less cohesive and numerically weaker groups into the stronger and larger ones is part of the trend of national consolidation. But because the Russians have been the main magnet for culturally weaker people, an assimilation into the Russian language and/or identity has tacitly been accepted as an important factor contributing to *sblizhenie*, and thus to the process of Soviet integration.

In general, *sblizhenie* has been a function of the on-going process of modernization and "internationalization" (ethnic and cultural mixing) of Soviet society. The essence of *sblizhenie* is a transfer of ethnic specificity from the "traditional sphere of material culture" to a new "spiritual and mainly professional" (i.e. modern) culture.[25] In plain words, it means a substitution of the new Soviet urban culture – comprised basically of Russian cultural content – for the traditional cultures of the non-Russians. Service in the armed forces is seen as an important part of this process. In practice the emergent new "Soviet man" has in fact been a version of the old Russian model, now modernized and dressed in Marxist-Leninist ideological clothing. This is the model that embraces the *assimilados* under a common umbrella-type identity.

The signposts of national consolidation reflect the prevalent socio-demographic realities in minority areas that have become increasingly visible in the USSR since the late 1950s. They are: a compact pattern of national settlement; a high concentration of the titular group in its national area; a high level of adherence to the national language; and safeguarding and development of a national culture and a "national exclusiveness." The long-range outcomes of the process of non-Russian national consolidation are obviously dysfunctional to Soviet national integration.[26]

The *sblizhenie* (rapprochement) process, on the other hand, is assumed to have been promoted by a whole range of "internationalist" phenomena: inter-regional migration, ethnic mixing at urban and industrial sites, mixed marriages and bilingualism (the native language plus Russian as the second language), or linguistic assimilation into Russian language. An "internationalist setting" is considered best for "nurturing the internationalist spirit," as the late General Secretary Yuri V. Andropov, speaking at the 60th anniversary of the USSR in December 1983, put it. Rural residence, on the other hand, is in most cases synonymous with a uni-national ethnic setting and villages are seen as the fulcrum of traditional "survivals."

The demographic indicators reviewed earlier testify to the new vitality of most non-Russian groups (a reversal of the 1926-1959 trends), and hence to the gains made by the national consolidation trend at the expense of *sblizhenie*. Politically this coincided with a relaxation of central controls, and a recognition of pressures for greater autonomy coming from the union republics that have emerged in the thirty years since the death of Joseph Stalin in 1953. It is only with the 1983 accession to the position of Secretary General of the CPSU of Yuri Andropov, and the arrival on the scene of Mikhail Gorbachev in 1985, that signs of a new policy have multiplied.

The old policy, despite the relaxation, denied that particular ethnic consciousness was growing among minority groups, and concentrated instead on emphasizing the *sblizhenie*. The new policy is more realistic: it recognizes, acknowledges, and studies the phenomenon of rising ethnic nationalisms, but at the same time it attempts to undermine their manifestations and to prevent their further growth. The first step has been to dismantle the autonomous perquisites the republics' ethnic party leaders were able to accumulate under the long reign of Leonid Brezhnev as a *quid pro quo* for personal allegiance to his leadership. A wide-ranging purge of regional *apparati* followed. It was made easier by the advanced age of most local leaders, and by their widely manifest venality and corruption. The post-27th CPSU Congress' new emphasis on "exchanging" cadres between the centre and the republics has made it more difficult for the local elites to act as spokesmen for their national interests.

Ethnic conflict in Soviet society has been officially recognized to exist in four major areas: (1) at the all-Union level between the interests of each national group and those of the Soviet Union as a whole and (2) in conflict between republics; (3) within the republics between immigrant (predominantly Russians) and indigenous groups; and (4) in the workplace in a multi-ethnic setting between individuals and/or groups of different nationalities.[27] Within this typology the military service can properly be assigned to the fourth category.

The place of a given national group on the integration spectrum between *rastsvet* and *sblizhenie* can best be assessed by estimating the degree of their attitudinal and/or functional conformity to the official Soviet value system and behavioural patterns. As defined for the purpose of the study on which this paper is based, attitudinal integration denotes the internalization of the official Soviet norms; functional integration, on the other hand, assumes outward conformity with the requirements imposed by these norms. The first implies the commitment to the preservation of the Soviet system and its stated goals, and is incompatible with lesser loyalties. The second does not preclude conflicting ethnic and political loyalties as long as these are held *in camera* and do not result in actions inimical to the system.

Attitudinal integration, seen as an end product of the process of *sblizhenie*, is the defining characteristic of the "Soviet People." Functional integration is seen as a first step towards *sblizhenie*; it is contingent on a set of conditions that reward conformity and make non-conformity impossible, difficult, or counter-productive for the individuals and the groups concerned.

For military purposes attitudinal integration is the ultimate goal of political-military indoctrination and the guarantee of loyalty under stress. But functional integration is an adequate substitute as long as it guarantees assured responses to command. The deployment and management of military manpower attempts to maximize the conditions that promote functional integration. At the same time, the thrust of the military political-education system is directed at inculcating attitudes in servicemen which would reflect the desired norms and values, and thus promote their attitudinal integration.

No Soviet opinion surveys are available that would measure the degree of commitment of its citizens to the official norms, let alone allow one to discern whether this commitment implies an internalization of norms and values, or merely testifies to outward conformity. But substitutes adequate for the purpose of this analysis are available in the form of statistical indicators of linguistic assimilation and bilingualism.

The use of language statistics for the purpose of measuring both types of integration is based on three assumptions. The first is that the official Soviet norms are derived from the Russian norms and value system. The second is that the linguistic assimilation of the non-Russians into the Russian language approximates their cultural assimilation into the Russian group. The third assumption is that bilingualism, i.e., the acquisition of a knowledge of Russian as a second language, approximates a citizen's readiness and capability to participate in Soviet life within the matrix of official norms, and is a symbol of functional integration.

Using language statistics as a measure of integration, approximately 59 percent of the Soviet population (155 million in 1979), could be considered integrated in attitudinal terms. In 1979 this group included the 137 million Russians and the 18 million non-Russians assimilated into the Russian language. The remaining 41 percent of the Soviet population (107 million), were the non-Russians who were in the process of consolidating their separate national identities. Accordingly, the ratio of attitudinally integrated "Soviet people" to culturally self-aware non-Russians was approximately three to two in 1979, a poor showing for the 60 years of intensive socialization, as pointed out even by Soviet specialists.[28]

But, in addition to the 14.4 percent of the *assimilados* among the non-Russians, 49.4 percent of them were bilingual, hence integrated in functional terms. Looking at the USSR as a whole, therefore, almost 83 percent of the population was integrated: a majority in attitudinal terms, others only functionally. The proportion of the non-integrated constituted only an approximate 17.2 percent of the people – a comfortable margin, it would appear, for political as well as military purposes.

Nevertheless, the situation was perceived as a major problem because this 17 percent included fully one-third of the non-Russians (36.2 percent of their total), who remained outside the integration picture. Moreover, the largest share of the non-integrated population was located either in the vulnerable western borderlands, or in the southeastern regions inhabited by ethnic groups whose birthrate was a long-range threat to the Russians' hegemonial position (see Table 2).

Military Implications

THE ANALYSIS ABOVE allows for an approximate assessment of Soviet national groups' reliability and/or functionality in military service. Applying its integration criteria, Soviet draftees can be divided into three main groups: (*a*) those integrated in attitudinal and functional terms; (*b*) those integrated functionally; and (*c*) the non-integrated. There is also a fourth group, that of (*d*) dissident elements.

Group *a* designates the Russians and Russified elements among the non-Russians. The latter category includes substantial segments of the other Slavs: Ukrainians and Belorussians, especially the expatriates among them and residents of areas in their republics where the interaction with the Russians has been intense, notably the urban and industrialized portions of their republics' eastern regions. Also included are major segments of the three major dispersed groups (Germans, Jews and Poles), and of practically all minority groups in the RSFSR, as well as individuals of all ethnic backgrounds who, for whatever reasons, have opted to Russify. The population base of group *a* draftees is the almost 60 percent of Soviet citizens who are attitudinally integrated, inclusive of the 14-plus percent of the non-Russians.

Group *b* comprises the non-Russians who have reached a level of modernization adequate to function within the "socialist" sector of Soviet life, as attested by their fluency in Russian, and who are willing to conform to the requirements of a Russian-dominated environment. Outwardly a conformist element, this group resists attitudinal integration because of a commitment to their own national identity,

TABLE 2

MAJOR NATIONAL GROUPS: ATTITUDINAL AND FUNCTIONAL INTEGRATION, 1979
(Measured by linguistic Russification and bilingualism—in thousands and percentage of total)

National Group	Total Nos. (000)	Attitudinal Integration (Russian as Native Language)		Functional Integration (Bilingual in Russian)		Non-Integrated (Do not speak Russian)	
		% of Total	Thousands	% of Total	Thousands	% of Total	Thousands
Ukrainians	42,347	17.1	7,214	49.8	21,089	33.1	14,017
Belorussians	9,463	25.4	2,404	57.0	5,394	17.6	1,665
Moldavians	2,968	6.0	178	47.4	1,407	46.6	1,383
Lithuanians	2,851	1.7	48	52.1	1,485	46.2	1,317
Latvians	1,419	4.8	68	56.7	805	38.5	546
Estonians	1,020	4.5	46	24.2	247	71.3	727
Georgians	3,571	1.7	61	26.7	953	71.6	2,557
Armenians	4,151	8.4	349	38.6	1,602	53.0	2,200
Azerbaidzhani	5,477	1.8	99	29.5	1,616	68.7	3,763
Uzbeks	12,456	0.6	75	49.3	6,141	50.1	6,240
Kazakhs	6,556	2.0	131	52.3	3,429	45.7	2,996
Tadzhiks	2,898	0.8	23	29.6	858	69.6	2,017
Turkmen	2,028	1.0	20	25.4	515	73.6	1,493
Kirgiz	1,906	0.5	10	29.4	560	70.1	1,336
Tatars	6,317	13.2	834	68.9	4,352	17.9	1,131
Chuvashi	1,751	18.1	317	64.8	1,135	17.1	229
Bashkirs	1,371	7.1	97	64.9	890	28.0	384
Mordvinians	1,192	27.4	327	65.6	782	7.0	83
Germans	1,936	42.6	825	51.7	1,001	5.7	110
Jews	1,811	83.3	1,509	13.7	248	3.0	54
Poles	1,151	26.2	302	44.7	514	29.1	335
Total Major Non-Russian Groups	114,640	13.0	14,964	48.0	55,023	39.0	44,653
Other Non-Russian Groups	10,028	est. 30.0	est. 3,008	est. 65.0	est. 6,518	est. 5.0	501
Total Non-Russians	124,668	est. 14.4	17,972	49.4	61,541	36.2	45,154
Russians	137,397	99.9	137,260	—	—	—	—
USSR Total	262,065	59.2	155,232	23.5	61,541	17.	45,154

and retains latent hostility towards the Russians that may emerge if Russification is pressed within their national enclaves. This group is derived from the bilingual elements among Ukrainians and Belorussians, Armenians and Georgians and others, including such Moslems who have mastered the required educational and linguistic skills. In numerical terms these people comprise the 60 million-plus bilingual non-Russians, i.e., an approximate 23 percent of the Soviet population, or almost one-half of all Soviet non-Russians. Because in some cases bilingualism statistics appear to be grossly inflated,[29] their actual numbers may in fact be smaller.

Group *c* recruits derive from the remaining 36 percent of the non-Russians who have not been integrated. They do not respond to attitudinal integration efforts because of the strength of their traditional cultures, and have not yet mastered either the linguistic skills or, in most cases, the educational skills to function adequately in the technically exacting Russian-speaking environment. As their functional skills improve, many from this group move into the *b* category. The base of group *c* is in the still overwhelmingly rural non-Russian population, which numbers close to 45 million people. The great majority of Moslems are to be found in this category, as well as the still surprisingly large proportions of other non-Russians who remain unilingual: almost three-quarters of Georgians and Armenians, Moldavians, and Estonians, and a sizable portion, still, of Ukrainians (one-third) and even Belorussians (close to one-fifth) (see Table 2). This group is non-integrated largely because of their adherence to a traditional way of life; but a few among them, such as the Estonians, have apparently made a conscious choice to refuse integration. Thus an overlap with the next and last category, *d*, must be assumed.

Group *d* includes "unreliable" elements. It has two components. One consists of national groups that the party regards as unreliable and treats as such: these, to the best of our knowledge, are the Baltic national groups, Western Ukrainians and Western Belorussians, Jews, and Crimean Tatars. Not all the nationals of these groups are dissenters and many are both well integrated and politically reliable, but the distrust has persisted. The second component consists of individual dissenters: national, religious and civil rights advocates, pacifists, and conscientious objectors. Many are indeed nationals of the distrusted groups but they come from all ethnic backgrounds, including the Russian. For obvious reasons it is not possible to assign a numerical value to this group, but it is not very large.

Taking into account the soldiers' desirable characteristics, such as political loyalty and functional capabilities, the *a* group has obviously been the preferred group for military recruitment, especially for the professional cadre. Group *b* has been adequate for most military purposes; group c conscripts have been least desirable. Because of their small numbers, group d recruits have not been a problem; they serve under restrictions, not infrequently under an especially hard special regime.

Up until and through the 1950s, the proportion of these groups in the draft age cohorts adequately met the needs of military deployment. But beginning in the 1960s several factors have combined to aggravate the military manpower situation:

1. Demographic trends reduced the supply of recruits from the preferred a group, while stimulating a population explosion in the least desirable c group. This meant that the supply of Russian youths — traditionally the backbone of the armed forces and the core of the officer cadre — has shrunk, while that of unskilled, non-integrated, non-Russian speakers from rural minority areas has increased.

2. There has been a catastrophic increase in alcoholism and an increase in mortality rates of men of prime military age; both factors have affected the a group more than any of the others.

3. The shortage of integrated, skilled and linguistically functional manpower has pitted the needs of the military sector against those of the economic sector, resulting in shortfalls for both. At the same time the requirements of modern warfare put a premium on a high level of technical competence, reliability, and initiative of individual soldiers and commanders.

4. Finally, the emergence of ethnonationalism, Russian and non-Russian, has affected the self-perception of all national groups and raised the threshold of ethnic conflict in the society at large as well as in the armed forces.

The reduction in the proportion of the young cohorts of group a in each year's military call-up, combined with an influx of non-integrated Moslem youths, has made it difficult to secure manpower for the technically more demanding services, to assure adequate re-enlistment of soldiers and of the professional NCO cadre, and to attract sufficient numbers of qualified officer candidates. It also led to a perception of a threat to the forces' Russian character.[30]

Most Western estimates of the shift in the proportion of recruits between the Slavic and the Moslem groups, seem to agree that the proportion of draft-age Russians will slide, by the end of the century, from one half of the total military manpower in the 1970s, to a little over 40 percent, while that of the Moslems will grow from 12 percent to between one-fourth and one-third of the total in the same period.[31]

This projected shift in the composition of military manpower obviously imposes major constraints on Soviet military planners; but it is not yet a disaster, as suggested by some Western analysts. It nevertheless requires a drastic reassessment of the role heretofore played in the forces by the recruits from the *c* group. Most of them will be Moslems, thus the problem has come to be known as the "Moslem" problem. It seems that such a reassessment of the Moslems' training and recruitment, and their future placement in the forces has already commenced.

The first task that the authorities have set for themselves has been to achieve the functional integration of the Soviet non-Russian population. The effort breaks down into three key aspects: teaching Russian, training in required technical skills and, last but not least, inculcation with proper patriotic attitudes.

The language problem of servicemen drafted from the *c* group has always been present in the SAF but was not openly discussed because of the highly sensitive nature of the problem. But beginning in the early 1980s — the onset of *glasnost* can readily be traced to Andropov — Soviet sources admitted that "more than half of the population in some republics" cannot speak Russian, and even that middle-aged people there seemed to know "Russian better than the young ones," selecting for special mention the Central Asian and Transcaucasian republics and Moldavia.[32] The military relevance of the problem was also openly articulated then for the first time, with numerous references to it in the media and military press of relevant republics.[33]

The remedial policies introduced in the late 1970s and early 1980s focused on the Moslem republics. They have consisted of: (1) measures to improve the study of the Russian language, directed explicitly at promoting a level of proficiency and vocabulary required in military service; (2) a campaign to recruit Moslems for officer schools, especially among the Uzbeks (who will account for an estimated 10 percent of military manpower by the end of the century); (3) propaganda efforts designed to create a new Soviet military ethos for the Moslems by glorification of their share in the Great Patriotic War; and (4) promotion of the development of national languages simultaneously with the emphasis on bilingualism, presumably to pre-empt an anticipated backlash to renewed pressures for linguistic Russification.

It is too early yet to assess the effect of these measures on the Moslems, but there is no evidence so far of a response, let alone enthusiastic response. Also, judging from the strength of Russian patriotic feelings among the professional military cadre (discussed below), an infusion of Moslem officers is not particularly welcomed in the forces.

The "Ethnic Security Map"

MANPOWER DISTRIBUTION IN the SAF is governed by an unwritten but nevertheless crucial ethnic key, which reflects both the differentials in the quality of education and technical skills of national groups, and the security perceptions of the leadership. The starting point for the application of the key is the requirement of an "internationalist" environment, established by the individual recruitment principle, and implemented under two basic official rules. These are, first, that no soldier should be stationed in his home area and, second, that each unit must be ethnically mixed.[34] Wartime mobilization provides the only exception to the multinational principle of military units. Formations filled with local reserves are of predominantly local national colouration; the national formations of 1941 were a case in point.

The first rule seems to have been generally followed. Military defectors firmly believe that stationing "ethnic" soldiers in hostile territory is done to enhance the troops' capacity for the suppression of local disturbances. A complementary practice has been to keep the troops in virtual isolation from the local population, especially when stationed in minority areas.

The multi-ethnic character of military formations is a sacrosanct principle, and the Soviet military press is full of descriptions of military units composed of members of many Soviet nations and nationalities who "happily" soldier together. But in practical application the principle has not necessarily resulted in equity representation. Group a and secondarily group b have been preferred for combat, elite, and specialized services, while representatives of group c and group d have virtually been relegated to auxiliaries, either because they lack technical competence or for security reasons.

The rules that govern the distribution of military manpower are established by the General Staff of the SAF; they are administered by Military Commissariats (*voenkomaty*), which exist at every administrative-territorial level from the district/town level, through province/city to the union republic. *Voenkomaty* are subordinated to the command of the military district in which they are located. The USSR is divided into 16 military districts; the districts are larger than many union republics and their boundaries do not coincide with the boundaries of the republics.

According to information obtained from émigrés, the General Staff estimates the numbers and profile of ethnic/educational/technical skills of each incoming conscript cohort, and then attempts to match the "buyers" (various services and their needs), with the "sellers" (the *voenkomaty*) for the distribution of the intake.[35] In making the assignments a *voenkomat* attempts to reconcile the policy directives and service demands with the manpower available. Its administrative personnel has a degree of discretion in making the assignments: they are thus subject to pressure by interested recruiters as well as by anguished parents.

Western estimates based on information from official and unofficial sources reveal that group *a* forms a large majority (an approximate 90 percent of the total) in elite and special mission combat services, and a significant majority (an approximate 80 percent of the total) in other combat services. Non-Slavic portions of these units are generally filled with group *b* elements. Moslems, on the other hand, and other non-integrated draftees, are concentrated in low-prestige non-combat units which are also a repository for political and national dissidents.

The shortage of and the need for group *a* recruits caused a drastic reduction in educational deferments in 1982. The deferments were revoked for all but a selected few higher educational institutions, thus releasing approximately one million "choice" young men for the draft. Only the educational institutions that were placed on a special list of the Council of Ministers of the USSR retained their deferment rights.[36]

What we know of the ethnic profile of the forces indicates a correlation between the representation of different ethnic groups in a given military unit and its combat role. The larger the share of Russians — and Slavs in general — in a given unit, the more important are the unit's combat functions. Émigrés who were interviewed expressed the conviction that *voenkomaty* had special instructions on the distribution of non-Russians in the armed forces in World War II, and also an instruction that required military formations to be built around a strong Slavic core.[37] There is also a general belief that both instructions retained their validity in the post-1945 period.[38]

The KGB Security and Border Troops are believed to be composed almost exclusively of Slav personnel; Russians predominate in the units stationed on the western borders and Ukrainians and Belorussians in units deployed in the east and southeast. Special elite services, such as the Strategic Rocket Forces, the Air Force and the Navy are reported to be overwhelmingly Slavic in ethnic composition; the non-Slavs, who are thought to constitute no more than 10 percent of their total complement, are concentrated mostly in support roles. To maximize the services' reliability, even members of the preferred Slavic group are chosen from among the "good" Komsomol (Communist Youth League) members. The airborne units are also predominantly Russian.[39]

The proportion of non-Russians is reported to be higher in the ground forces. The Army's combat formations — armour, artillery and infantry – allow for a substantial proportion of the units' strength to be non-Slav, mostly recruited from the *b* group. Non-Slavs, and particularly the members of the *c* group, predominate in non-combat formations, and especially in construction and railroad troops. An estimated one half of the strength of construction battalions (*stroibaty*) are composed of Central Asian Moslems, about 20 percent are Slavs, and the balance is made up of Caucasians, Balts, Jews and other non-Slavs. Surprising as it may seem, a strong Moslem contingent serves in the internal security troops of the Ministry of Internal Affairs (MVD), mostly on prison guard duty. Their dislike for the Europeans (who form a majority of political prisoners) and their poor knowledge of Russian, make them reliable for security duty.[40]

Data from émigrés and defectors are confirmed by other information available to Western analysts. In a detailed study Robert Martin concludes that the "national security force," i.e., the five combat services plus the KGB Border Guards, were roughly 80 percent Slav and 20 percent non-Slav in composition. In contrast, more than two-thirds of the soldiers in railroad and construction troops and approximately one half of the MVD security troops were Moslem. Martin calls the non-combat troops an "ethnic sponge" and speculates on the extent to which these types of units will be able to absorb Moslem surpluses in the future. His view is that, given demographic trends, the "sponge's" absorption capacity is limited and that it will not be possible to maintain the high Slavic ratios in elite and combat units in the future.[41] Thus Soviet military administrators have little choice but to attempt to motivate and to train young Moslems for effective combat service. First steps have already been taken in this direction. But the obstacles to the implementation of this policy lie not only in the Moslems' cultural alienation, but also in the unwillingness of the Russian professional cadre to allow for the dilution, by the Moslems, of a predominantly Russian character of the cadre and of the elite forces.

Unlike the soldiers, members of the professional cadre are volunteers. Admission to officer schools requires high-level educational and technical skills and fluency in Russian. Moreover, for a non-Russian, a decision to become an officer is synonymous with a decision to Russify, because of the Russian character of the forces and the deliberate maintenance of many of the traditions and practices of the Imperial Russian officer corps. The objective requirements and subjective perceptions both severely limit the intake of non-Russians into officers' schools. The inevitable consequence has been that the professional officer cadre is composed overwhelmingly of ethnic Russians; the non-Russian officers are mostly recruited from among ethnic elements already Russified or prone to Russification.

Western estimates of the ethnic composition of the officer corps are based on analysis of names, because no hard information is ever given on the subject. It is generally agreed that approximately 90 percent of the senior officers are of Slavic origin, and that Slavs also predominate in the junior ranks. A recently completed analysis of over ten thousand names of officers collected for the period 1976-78 revealed that, over all, 92.75 percent of the sample consisted of Slavic names, with only 7.46 percent non-Slavic, with the ratio of 91.59 to 8.41, 94.76 to 5.26, and 94.19 to 5.84, respectively, for the names of the ground forces, naval, and air and air defence forces' officers. The study also confirmed the perception that the share of Slavic officers was higher among flag and general officers than among junior ranks.[42]

The analysis of the names of naval officers showed them to be overwhelmingly Slavic. The share of Slavs was highest on ballistic missile submarines, and next highest on warships and among naval infantry and aviation; it was lowest on coastal patrol vessels.[43] Information from émigrés confirms this analysis. According to them naval officers were mostly either Russian or Ukrainian. A former instructor in a naval officer school reported that there was a list of more than 50 minorities who normally were not admitted to naval officer schools; the list included Jews, Germans, Crimean Tatars, and Soviet citizens of foreign origin.[44]

The analysis of a large sample of names cited above also revealed that almost all major non-Slavic groups were represented in the officer corps, particularly at the junior level, but that their total in the sample did not exceed 7.5 percent though they formed one quarter of the Soviet population. The degree of representation differed for particular groups, however. Armenians and Jews were overrepresented in comparison with their share of the population, while Moslems were substantially underrepresented (3 percent of the sample as compared to 17 percent of the population and over 20 percent of the young cohorts). Still, numerically, their group was the largest among the non-Slavic officers. Another interesting revelation was that there were more Moslems among the junior than among the senior officers, while the reverse was true for the Jews.[45]

The non-commissioned officer cadre, the traditional backbone of any army, is acknowledged to be a weak link in the SAF. This type of career has not attracted sufficient numbers of volunteers despite the fact that a new career rank of warrant officer was established in November 1971. Consequently, a large proportion of NCOs are conscripts selected from among each incoming cohort. Conscript NCOs are given six months' special training and are then posted as NCOs for the duration of their hitch. The evidence of émigrés indicates that from the point of view of ethnic composition, draft NCOs are mostly Slavs, and career NCOs and warrant officers are predominantly Slavs. Ukrainians are a preferred national group for the NCO cadre and are said to predominate among them. There are almost no Moslems in the group. The NCO ethnic colouration is explained both by the selection criteria and by the pattern of re-enlistment that seems to be particularly high among soldiers of Slavic background who come from rural or small-town environments and find professional military service a social advancement. There is no comparable appeal for the non-Russians, Moslems in particular, because of the Russification that such a decision entails.[46]

All training in the service is conducted in the Russian language, and the use of any other language, even informally, is officially discouraged. As the émigrés point out, it is not only the question of the non-Russians learning Russian that concerns the authorities, but the ability of political officers and security agents among the servicemen to understand what the soldiers are talking about among themselves. A substantial number of the recruits in each call-up cohort speak little or no Russian, and the complaints that are now made openly in military sources indicate that the problem not only exists but also negatively affects the military training and socialization policies.

Nevertheless no concessions are made to ethnic soldiers who do not understand the language of command, and no special instruction in the language is provided for them, although in the 1980s an increased emphasis has been placed on the teaching of Russian to the minorities in pre-induction training. Instead, Russian soldiers are supposed to help non-Russian soldiers informally, thus manifesting their "fraternal friendship." Any such encroachment on the soldiers' limited leisure time is highly resented by both sides, and has contributed to ethnic conflict in the ranks.[47] Most ethnic soldiers eventually manage to acquire a minimal working knowledge of Russian that enables them to survive the service. Because of their polyglot nature and lesser importance, the Russian character of construction battalions is less pronounced. For this reason service there is preferred by many non-Russians.

The "School of the Nation"

THE SOVIET ARMED Forces' role in educating Soviet citizens "in the spirit of deep loyalty to the Socialist Motherland, to the ideas of peace and internationalism and to the ideas of the friendship of the people" was singled out by the late General Secretary of the CPSU, Leonid Brezhnev, as the main quality that makes the SAF different from its "bourgeois" counterparts.[48] Soviet sources never tire of emphasizing the importance of military service for the process of *sblizhenie* and for the "upbringing" of "Soviet people." Thus the socialization role performed by the forces continues to be of major importance and, contrary to expectations, not only has not disappeared but actually gained in intensity as socialism has "matured."

Effective combat preparedness, that would combine proper attitudes and morale with necessary military skills, has been the desired end product of military socialization. But the effort to foster the proper *Weltanschauung* has been undermined by "incorrect" attitudes brought in by the conscripts from their home environment. The apparent prevalence of such attitudes among young soldiers testifies both to the tenacity of traditional views and to the failure of the many years of Soviet socialization. If one is to believe Soviet military press, the struggle with such attitudes was at the centre of attention of the indoctrination efforts in the early 1980s.

In the 1970s and 1980s, for example, the thrust of military-political education was directed at what Soviet leaders perceived as "bourgeois," pro-Western, and "cynical" attitudes held by "some" young people, and ideological education of youth was the subject of numerous conferences and resolutions.[49] Special socialization campaigns were mounted to commemorate past events. None was more important from the military point of view than the 40th anniversary of the Soviet victory in the Great Patriotic War. It opened with a round of intense appeals to "improve" young people's "class consciousness," and special concern was expressed throughout "because elements of political naiveté have not disappeared among some segments of our young people, and there were cases when the edge of vigilance was dulled, and pacifist attitudes [emerged]."[50]

The "struggle for the minds" of young Soviet soldiers has always been in the forefront of the socialization efforts in the SAF. This struggle, in its various aspects, has been analyzed and documented by Herbert Goldhammer in his pioneering study, *The Soviet Soldier*.[51] Here only most important salient points will be noted, such as the current themes, and the recent emphasis on the need to intensify the indoctrination effort. Several reasons were brought forth to justify this need. The forces' internationalist role as the instrument of *sblizhenie* at home and abroad was cited as the most important:

> The necessity to strengthen further the international indoctrination of the Soviet people and the Army and Navy personnel . . . is dictated by two interrelated aspects. In the first place, under the conditions of developed socialism, the integration of Soviet nations and nationalities is being accelerated. . . . Secondly, in inculcating Soviet citizens with a spirit of internationalism, the party has to take into account phenomena and processes that have characterized the development of world

socialism. To further successfully the [world] revolutionary process it is essential to understand correctly the relationship between national and international interests. . . .[52]

Another reason given for the need to improve the socialization effort in the forces was the higher quality education the soldiers have had, as well as the more technically complex character of modern warfare, both of which placed new demands on the quality of political education and on military training. Last but not least, an intensified "psychological warfare" conducted against the USSR by the West was deemed to require a suitable response.

The military political education in the 1970s and 1980s emphasized several major themes. There was an appeal to "Soviet Patriotism" which was largely filled with Russian historical and cultural content. There was also an emphasis on "Internationalism." In the domestic context the code word was "Friendship of the Peoples" (*druzhba narodov*), denoting the unity of the multi-ethnic Soviet society; for the soldiers in the forces the other key word was "Brotherhood in Arms" (*bratstvo oruzhiia*). For foreign policy purposes "Socialist Internationalism" was a governing slogan. It signified the common adherence to Marxist-Leninist ideology and a class-based unity of interests between all Soviet nations and nationalities, all members of the "socialist community," all the communist parties, and all world-wide "progressive" forces. "Brotherhood in Arms" was the term applied to describe the relations between the armies of member states of the Warsaw Pact military alliance. Hatred of the enemy, described as "imperialists" or "fascists," was an integral part of both the patriotic and the internationalist themes.

The theme of "Soviet Patriotism" had as its leading component the glories of Russia's heroic pre-revolutionary past, as well as the Russians' leading role in the "Great October Revolution" and in the "Great Patriotic War." A share of the glory was reserved also for the non-Russians, but always as junior partners of the ubiquitous Russian elder brother, and always in proportion to their place in the All-Union scheme of things. War memories, combined with the message of hatred for the "fascist" enemy, were the most common and the most important theme. The memories were brought to life by contacts with living veterans, by cultivating regimental exploits and traditions, and by glorifying partisan and military heroes. The emphasis was on motivating individual behaviour of the soldiers and creating models for the performance of "combat collectives."

A guide for conducting political classes on the subject was contained in a 1979 issue of an authoritative military journal. The first theme it developed was that of the special role played by the Russians. This was followed by the theme of how the love for one's particular region is transmuted into the love for "the great multinational Motherland." The guide was capped by a list of heroes who distinguished themselves in the war, to be extolled as role models. The list enumerated over 11,000 heroes listed by national groups in a descending order, according to the given group's supposed share in the defence effort. All the union republic nations were enumerated, with the three Slavic groups leading (the Russians first) with 95 percent of the total number of the "heroes."[53] The numbers assigned to the Moslems were small in proportion not only to their weight in the population, but also to what had been their actual participation in the war effort.

The theme of fraternal friendship in wartime easily translates into the peacetime theme of each unit constituting "a friendly multinational family." The unity of such a "family" centres on their common devotion to the socialist Motherland and is considered indispensable for victory in any war which the "imperialists" may want to "unleash." It is a given in Soviet socialization, incidentally, that if there is a war, it will be started by the "imperialists." Because of their "peace-loving" nature "socialist" countries are incapable of starting a war; they can only respond to "imperialist aggression."

The dual roles assigned to the SAF, that of a professional fighting force and that of a school of ideological indoctrination, are neither compatible nor complementary. The intensive and sustained effort at political education tends to be counterproductive when combined with intensive military training in competition for a soldier's or officer's time, attention, and quality of performance. Although there is an obvious value in the soldiers' indoctrination in undivided loyalty to the state they serve, the Soviet effort has suffered from an internal conflict between the "internationalist" message and the Russian reality, which fails to make it fully convincing either to the Russian conscript, who is still the core of the military manpower, or to the non-Russians. In that context, the internationalist message appears to be just a thin veneer covering what is basically the traditional Russian military ethos. But it should be noted that, although the effort to include the non-Russians in the country's heroic traditions has not been particularly effective, it has been genuine, because of its importance in developing a supra-national revolutionary legitimacy for domestic as well as foreign policy purposes, and to justify the USSR's extension of political influence abroad.

Thus there are latent contradictions in the message aimed at the soldier, and in the demands directed at him. These have been difficult to resolve. The Soviet soldier is asked to think and to behave as a good Russian, but is pressed at the same time to be an ardent internationalist. He is expected to develop a high level of competence in military and technical specialization, yet at the same time his time and attention are repeatedly diverted in order to make him into a political activist. The effectiveness of the political message is further undermined by the poor quality of its content and by its crude form: it remains formal and heavy-handed, and frequently has little relevance to verifiable realities. On the basis of information available an observer is left with an impression that most soldiers absorb the message for which they have a predisposition, while rejecting everything else. In the case of the conflict between the "national" and the "international," the Russians simply ignore the "internationalist" veneer, while the non-Russians treat the exercise with a strong dose of cynicism.

There are problems also in professional training. The requirements of modern warfare place a premium on individual initiative by soldiers, NCOs and junior officers on a battlefield, a new theme that has received considerable attention in Soviet military literature of the 1970s and 1980s. But the still very traditional training depends on blind obedience to orders, and on memorization and conditioned reflexes. Sticking one's neck out has not been "healthy" either in the ranks or in society at large. Thus the preaching of the need for "initiative" that has been accelerated since Gorbachev's accession so far seems to be falling largely on deaf ears among men as well as officers.

There is evidence, nevertheless, that certain key perceptions and stereotypes hammered in by the indoctrination are being readily absorbed. One is the commitment to the defence of the country, especially in the light of the experience of World War II, the scars of which still lie heavily on the memory of the Soviet population. Another is the perception of and pride in the strength of the Soviet Armed Forces and the USSR's superpower status. Emigrés confirm that servicemen are proud of their country's might and are convinced that the SAF is stronger and better trained than any other army, and that its weapons are second to none. It is now clear that the frustrating years of combat in Afghanistan have undermined these perceptions.

Ethnic Attitudes in the SAF

THE NATURE OF the perceptions and attitudes which are prevalent in the barracks can be glimpsed from discussions of training needs and problems and from criticisms which sporadically appear in the military press. Official media tend to emphasize the positive side; so any criticisms, especially if repeated, are indicative of major problems.

The existence of "undesirable attitudes" among soldiers is well documented, as is a phenomenon of "microgroups" which spontaneously appear in the barracks. According to official criticisms many of these groups claim for themselves a "privileged position" in a unit, or else present a "closely knit front" directed against military superiors; both types undermine military discipline. There is evidence also of "manifestations of negative traditions" that result in "clannishness" and in the use of "insulting nicknames."[54] Social cleavages in the forces that result in the formation of such groups and attitudes develop along three main lines: conflict between "new" (fresh recruits) and "old" soldiers; animosity between educated and uneducated conscripts; and antagonisms which develop along ethnocultural lines. Ethnic perceptions are contributory to all three conflicts.

Over the years Soviet military sources made only cryptic references to ethnic conflict in the ranks. Only since the early 1980s has its existence been openly acknowledged, presumably because of the increase in its intensity and the concern over the proliferation in the forces of ethnic-based ties and alliances. An official survey research apparently revealed that about one half of soldiers' friendships early in the service were based on national and/or regional ties, and that even for seasoned soldiers such ties still constituted a basic motivation in 35 to 40 percent of their in-service connections.[55] Information from émigrés not only confirms but adds to the picture. It seems that informal ethnocultural groups are formed primarily for mutual protection, but they also serve to express ethnic antagonisms. Such antagonisms are enhanced by the practice of hazing the junior by the senior soldiers, by the crowded nature of life in the barracks, by the brutalization characteristic of military life, and by ethnic stereotypes — embedded in soldiers' perceptions — that form the basis for their treatment of each other.

Each national group is credited with specific characteristics and attitudes. Ukrainians are believed to be "very nationalistic." Baltic soldiers are seen as the most "European" and the most aloof but competent soldiers; they are nicknamed "fascist" (the worst possible insult) because they hate the Russians; they stand up for each other's rights, and are disliked but respected. Georgians and Armenians are said to be as "insular" as the Balts, and always ready to support "their own," regardless of merit or consequences. Volga Tatars also are reported to stick together and to be hostile to other groups.

Moslems are generally least functional. Most of them cannot speak Russian and lack technical education. They suffer if they try to maintain the observance of Islamic injunctions such as prayers or keeping to the diet. Their obvious cultural alienation and different physical features invite ostracism. They are regarded as inferior (the widely used epithet "black asses" expresses the contempt) and are

subject to hazing and discriminatory treatment. They respond in
kind whenever able to do so, in their role as senior soldiers, for
example.[56]

All evidence points to conclusions that ethnic conflict is endemic
in the ranks. But, because it has always been there, it is seen as
"normal," and only the excesses are subject to concern. The two
main ethnic cleavages are between Russians and non-Russians, and
between Moslems and Europeans. But there are also specific national
feuds. Armenians, for example, fear and hate the Azerbaidzhani
Turks, and are in turn disliked by all other national groups of Transcaucasus; there are intra-Moslem antagonisms as well, although they
all pull together when attacked by Europeans. Soldiers' fights based
on national antagonisms are sporadically reported. Soviet deserters
from Afghanistan describe fighting between Ukrainians and Russians,
between Russians and Tadzhiks, between Turkmen and Tadzhiks,
between Turkmen and Tatars, and others.[57] Similar stories are
reported in *samizdat* and repeated by word of mouth, and are now
well-documented by a study based on a survey conducted with Soviet
veterans of the Afghan war.[58] Conflicts in the ranks frequently spill
over into conflicts with the local population, particularly in minority
areas in the western borderlands.

Official concern over the situation has lately resulted not only in
open discussion but in proposing remedies, apart from and additional
to an improvement in political education. There has been discussion
of the need to provide minority soldiers with some cultural amenities
(no practical steps seem to have been taken, however), and calls to
"respect the national dignity" of each soldier, and to avoid negative
stereotyping.[59] The need to combat soldiers' religious prejudices has
been related to ethnic perceptions. It has been connected also to the
rise of pacifism among the young, a new complaint and apparently a
matter of special official concern.[60]

In contrast to the ethnic mosaic in the ranks, the officer cadre is
very much the bearer of the "Russian message" — in composition as
well as in attitudes — and sets the tone for the armed forces as a
whole. The cadre's attitudes appear to be centralist and Russian
nationalist. Not only do the officers have little sympathy for nationalist demands of the minorities, but they also clearly equate *sblizhenie*
in the ranks with Russification. Thus they cannot be expected to be
happy with new initiatives to recruit Moslem officers, or to make cultural concessions to minority soldiers in the ranks. As noted earlier,
the military press condemns, from time to time, "incorrect attitudes"
towards ethnic soldiers.

A 1980 issue of the forces' newspaper carried an extraordinarily
explicit article warning against the excesses of Russifying zeal. "In a

socialist state," it warned, "there is no place for even the smallest expressions of discrimination against any nation and nationality," adding that "what counts" in an assignment of service duties is the "ideological-political and moral maturity" of an officer, as well as his military preparedness, and not his "national origins." The article concluded, nevertheless, that the national question was a political question, and that it was not an "easy matter" to secure a "proper moral climate" in the ranks.[61]

Conclusions

THE MULTI-ETHNIC COMPOSITION of the USSR population, the demographic trends of the last two decades, and the growth of national self-assertion of Soviet minorities made possible by the post-Stalin evolution of the Soviet political system, all have made the growth of ethnic conflict in the SAF inevitable. This has been aggravated by the continuation of the Russian character and traditions of the forces and by the Russian ethnic origins and Russian nationalist attitudes of the professional cadre.

As we have seen, the existence of ethnic antagonisms in the ranks is seen to be a political problem. But it is not a new problem, because the conflict has always been there, especially in the Soviet period. It is thus regarded as "normal," as are the policies and mechanisms designed to neutralize its potentially negative impact on the forces' reliability and effectiveness. What is new, perhaps, is the conflict's greater depth and intensity. But it should be noted that in the past it did not compromise the effectiveness of the Soviet military effort at crisis points, not even in World War II, despite the fact that minorities constituted a substantial part of the mass defections in the first months after the July 1941 Nazi attack on the Soviet Union.

The military service undoubtedly plays an important part in the promotion of functional integration of all Soviet minorities. It also contributes to attitudinal integration of the elements among them most susceptible to Russification. The political education system does seem to have succeeded in promoting the most basic loyalty to the "Motherland" and to its defence among all soldiers, excluding only the members of the most antagonistic and politically most conscious minorities, and the dissidents. For the rest, the "ethnic security map" in the distribution of military manpower maximizes the reliability of the Soviet Armed Forces, and goes a long way to assure their effectiveness in carrying out their national as well as their internationalist mission.

The least integrated elements constituted the fastest growing component of future Soviet military manpower, and recent information only confirmed the worst expectations. A 1988 Soviet source revealed that 37 percent of the year's draft cohort was composed of youths from Central Asia and the Caucusus, as compared to their share of 28 percent of the total in 1980, and 17 percent in the seventies,[62] thus casting doubt on the continued maintenance of the Soviet forces' Russian characteristics. In the long run some accommodation undoubtedly will have to be made for what is contemptuously referred to by some Soviet officers as the "yellowing" of the national complexion. But it is doubtful, in terms of historical experience and demographic, cultural, and political trends, that the new policies, or any policies, would succeed in Russifying the Moslems and other large, non-integrated national groups.

In the meantime, a determined effort at "internationalization," mounted by the Gorbachev administration, appears to testify to the continuing unwillingness of the leadership and of the Russian majority to face the problem. Overall, there has been a renewed effort to accelerate *sblizhenie*, and to forge new ties across ethnic and cultural boundaries as well as to promote cross-ethnic-settlement. On the military front, Gorbachev announced in December 1988 his decision to reduce the size of the Soviet Armed Forces by half a million men. The decision appears to have been motivated as much by the desire to maintain the Russian character of the forces, as by the need to reduce the cost of the military establishment, and to promote relaxation in Soviet relations with the West. Despite an avowed aim to decentralize the country's administration, there were no signs pointing to a revival of territorial militias. Such military decentralization is an unlikely prospect, despite an ever stronger articulation by the non-Russians of their national demands. It is unlikely because it would contradict the Leninist legacy of central control over the military and because it is strongly opposed by the senior cadre of the Soviet Armed Forces.

Notes

1. Out of 11 army commanders in 1914 only three had Russian names; of the remaining eight commanders five had German names (reflecting the importance of Baltic Germans in the Imperial Army, as in the Imperial bureaucracy in general), and the other three were of Bulgarian, Flemish and Polish origin. See N. Stone, "The Historical Background of the Red Army," in *Soviet Military Power and Performance*, ed. J. Erickson and E.J. Feuchtwanger (London, 1979), p. 6. In contrast, all estimates of the ethnic origin of Soviet general officers since World War II (based on name analysis) agree that over 90 percent have been Slavs, that most have been Russians, and that the share of ethnic Russians in high command positions seems to have actually increased in the 1970s. See T. Rakowska-Harmstone, "The Soviet Army as an Instrument of National Integration," in Erickson and Feutchwanger, eds., *Soviet Military Power and Performance*, pp. 133, 142-44; T.J. Colton, *Commissars, Commanders and Civilian Authority: The Structure of Soviet Military Politics*

(Cambridge, Mass., 1979), p. 261; Allen Hetmanek, Bruce Thompson, and Richard Trout, *Ethnic Composition of the Soviet Officer Corps (U)*, September 1979, a Department of Defense intelligence document.

2. C. Bellamy, "Seventy Years On: Similarities between the Soviet Army and its Tsarist Antecedent," *RUSI Journal for Defence Studies* 124 (September 1979), pp. 29-37; Stone, "The Historical Background of the Red Army"; C.N. Donnelly, "The Development of Soviet Military Doctrine," *Military Review* 62 (August 1982), p. 38-51.

3. Cynthia H. Enloe, *Ethnic Soldiers: State Security in Divided Societies* (Athens, Georgia, 1980), p. 15.

4. Susan L. Curran and Dimitry Ponomareff, *Managing the Ethnic Factor in the Russian and Soviet Armed Forces: An Historical Overview*, Rand Corporation R-2640/1 (Santa Monica, CA., July 1982), pp. 1-7.

5. V.I. Lenin, *Collected Works* (London, 1960-1970), Vol. 26, p. 449.

6. J.V. Stalin, *Marxism and the National Question* (New York, 1942), p. 158.

7. Richard Pipes, *The Formation of the Soviet Union: Communism and Nationalism, 1917-1923*, rev. ed. (Cambridge, Mass., 1964), p. 286.

8. I.I. Mints, ed., *Boevoe sodruzhestvo sovetskikh respublik 1919-1922* (Moscow, 1982), pp. 161-63.

9. Ibid.

10. Ibid., p. 25.

11. Cited in P. Rtishchev, "Leninskaia natsional'naia politika i stroitel'stvo sovetskikh vooruzhennykh sil," *Kommunist vooruzhennykh sil*, No. 9 (1974), p. 6.

12. N.A. Kirsanov, "Kommunisticheskaia partiia – organizator dobrovol' cheskikh formirovanii Krasnoi Armii v gody Velikoi Otechestvennoi Voiny," *Voprosy istorii KPSS* No. 11, 1976, p. 9.

13. Ibid., n. 46, p. 68.

14. Ibid., p. 69.

15. A.P. Artem'ev, *Bratskii Boevoi Soiuz narodov SSR v Velikoi Otechestvennoi voine* (Moscow, 1975), p. 39.

16. "Warsaw Pact: The Question of Cohesion," Phase II, Vol. 3, Chapter II, 3. B, p. 26.

17. Ibid., Chapter II, 3, C, pp. 30-45.

18. Ibid., Chapter II, 3, pp. 26-27.

19. Artemev, pp. 53-54.

20. A.F. Danilevskii, *V.I. Lenin i voprosy voennogo stroitel 'stva na VIII s'ezde RKP (b)* (Moscow, 1964).

21. Murray Feshbach, "The Soviet Union: Population Trends and Dilemmas," *Population Bulletin* 37 (August 1982), p. 7.

22. Ibid., pp. 10-11.

23. Murray Feshbach, "Trends in the Soviet Muslim Population: Demographic Aspects," in *The USSR and the Muslim World* ed. Yaacov Ro'i (London, 1984), p. 94; also Mikhail S. Bernstam, "Demographic Depression in the USSR and the Welfare State: Their Relevance to Russian Nationalism," in *The Last Empire: Nationality and the Soviet Future*, ed. Robert Conquest (Stanford, CA., 1986), Tables 2 and 4.

24. Teresa Rakowska-Harmstone, "Gorbachev's Nationality Policy," a paper presented at the 20th Convention of the American Association for the Advancement of Slavic Studies, Honolulu, Hawaii, November 1988.

156 Ethnic Armies

25. See Teresa Rakowska-Harmstone, "Minority Nationalism Today: An Overview," in Conquest, ed., *The Last Empire*.
26. See T. Rakowska-Harmstone, "The Dialectics of Nationalism in the USSR," *Problems of Communism* 23 (May-June 1974), pp. 1-22; H. Carrère-d'Encausse, *Decline of an Empire: The Soviet Socialist Republics in Revolt* (New York, 1979); and G. Warshofsky Lapidus, "Ethnonationalism and Political Stability," *World Politics*, 36 (July 1984).
27. I.S. Gurvich, "Osobennosti sovremennogo etapa etnokul'turnogo razvitiia narodov Sovetskogo Soiuza," *Sovetskaia etnografiia*, No. 6 (November-December 1982), p. 16.
28. Iu. V. Bromlei, "Etnograficheskoe izuchenie sovremennykh natsional'nykh protsessov v SSSR. K 50-letiiu ordena Druzhby Narodov Instituta Etnografii AN SSSR," *Sovetskaia etnografiia*, No. 2 (1983), p. 8.
29. Uzbekistan, where the proportion of the bilinguals increased by 34.8 percent between 1970 and 1979, as compared to between 10 and 14 percent increases in the other three Central Asian republics, is a notorious example.
30. J.A. Azrael, "Emergent Nationality Problems in the USSR," RAND Corporation, R-2172-AF, September 1977, p. 16; and S. Enders Wimbush and Dimitry Ponomareff, "Alternatives for Mobilizing Soviet Central Asian Labor: Outmigration and Regional Development," *RAND Corporation Project Air Force Report*, R-2476-AF (November 1979), p. 5.
31. Robert Martin, "Ethnic Minorities in the Soviet Military: Non-Combat Units as an Ethnic 'Sponge,'" paper given at a meeting of the International Studies Association, October 20-22, 1982, Carlisle, Pa. (unclassified), p. 24.
32. Iu. V. Bromlei, "O nekotorykh aktual'nykh zadachakh etnograficheskogo izucheniia sovremennosti," *Sovetskaia etnografiia*, No. 6 (November-December 1983), pp. 20-21.
33. "Warsaw Pact: The Question of Cohesion," Phase II, Vol. 3, *passim*.
34. A. Skryl'nik, "XXVI s'ezd KPSS i internatsional'noe vospitanie voinov," *Voenno-istoricheskii zhurnal*, No. 11 (1981), p. 7.
35. S. Enders Wimbush and Alex Alexiev, *The Ethnic Factor in the Soviet Armed Forces*, R-2787/1 (Santa Monica, CA.: Rand Corporation, March 1982). The book is based on interviews with 130 Soviet ex-servicemen.
36. Alex Beam, "Why More Soviet Students Will Be Wearing Combat Boots," *Business Week* (2 August 1982), pp. 38-39, and *Novaia Gazeta* (New York).
37. Robert Bathurst, Michael Burger, and Ellen Wolffe, *The Soviet Sailor: Combat Readiness and Morale*, KFR383-82 (Arlington, Va.: Ketron Inc., Rosslyn Center, 30 June 1982).
38. Wimbush and Alexiev, pp. 5-6.
39. Ibid., pp. 15-17, and Bathurst *et al.*, p. 6.
40. Wimbush and Alexiev, pp. 17-23.
41. Martin, "Ethnic Minorities in the Soviet Military."
42. Allen Hetmanek, Bruce Thompson and Richard Trout, *Ethnic Composition of the Soviet Officer Corps* (U); a Department of Defense Intelligence Document prepared under an inter-agency agreement for the Soviet/Warsaw Pact Division, Directorate for Intelligence Research, Defense Intelligence Agency (September 1979).
43. Ibid.
44. Bathurst *et al.*, pp. 50-52.
45. Hetmanek *et al.*, pp. 9, 11, and 12.
46. Wimbush and Alexiev, p. 27 and Bathurst *et al.*, pp. 49-50.

47. See, for example, *Kommunist* (Baku, in Azeri) (9 January 1982), lead editorial, translated in *JPRS* 80867 (20 May 1982), p. 2; N. Timofeev, "Klub nazyvaetsia 'druzhba,'" *Kommunist vooruzhennykh sil*, No. 1 (January 1983); *Sovet Maktabi* (Tashkent, in Uzbek), No. 2 (1982), pp. 3-8, translated in *JPRS* 81843 (24 September 1982), pp. 54-55; A.D. Lizichev, "Postoianno sovershenstvovat' patrioticheskoe i internatsional'noe vospitanie," pp. 19-26, in *Sovetskaia Armiia — shkola druzhby i bratstva*, (a report from the Riga Conference, 28-30 June 1982) (Moscow, 1982).

48. Secretary General Brezhnev at the 25th Congress of the CPSU (24 February 1976).

49. E. Teague, "New Head of Komsomol Appointed," *Radio Liberty Research*, RL-488/82 (6 December 1982), also reported in *Rad* BR/109 (20 June 1984) and *Izvestiia* (6 November 1984).

50. A. Skrylnik and N. Tarasenko, "Narod i Armiia," *Pravda* (16 August 1985).

51. Herbert Goldhammer, *The Soviet Soldier* (London, 1975).

52. A. Skryl'nik, "XXVI s'ezd KPSS i internatsional'noe vospitanie voinov," *Voenno-istoricheskii zhurnal*, No. 11, 1981, pp. 5-6. My emphasis.

53. *Kommunist vooruzhennykh sil*, No. 3 (February 1979), pp. 79-86.

54. See, for example, Maj. Gen. M. Yasiukov writing in *Voenno-istoricheskii zhurnal*, No. 4 (April 1979), pp. 10-17; the editorial in *KVS* No. 13 (July 1979), pp. 3-8.

55. A 1980 source quoted by Deane, pp. 196f.

56. Robert Bathurst and Michael Burger, *Controlling the Soviet Soldier: Some Eyewitness Accounts*, The Center for Strategic Technology (College Station, Texas, April 1981), pp. 3-7; Wimbush and Alexiev, pp. 47-59.

57. *Posev* 39 (February 1983), pp. 18-21, an interview with a nineteen-year-old Russian from Omsk.

58. Alexander Alexiev, *Inside the Soviet Army in Afganistan*, R-3627-A (Santa Monica, CA, May 1988).

59. M. Pletushkov, "Soiuz nerushimyi respublik svobodnykh," *Znamenosets*, No. 9 (1982), p. 24; Maj. Gen. V. Samoilenko, "Defending Socialism — Historical Experience and the Present Day: Friendship of Peoples Triumphs," *Krasnaia zvezda* (March 7, 1985), pp. 2-3, translated in *CDSP* Vol. 37, No. 11, p. 21.

60. F.I. Dolgikh and A.P. Kurantov, *Kommunisticheskie idealy i ateisticheskoe vospitanie voinov* (Moscow, 1976), pp. 180-85.

61. N. Shumikhin, "Armiia mnogonatsional'nogo Sovetskogo gosudarstva," *Krasnaia zvezda* (9 October 1980).

62. Ann Sheehy, "Interethnic Relations in the Soviet Armed Forces," Radio Liberty Research, RL 421/88, 15 September 1988, p. 1.

BILINGUALISM AND MULTICULTURALISM IN THE CANADIAN ARMED FORCES

RICHARD A. PRESTON

CANADA HAS BEEN officially described as a bilingual and bicultural country, and during the administration of Prime Minister Pierre Elliott Trudeau, it also became called "multicultural." This is in sharp contrast with the United States which is basically unilingual (English-speaking) and unicultural. The United States began as a group of English colonies in which most non-English settlers became assimilated and which, during colonial times, had already developed distinctly American cultural features. After the Revolution, immigrants of diverse origins were absorbed by what was described as the "melting-pot." Canada, on the other hand, was in effect founded by two peoples, the French and the English. After the British conquest of New France, directions from the British government and pressures by a minority of new arrivals, mainly Anglo-American merchants, suggested a possible future for Canada not dissimilar from that of the United States. But Canada's first two governors, Generals James Murray and Guy Carleton (Lord Dorchester), wanted to conciliate the French-Canadian inhabitants by making concessions. The policy of cultural tolerance initiated by Murray and Carleton was codified in various acts passed by the British Parliament, starting with the Quebec Act of 1774 and leading up to the British North America (BNA) Act of 1867 which enacted Confederation and created the Dominion. The Quebec Act in particular re-established French civil law in Quebec and permitted members of the Catholic Church to hold office, while the Constitutional Act of 1791 introduced the principle of Canada's having provinces with different linguistic and cultural bases. Francophone cultural rights were further reinforced by the BNA Act.[1] These acts safeguarded French Canada's basic institutions and helped to preserve and perpetuate French culture in British North America. Nineteenth- and twentieth-century immigrants to Canada, partly because of the cultural diversity existing in the country due to the presence of the two so-called "founding peoples" or "charter groups," and possibly also as a deliberate rejection of the American philosophy and practice of "Americanizing" newcomers, were — in theory at least — permitted to retain their cultural distinctiveness.

Canada's diverse ethnic make-up has been recognized in recent decades. For the two founding peoples, the federal government adopted an official policy of bilingualism and biculturalism. The addition of a policy of multiculturalism is a concession to those other Canadians who do not belong to either of the charter groups, but since it does not include language rights, a significant protective factor in cultural retention, it may be a symbolic rather than real concession.

One aim of the 13th RMC Military History Symposium was to explore cultural and linguistic diversity in armed forces elsewhere, as a background for the study of the impact of policies of bilingualism and biculturalism, and also of the concept of multiculturalism, on the Canadian forces. This chapter focuses on the history of language problems in those forces and on the future prospects for bilingualism and multiculturalism in them.

WE MUST BEGIN with a reference to the impact on the country's defence system of what used to be called Canada's "racial problem." As indicated in the introduction to this book, in Canada the word "race" has had, and to some extent still has, a quite different meaning from what is commonly understood by the same word in the United States. "Race relations" and "racial questions" in Canada used to refer to English-French issues. One of the most serious of these was the problem of the representation of French Canadians in the country's armed forces. The two world wars of our century clearly demonstrated this problem. Although at the time of the First World War, French Canadians made up almost one-third of the Canadian population, they constituted only 12.6 percent of the effectives in the Canadian Army. In the Second World War that percentage rose, but only to 19 percent. In both wars francophones, as French Canadians are now often called, were even fewer in the other two services.

Part of the explanation for this state of affairs lay in the nature of the Canadian forces at the time: the Army did have a few French-speaking units, but in the Navy during both wars, and also during World War II in the Air Force, French-Canadian volunteers had to serve in anglophone units. (The RCAF's 425 Alouette Squadron was a minor exception, but its ground staff included anglophone, and even British, personnel.) In the Second World War (unlike the First) there were hastily devised efforts to provide francophones in the various services with English-language instruction. In both wars the imposition of conscription, when it was believed necessary, led to political crises that left legacies of racial bitterness.[2]

This wartime record must be set against the history of the employment of French Canadians in military service in times of peace. The few who had sought to serve in the peacetime Navy had to become Anglicized. The RCAF similarly had no provision for French Canadians to use their own language. Although this was largely a result of contemporary Canadian attitudes, the Navy and the Air Force carried those attitudes to extremes. One reason for this may have been that both of those services were very closely affiliated with their British counterparts in which there were few precedents for the recruitment of non-English-speaking personnel. Furthermore, the Navy and the Air Force were technical services, and ships and aircraft seemed to need crews that used one language.

On the other hand, francophone under-representation in Canada's professional military forces, and the lack of accommodation for their linguistic and cultural needs, was not based on any characteristic of the Canadian Militia. Part of the explanation again probably lies in the fact that the British Army, which had served as a role model for this militia for generations, had had extensive experience with troops recruited from non-British cultural groups who could function in their own linguistic units.

French Canadians had had a militia tradition going back to the seventeenth century, and they had a record of service and participation in the administration of the Canadian Militia after the British Conquest. It might be recalled that small French-Canadian militia units had contributed to the defeat of the Americans at Châteaugai in 1814 during the War of 1812. Then in 1856, when the Militia of the United Province of the Canadas was put on a permanent footing, the first unit organized was one of French-Canadian artillery.[3] When George-Etienne Cartier, John A. Macdonald's French-Canadian lieutenant, brought in the Militia Bill of the newly confederated Canada in 1868 and argued in a five-hour speech that a military force was the indispensable "crown of the edifice" of a nation,[4] three of the first nine Military Districts that he set up were in Quebec; two of those were French-Canadian. Two later Ministers of Militia who held office for long periods were French-Canadian; and in the nineteenth century the Deputy Minister, the civilian administrative head of the department, was always a French Canadian. One of the three new infantry schools organized in 1883 was French-Canadian. In that same year another French Canadian, Lieutenant-Colonel J.A. Ouimet, MP, told the House of Commons that the Canadian Militia was a "national institution" and that it was the best means of "creating among our people a national feeling, a real Canadian feeling."[5] Later, two British General Officers Commanding the Canadian Militia,

Major-Generals Ivor Herbert (1890-1895) and Edward Hutton (1898-1900), who spoke French fluently, went out of their way to encourage French-Canadian interest. The latter aimed at forming a Canadian "national army," and he told English-Canadian officers that they ought to learn French.

However, despite these suggestions of the possibility of significant French-Canadian participation in the Canadian Militia, there was, in fact, declining interest. In 1870 there were fifteen French units and sixty-four English. By 1914 there were still only fifteen French units, but the number of English units had risen to eighty-five; and some of the nominally French units had recruited English-speaking personnel.[6] Some anglophone polemicists have said that the reason for this low participation is that French Canadians are "anti-military."[7] But in 1978 John Meisel took an opinion poll that showed French Canadians actually more supportive of the use of armed force to maintain public order (which was at that time the crucial issue) than comparable English-speaking groups. Although Meisel had some doubts about the validity of the findings,[8] history shows that the characterization of French-Canadian society as traditionally "anti-militarist" is unsound. New France was, as W.J. Eccles suggests, a military state in which by 1690 the *habitants*, that is, the colonists, were organized into a militia and were determined and able to protect their communities against Iroquois and Anglo-American raids. The militia also gave effective support for the French royal forces in Canada because they were, in some ways, more suitable for North American warfare than were troops sent from Europe.[9] We have already mentioned a French-Canadian contribution in the War of 1812. Later, the recruiting of the Papal Zouaves and the record of the Royal 22nd (the "Van Doos") suggest that with the passage of generations French Canadians did not lose their early potential for, and interest in, things military.

However, when the voluntary principle was re-confirmed for the Canadian Militia after Confederation, French Canadians proved less inclined than their anglophone fellow citizens to join it. To explain this Sir Etienne-Paschal Taché, one of the French-Canadian architects of Confederation, argued that the voluntary principle was alien to French Canadians.[10] If he meant that they would have accepted compulsion, it was a strange suggestion when viewed in the light of earlier and later experience. French Canadians had, it is true, been accustomed to compulsory service during the French colonial regime, but they had strenuously objected when, after more than a decade without it, the British reintroduced compulsion during the American War of Independence. Military service, whether compulsory or voluntary, was apparently unpopular with them.

Limited French-Canadian interest in the post-Confederation Militia was, then, a consequence of circumstances rather than antimilitarism or lack of familiarity with a volunteer system. The fact was that Cartier and his successors, who were in a position to do something about it, had done little to make the participation of their fellow French Canadians in the Militia meaningful. Part of the problem was that the Militia's ostensible purpose was to support, and eventually replace, the British garrison as a bulwark against the United States. But many Canadians, English as well as French, doubted whether that defence was feasible. Perhaps more important was the fact that for Canadian governments the Militia was merely a cheap source of political patronage, especially in Quebec. For individuals, it was primarily an opportunity to gain social prestige. As Desmond Morton has shown, it was a rather expensive voluntary society for its officers who modelled themselves on the British Army, adopting its military finery, feathers, kilts, and all.[11] But in the eyes of many French Canadians these British uniforms were the dress of the conqueror. It is revealing that, in 1870 at the time of the Fenian raids, when French Canadians who had been inspired by their expedition to serve the Pope proposed that French recruits enlisted to oppose the would-be invaders from the United States should wear Zouave dress, a French colonial garb with North African-type baggy pants which for Canadian winters was not quite as impractical as the much beloved kilt, the Militia Department turned it down because it was "un-British."[12] Another factor in the French Canadians' lack of interest in the Militia may have been its frequent use to aid civil authorities during labour strife or riots. Calling out the Militia was preferable to using the British regulars. Clashes between the French and the Irish in Montreal were a frequent source of trouble during the early part of the nineteenth century. There is, however, little evidence that use of the Militia to suppress them had serious ethnic or political overtones as far as French-English relations are concerned. It was more likely a means of protecting middle-class property without concern for the ethnic affiliation of its owners.

In the fourth quarter of the nineteenth century the ostensible purpose of the Canadian Militia began to change from the defence of Canada against the United States to the provision of reinforcements for British imperial defence. French Canadians had even less interest in this than they had had in a questionable stand against an unexpected American invasion. Many still took Militia commissions, but some of these individuals were already, or would often become, assimilated or even Anglicized. Promotion examinations introduced by General Officer Commanding the Militia Herbert in the early 1890s, conducted in English, drove away many French-Canadian junior officers whose command of English was deficient.

As for other ranks, many units of the the Canadian Militia were notoriously understrength. COs customarily made up numbers for annual camps by hasty last-minute recruiting, and French-Canadian units brought in the largest number of quite unsuitable men in this way. Furthermore, whereas city units — which were maintained partly because they were useful for preserving civil order — were much more efficient than rural units which rarely drilled between camps, French Canada had only two such city units. It also had no engineer or artillery units (the one established in 1856 not having survived), allegedly because French-Canadian education did not provide the necessary technical background.

Canadian participation in the South African War, which many French Canadians regarded as a war aimed at the subjugation of a people on the pattern of the British conquest of New France in the eighteenth century, strengthened French alienation from the Militia.[13] The conscription crises in the two world wars, partly inflamed by clumsy administration and unrelated non-military policies, reinforced a decline of French-Canadian interest in the military that had been discernible for a long time.[14] Although very many French Canadians served magnificently in both wars, a majority of their francophone compatriots, while prepared to acknowledge a need for home defence, opposed overseas service, especially if it was to be compulsory. Some historians now assert that full Canadian national participation in both world wars was not realized primarily because French Canadians felt that they were second-class citizens in their own country and also in its armed forces.

WHEN THE END of World War II brought a severe reduction in the wartime forces, the Navy and the Air Force continued their traditional monolingualism. But the Army, in an effort to retain a French component, established its battle-honoured "Van Doos," the Royal 22nd Regiment, as a regular rather than as merely a Militia unit. It also announced an optimal quota of 30 percent French for the infantry, and 15 percent for the technical corps (which quotas were often not met). But only in the Royal 22nd was the working language French. In 1946, in further recognition of an acknowledged need, the Army opened a school in Quebec to give basic military instruction in French to French-speaking recruits. That school was soon expanded to teach French to English-speaking officers and NCOs, so that they could train francophone recruits. The next year the General Staff inaugurated a program of French instruction for Headquarters personnel. A little later it began similar program in other parts of the country. But the working language of the services was still English and at that time there was little interest in proposals that the forces should move deliberately towards bilingualism to secure French-Canadian support.

Brooke Claxton, the second postwar Minister of National Defence, was sympathetic to the idea of an increase in French participation in the forces; and General Charles Foulkes, Chief of the General Staff, told the Defence Council that it would be useful for anglophone Army officers to be able to speak French. These expressions of interest were, however, not acted upon until the Korean War, followed by the warming up of the Cold War, necessitated a rebuilding of the Canadian forces. It was then found that the Army could not accept many of the French-Canadian recruits who, partly because of heightened anti-communist sentiments and partly because of economic distress, now offered themselves in larger numbers. The problem was that these recruits lacked English. Canadian authorities began to fear that, in the event of an even greater emergency, unless French Canadians had come to participate more fully in the peacetime forces, attempts to conscript them might lead to even more serious disruptive crises than those which had flared up in the previous wars.[15] That prospect led Canada's military and political leaders to give serious consideration to making the forces more attractive to French Canadians.

It was believed that French Canadians were reluctant to join the permanent forces, not only because they and their families would be liable to spend their whole lives in an alien cultural environment, but also because the servicemen themselves would very probably have to serve under monolingual anglophone officers. Therefore, in addition to the provision of French-language schools and cultural institutions at Canadian military bases, steps were taken towards increasing the number of French-speaking officers in all three services.[16]

At the time the primary, though not the largest, source of officers for the Canadian forces was the Canadian Services Colleges. The Royal Military College of Canada (RMC) in Kingston, Ontario, after a wartime closing, had been re-opened in 1948 as one of two tri-service Canadian Services Colleges designed to produce officers who were not obliged to serve in the regular forces. In 1948 RMC was still predominantly anglophone. The other Canadian Services College, Royal Roads — originally a naval institution and then for one year operated jointly by the RCN and the RCAF — was, like RMC, also in an English-speaking part of Canada (in Victoria, British Columbia). Royal Roads prepared cadets for further training in the Royal Navy as a preparation for service in the RCN, or alternatively for entry to the third year at RMC. As a result of the shortage of officers for the Korean War, a Regular Officer Training Plan (ROTP) was introduced in 1951 for both the Canadian Services Colleges and the country's civilian universities, English and French. Cadets who elected to join the regular forces under this scheme were given generous financial support for four years during their academic education. Soon after the introduction of this plan, RMC and Royal Roads became almost exclusively devoted to the production of career, rather than of reserve, officers.[17]

The Société Saint-Jean-Baptiste and a French-Canadian MP, Léon Balcer, a wartime naval officer, then began to campaign for a third Canadian Services College, this time in the province of Quebec where it would serve young French Canadians in the same way as RMC and Royal Roads were serving anglophone Canadians. Some Conservative MPs in the parliamentary opposition, aware of their party's need to improve its image in Quebec, said that if they won power they would establish such a military college. To upstage them, four days before two closely contested by-elections in Quebec, Liberal Prime Minister Louis St. Laurent announced the immediate opening of what came to be called the Collège Militaire Royal de St-Jean (CMR).

CMR recruited cadets at an academic level equal to junior matriculation in Ontario, that is, a year before the level for entry to RMC and Royal Roads. This was an adjustment to suit the educational systems of the Province of Quebec and other provinces where there was no equivalent of Ontario's senior matriculation, the so-called Grade XIII. The new college, as first announced, was to offer only a preparatory year to enable CMR cadets to enter RMC's first year; but before its initial year had ended, the program was extended to allow students to cover, like those at Royal Roads, the first two years of the four-year RMC course.

Although CMR was primarily intended as a means of bringing in more French Canadians, it was to be bilingual, 40 percent of its recruits were to be anglophone, and its courses were to be given in both languages. Moreover, it was to stress bilingualism. In place of traditional academic language courses that taught grammar, composition, and literature, CMR introduced the direct or audiolinguistic method to teach conversational speech and comprehension. From the outset, therefore, it had considerable success in second-language training, especially with French Canadians. But the CMR program and the French environment of St-Jean undoubtedly also helped its anglophone cadets to make good progress in their second language. So, although CMR is sometimes thought of as a francophone institution, and that might have been a hope of some French-Canadian nationalists, its creation was in fact a significant step towards bilingualism in the Canadian forces.[18] It is, however, indicative of the limited interest that French Canadians still had in military careers that in order to fill the first CMR class with suitable recruits, the proportion of anglophones to francophones had to be 60:40 and not 40:60.

In 1952, after a critical report by Commander Marcel Jetté, RCN, who had been assigned to investigate why French Canadians did not join the Navy, the RCN established schools to teach English to French-Canadian sailors and French to anglophone officers.[19] But further representations by Jetté, and also by senior French-Canadian army officers (notably Brigadier J.P.E. Bernatchez, an RMC ex-cadet) all advocating that bilingualism should be extended in the forces, were ignored by their superiors.[20] Furthermore, throughout the 1950s and 1960s, RMC and Royal Roads, while paying lip-service to the need for anglophone Canadian officers to acquire French, did not do enough about it to meet the current need. In 1962 Professor Gerald Tougas, head of the RMC French Department, reported that only 2 percent of RMC's English-speaking graduates were fully bilingual by the time they were commissioned.[21]

Four years earlier, when about 28 percent of all Canadians were French-speaking, French Canadians still constituted only 15 percent of all army lieutenants, 12 percent of captains and majors, 9 percent of the lieutenant-colonels, and a mere 8 percent above that rank. This was ample evidence of the disadvantages that the francophones who had entered the Army faced in promotion.[22] Francophones were even less well represented in the higher ranks of the other two services. In 1963 the Glassco Royal Commission on Government Organization, which drew attention to the continued shortfall of French Canadians in the higher levels of all federal government services, took special notice of this circumstance in the Canadian forces.[23] Five years later, when the Commission on Bilingualism and Biculturalism was severe in its criticism of the government's inability to communicate with the French-Canadian members of the public in their own language, it drew attention to the predominance of anglophones in the forces.[24]

This situation began to change when Prime Minister Pierre Trudeau's Official Languages Act, passed in 1969, required all government departments to be able to reply to the public in the language, English or French, in which they were addressed. In 1971 a Defence White Paper applied this policy to the military, saying that they had a major role to play in promoting national unity by reflecting the bilingual and bicultural nature of the country.[25] About the same time RMC was informed that it must become what some called "a mirror image of CMR," that is to say an English-based bilingual institution, so that all of its graduates would become functionally bilingual by the time they graduated and were commissioned.[26]

THIS ACCOUNT OF progress towards bilingualism in the Canadian forces must be supplemented by some consideration of what can be learned from language problems in military forces elsewhere. From the classical period on, there had been many armies in which men of different cultures, who spoke different languages, served together; and such armies had often been successful in war. But when bilingualism was suggested for the Canadian forces, those historical precedents carried little or no weight.

Instead, the idea evoked much skepticism. There was a deep conviction, reinforced in the Western World since the American and French revolutions, that the most effective military forces were those which consisted of citizen volunteers who shared a common patriotism and a national culture, including a common language. That conviction applied also to the professional forces that were the peacetime nuclei of citizen armies to be called out in the event of a major war. It was also held that in modern war an army, now more than ever before, must use a single language for internal communications. Some English-Canadian ex-officers, recalling their own experience in World War II, were inclined to say, "If the balloon goes up, they [French-Canadians in the forces] will have to speak English." For these officers bilingualism in the Canadian forces was a dangerous policy. The trend towards what was called the "open battlefield," with its instant radio contacts, was said to confirm this belief, although in fact it might be argued that, on the contrary, an open battlefield might require the use of whatever language was most familiar to the particular combatants.

The experience of multicultural and multilingual armies in the nineteenth-century empires gave some qualified support for the view that a single language of communication was essential. Multilingual armies overcame the problem of the multiplicity of languages by the use of a *lingua franca*. Normally this *lingua franca* was the language of officers commissioned from the empire's politically dominant ethnic group. But where the number of minorities was large, they were often recruited into units that were linguistically homogeneous, but in which the officers and NCOs were bilingual.

Where the number of different minorities was particularly large, as in the British Indian Army, there sometimes had to be a second *lingua franca* in addition to the language of the officer corps. In India the British made use of Hindustani which was understood by many different peoples in northern India, especially in the larger cities. It is a mixture of Hindi, the literary language of the Hindus, and Urdu, the literary language of the Moslems, languages which have some features in common. (Hindustani was, in fact, known as the "language of the camp" because the Moslem emperors, who had ruled India before the British, had used it in their forces in the same way.) In British India this practice was accompanied by the creation of an intermediary Indian officer corps which held vice-regal, as opposed to king's, commissions. Linguistic and hierarchical practices of this kind served quite effectively in armies when war was less technical than it is today. They were suitable for imperial armies.[27] The question to be answered is whether they are suitable for modern, technologically advanced, democracies.

A little-known NATO experiment of multilinguistic cooperation in armed forces has some bearing on this question of its practicability in modern war. It began in 1963-64. The Alliance was considering the creation of a multi-lateral force (MLF), or an Atlantic nuclear force (ANF), in which several NATO nations would cooperate. Those ideas never got off the ground because of international opposition. The French, as well as the Soviets, believed them to be merely a means to give the West Germans a finger on the nuclear trigger. However, in connection with it, the U.S. Navy offered to supply a submarine for a modified experiment in what it called "mixed manning."

When the possibility of a mixed-manned nuclear Polaris submarine seemed to be still-born, the Americans then offered a destroyer for a non-nuclear mixed-manning surface experiment. The USS *Claude V. Ricketts*, formerly the USS *Biddle*, was in commission from June 1964 to December 1965 with a mixed crew of Americans, Germans, British, Greeks, Italians, Dutchmen, and, up to the eve of sailing, Turks. (For some reason there were no Canadians.) *Ricketts* cruised the Caribbean, the Atlantic, the North Sea, and the Mediterranean, and also exercised with the U.S. Sixth and Second Fleets.

Mixed manning on *Ricketts* gave rise to problems related to rations and discipline. To meet national aspirations, there were twice as many petty officers as a ship of that size needed. Some of them were unhappy with their accommodation and also because, it was alleged, they had to chip paint. Nevertheless, *Ricketts*' American captain believed that he had proved that mixed manning was militarily feasible, but the experiment was not repeated.

From our point of view, what is important is that the language of operation on *Ricketts* was English. Before the ship was commissioned, English lessons were given to those crew members who needed them. Notwithstanding, there is some indication that, even after these lessons, communication was not always effective.[28] NATO's experimentation with mixed manning thus did not provide much support for policies of multilingualism in armed forces. Instead, it appeared to confirm the beliefs of those who argue that there must always be a single language of operation.

Further possible effects of cultural, including linguistic, differences in armed forces can be derived from an examination of other recent developments. During the 1970s sociologists began intensive study of "ethnic groups," also called "cultural minorities." Many of those sociologists were primarily, and in some cases obsessively, concerned with oppressive imperialist policies before decolonization and also with problems in the development of new states recently freed from colonial rule. A major difficulty for the new states was how to shape new nations from a conglomeration of ethnic and linguistic groups brought together by an imperial power with scant respect for tribal boundaries. The role of the military in such efforts obviously needed investigation and synthesis.

In 1980, Dr. Cynthia Enloe published a seminal book, *Ethnic Soldiers*, that provided the first systematic and comprehensive analysis of the question of ethnicity in the military. She assumed that this interplay is not confined to those times and places where there is evidence of oppression, as some earlier research had seemed to suggest, but that it must be related more generally to the political development of any state in which different ethnic groups co-exist.

Starting from her earlier research on Scottish clans and a resultant fascination with Scottish regimental mutinies, Enloe analyzed the way imperial authorities exploited cultural minority groups to maintain and extend their control, for instance by the use of so-called "martial tribes" and a policy of "divide and rule."[29] But she had a "growing unease" with the widespread notion that militaries in modern societies are "prime forces for supra-ethnic integration,"[30] that is to say, that they can help to build new nations from states consisting of many different peoples.

She also noted that there are a few exceptions to the application of a general principle that the organization of the military is always designed primarily to maintain the existing distribution of power. She noted that some countries, including Canada, are attempting to reverse the present trend towards ethnic disintegration, and that these countries are different from others in one important respect: they are not faced with incipient insurgencies.[31]

There is, indeed, some question whether military organization in Canada in the nineteenth century had been used to maintain the power of a dominant English element of the population in the same way it was used, for instance, in India. As French Canadians took part in the political process in a more significant way than did Indians in the sub-continent, a difference is readily apparent. Secondly, as noted above, the use of the Militia to control disturbances in Montreal, though it might be seen as a way to ward off disorders that could lead to political instability, was more to protect the middle class, French as well as English, than to assert racial domination. Moreover, efforts to increase French-Canadian participation in defence programs and institutions and in other parts of government administration were more in line with what political scientist Donald Smiley has called "consociational democracy,"[32] that is to say, the sharing of power, than with the maintenance of an elite domination.

Therefore, more relevant to an understanding of the Canadian situation are the experiences and linguistic policies of other multicultural consociational democracies, for instance, Belgium, Switzerland, and (in a strictly limited sense) the internal ethnic divisions within the dominant white minority in South Africa. It may be significant that in Belgium, where Flemings were less attracted to military service than were French-speaking Walloons, representation in the military officer corps was kept for many years on a 50-50 quota basis, but military leadership passed from the Walloons to the Flemings some half-century ago. Similarly, in the dominant white government of South Africa, where English-speaking personnel were predominant in the military in both world wars, but where a policy of publishing official documents in both English and Afrikaans was introduced quite early, dominance in the army has now passed to the Afrikaaners. These generalizations, which might have ominous significance in the eyes of anglophone Canadians, are however based on inadequate information. More research needs to be done to explore their relevance, especially as to whether the transfer of a dominating influence is a consequence of language policies, or of other circumstances.[33]

The question whether more equitable representation in the Canadian armed forces can be, as is apparently hoped, nation-building, or may instead be a re-arrangement of military organization and political power in favour of French Canada, is one about which there may be considerable difference of opinion. Enloe concluded her study by saying that ethnic manipulations in militaries will decline only when the basis for the existence of the state concerned is no longer social segregation and coercion.[34] But this does not suggest much about the immediate future of policies to preserve language and other cultural distinctions.

CANADA'S PRESENT MOVE towards bilingual forces is both on a much bigger scale, and quite different from most other experiences. The Department of National Defence established a Director of Language Training in Headquarters, charged with implementing a program of language instruction to produce the personnel needed to fill a large number of appointments designated as bilingual. All military orders, official documents and signs, across Canada, must be in both languages. A large translation staff was established.

Crucial to the long-term success of the Canadian program was the introduction of bilingualism into officer education and training at the cadet level, which was seen as the key to attracting more French Canadians into the ranks. It was announced in 1971 that by the time the incoming RMC recruit class graduated in 1975 it must be bilingual; but it was also said that there must be no consequent reduction of either academic standards or military training. The ultimate objective was to make the Canadian officer corps, as a whole, bilingual.

This was, of course, easier to declare in principle than to put into effect. The first RMC class actually to go through the whole program did not graduate until 1981, six years behind schedule. Adding many compulsory and some optional parallel courses in French to the curriculum had required almost a doubling of the faculty. A new building for a Second Language Centre had had to be constructed, and a staff of thirty language instructors appointed. Time for the addition of five hours of language instruction each week had to be obtained by shortening each class time by five minutes, increasing the number of weeks of classes and utilizing summer training time more effectively. Cadets who failed to become functionally bilingual by the time they graduated had to take further language training the following summer.

The Commission on Bilingualism and Biculturalism had recommended that there should be two military colleges, one basically English-speaking, and the second French-speaking, each giving a full four-year academic program including engineering.[35] But even though financing for second-language training seemed to have a bottomless purse, the duplication of a third-and fourth-year engineering program at CMR (which had extended its course by two more years to give degrees in Arts, Canadian Studies, and Management) was seen at that time to be unattainable financially. French-Canadian cadets who wanted to become engineers must still attend RMC for their last two years, transferring there from CMR if they did not originally go to Kingston as recruits. This input of francophones helps RMC's institutional bilingualism and the promotion of bilingualism among its anglophone cadets. Because all students have a right by virtue of the Canadian Charter of Rights and Freedoms, to be instructed in their own language, all compulsory courses at RMC must be given in both English and French. By 1981 RMC could claim that 95 percent of compulsory courses were being given in both languages.[36]

To provide a suitable environment for language instruction in French for anglophones, and to make French-Canadian recruits and third-year transfers from CMR feel more at home in an anglophone community, substantial grants were made for French cultural acquisitions, including cable TV. The running of the cadet wing became completely bilingual, operating in alternate weeks in one or the other language. Promotion to certain cadet ranks requires functional competence in both languages. RMC's objective of institutional bilingualism resembles what is being adopted all across Canada in other fields of government service, to satisfy the ends of bilingual policy without causing anglophones to fear that every Canadian is expected to become bilingual.

In order to increase the flow of recruits from francophone Quebec, ROTP funding was offered to candidates taking approved final-year courses in the Collèges d'Enseignement General et Professionnel – the CEGEPs that had replaced the old Classical Colleges during Quebec's Quiet Revolution in order to modernize Quebec education with the addition of science and technical courses. After being financed through their last year of CEGEP education, many of these cadets were expected to enter RMC. To familiarize them with what they could expect, they were taken there on visits during their CEGEP-ROTP year.

However, some of the CEGEP-ROTP recruits preferred to go on to CMR rather than to RMC. Furthermore, fewer of the second-year CMR cadets than expected were willing to transfer to RMC, even though it meant losing the education as an engineer which they had originally sought. When it was found that so many French-Canadian cadets preferred to go to CMR, the proportion of French Canadians there was raised from 60:40 to 70:30.

CMR and Royal Roads are now seeking to give complete degree courses in selected special fields in engineering. They find that, as a majority of cadets want to be engineers, when they are without an engineering faculty their third and fourth years are left with too few senior cadets to provide for a sound military training program. If these *curriculum* expansions should take place, even though RMC remains, and Royal Roads becomes, institutionally bilingual, it might seriously affect the bilingual programs at both schools. As has been shown, the input of francophones into the RMC program has been an important factor in promoting its bilingual system and so in furthering the second-language competence of its anglophones. It is also claimed to be an important element in preserving unity in the officer-production system. As most French-Canadian cadets might prefer to take engineering at CMR, that would deprive the other two colleges of an adequate intake of francophones and so would jeopardize anglophone bilingualism in the forces.

The Canadian forces' program of institutional bilingualism, including that in the Canadian Military Colleges which is the heart of the whole undertaking, is designed to bring more francophones into the forces by replacing monolingual communication by a degree of bilingualism. Some units, including three naval vessels, were designated bilingual, and everywhere francophones were to be encouraged and utilized. The program is, of course, very expensive. It can be said to impose on anglophones the same impediment to their promotion prospects that French Canadians have long endured, that is, "the learning of a second language." It thus is a form of what is known in the U.S., in another connection and application, as "affirmative action."

Insofar as anglophones may resent this program because it demands what they see as an "unnecessary" effort on their part that may disadvantage them in their careers, it may be detrimental; and how can a bilingual capacity be retained by individuals who have little opportunity to use it later for long periods? Thus, while making more French Canadians available for the defence of Canada, this policy might, at the same time, exacerbate French-English relations and diminish anglophone willingness to serve. It may also come to be seen as a threat to military professionalism and as an expensive infringement on military efficiency.

On the other hand, making the Canadian forces more representative of both races could contribute to the building and preservation of Canada. Ultimately that result will probably be decided by the nature of future demands upon Canada's bilingual forces, i.e., whether for prolonged peace-keeping and deterrence or, in an unpleasantly near future, for a major war. It may be that this bilingual program is, in fact, only possible now because Canada's peace and security are guaranteed by the United States, and because no war seems imminent. If the deterrent posture of the Cold War is long continued, institutional bilingualism might be the only way in which full national support for Canada's defence can be obtained. But if much further relaxation of international tensions occurs, financial support for an expensive program of bilingualism may wither.

No POLICIES OR proposals for making the Canadian forces reflect the multicultural nature of Canadian society are in any way comparable with the English-French bilingualism program. But some of the arguments in the debate about French-English bilingualism cast light on this question. There are grounds for saying that language is the chief vehicle of cultural attributes and that its loss inevitably weakens, and ultimately will destroy, the special features of a cultural group. The recent increase in the intensity of the movement for separatism in Quebec, and for language rights and also for bilingualism and biculturalism elsewhere in Canada, has been promoted in part by the facts that the French-Canadian birthrate, once the highest in the Western World, is now the lowest, and that the tendency is for new immigrants to Quebec to prefer to learn English, the language of the vast majority of North Americans, rather than French. These circumstances may indicate that within the foreseeable future the French language may die out on this continent with the consequent demise of French cultural traditions. Hence, a determined effort is needed to attempt to preserve it.

On the other hand, some opponents of bilingualism, in Canada generally and in the armed forces in particular, argue that the French-Canadian claim that preservation of their language is essential to the preservation of their culture is unsound. These people state that language is an acquired characteristic and that some peoples, for instance the Scots, have maintained distinctive cultural features without it. It may be that the Ukrainians in Canada are now doing the same thing.

There is in fact some evidence in military forces that cultural characteristics may be retained without the preservation of a language. In the eighteenth century the British government approved the adoption of clan kilts and tartans for Scottish regiments in the British Army. These are now an important source of morale. But these symbols may, in fact, not depend entirely on cultural and inherited differences. This is suggested by the record of what is perhaps the most famous Scottish regiment of all, the Black Watch, which has affiliated regiments in Scotland, Canada, and Australia. The Watch was not originally a single clan regiment but was recruited by the British from among unrelated individuals from various sources. Its first colonel, the Earl of Crawford, was a Lowlander. The regiment was originally used to keep order among the restless clans. Its recruiting has been described as having been based on the principle that "it takes a thief to catch a thief." Its Scottish clan affiliation is thus adoptive, rather than inherited. Without a particular clan affiliation, the Watch earned its great prestige by its glorious war record and by a high morale which was in part based on symbols.[37] There are in the Canadian forces today many men who proudly wear the kilt of Canadian Scottish regiments whose forebears, coming from the steppes or from elsewhere than the Highlands, spoke tongues other than Gaelic. One Canadian Scottish regiment has a black piper. In these cases it is the symbol that counts, not ethnicity or language.

There is as yet little indication that Canada's ethnic groups will press for language privileges, will long retain their ancestral languages, or will request the creation of military units that are ethnically homogeneous. However, Canada has to some extent inherited the British practice of associating regiments with localities as a means of strengthening morale. Recruitment from areas where ethnic groups reside might, in the future, become a source of morale-building strength for the Canadian forces if ethnic symbols are carefully utilized. So far, however, multiculturalism is far less significant than bilingualism as a problem for the Canadian forces of today or tomorrow.

Notes

1. On this subject see the presidential address G.F.G. Stanley delivered to the Canadian Historical Association in 1956: "Act or Pact: Another Look at Confederation," *Annual Report of the Canadian Historical Association*, 1956, pp. 1-25. In the late 1960s and early 1970s, D.G. Creighton, Ralph Heintzman, and David Hall debated whether and to what extent Confederation implied a Canada-wide acceptance of bilingualism and biculturalism. See D.G. Creighton, "John A. Macdonald, Confederation, and the Canadian West," reprinted in *Minorities, Schools, and Politics*, ed. R. Craig Brown (Toronto, 1969), pp. 1-9; Ralph Heintzman, "The Spirit of Confederation: Professor Creighton, Biculturalism, and the Use of History," *Canadian Historical Review*, 52 (Sept. 1971), pp. 245-75; and David Hall, " 'The Spirit of Confederation': Ralph Heintzman, Professor Creighton, and the Bicultural Compact Theory," *Journal of Canadian Studies*, 9 (Nov. 1974), pp. 24-42.

2. Jean Pariseau, Etude No. 1, "Le bilinguisme et le biculturalisme au Ministère de la Défense Nationale, 1946-1973" (Ottawa: QGDN, 22 Dec. 1980), pp. 6-15. I am indebted to the author and the Director of the Canadian Forces' Historical Section, Dr. W.A.B. Douglas, for access to this work and to other works by Captain Pariseau, Etude No. 9, "Le bilinguisme et le biculturalisme au sein des institutions d'enseignement supérieur du MDN" (Ottawa: Service historique, QGDN, 20 May 1983), and Etude No. 24, "Le Commissaire aux langues officielles et le Ministère de la Défense Nationale, 1970-1980" (Ottawa: Service historique, QGDN, 12 March 1981).

3. Desmond Morton, "French Canada and War, 1868-1917: The Military Background to the Conscription Crisis of 1917," in *War and Society in North America*, ed. J.L. Granatstein and R.D. Cuff (Toronto, 1971), p. 86. See also Morton's "French Canada and the Militia, 1868-1914," *Histoire sociale* 3 (April 1969), pp. 32-50; and his *Canada and War: A Political and Military History* (Toronto, 1981).

4. John Boyd, *Sir George-Etienne Cartier: His Life and Times: A Political History of Canada from 1814 until 1873* (Toronto, 1914), p. 291.

5. Canada, Parliament, *Commons Debates 1883* 1, April 19 (Ottawa, 1885), p. 725.

6. Morton, "French Canada and War," pp. 86-90; *Canada and War*, pp. 21f.

7. Warren L. Young, *Minorities and the Military: A Cross-National Study in World Perspective, Contributions in Ethnic Studies*, no. 6 (Westport, Conn. and London, 1982), pp. 18f.

8. John Meisel, "Values, Language, and Politics in Canada," in *Advances in the Study of Societal Multi-lingualism*, ed. Joshua A. Fishman (The Hague, 1978), p. 082.

9. W.J. Eccles, "The Social, Economic, and Political Significance of the Military

Establishment in New France," *Canadian Historical Review* 7: 1-22; Jean-Yves Gravel, *Le Québec et la guerre, Etudes d'histoire du Québec*, no. 7 (Montreal, 1974), p. 4.

10. Un vétéran de 1812 [E.P. Taché], *Quelques réflexions sur l'organisation des volontaires et de la milice de cette province* (Québec, 1863), p. 5.
11. Morton, *Canada and War*, p. 21; Jean-Yves Gravel, *L'armée au Québec, 1829-1900: un portrait social* (Montreal, 1974); L. Gustave D'Orsonnens, *Considérations sur l'organisation militaire de la Confédération canadienne* (Montreal, 1874), p. 50.
12. D'Orsonnens, p. 49.
13. Morton, "French Canada and War," pp. 89-90.
14. J.L. Granatstein and J.M. Hitsman, *Broken Promises: A History of Conscription in Canada* (Toronto, 1977); J.Y. Gravel, "Le Québec militaire, 1939-45," in *Le Québec et la guerre*, pp. 80-84.
15. J. Eayrs, *In Defence of Canada*, Vol. 3: *Peace-making and Deterrence* (Toronto, 1972), pp. 132-36.
16. Pariseau, Etude No. 9, pp. 2-27.
17. Richard A. Preston, *Canada's RMC: A History of the Royal Military College* (Toronto, 1969), pp. 332-49. A small "Reserve Entry" was restored a few years later.
18. Jean-Yves Gravel, "La fondation du collège militaire de Saint-Jean," in *Revue de l'histoire de l'Amérique française*, 27 (1973), 257-80.
19. Eayrs, 3, pp. 132-33.
20. Pariseau, Etude No. 1, pp. 19-26.
21. G. Tougas, "Report on the Teaching of French and on the Position of French-speaking Cadets in the Services Colleges," RMC Faculty Council Minutes, April 1962.
22. Eayrs, 3, pp. 135-36.
23. Canada, Royal Commission on Government Organization 1, *Management of the Public Service* (Ottawa, 1962), pp. 75-76.
24. Canada, Royal Commission on Bilingualism and Biculturalism, *Report* 3 (Ottawa, 19 Sept. 1969), p. 340, para. 1003.
25. Canada, Department of National Defence, *White Paper on Defence: Defence in the 70's* (Ottawa, 1971), pp. 3-4, 47.
26. CDEE Directive No. 4/71, "Bilingualism at the CMCs," 24 Feb. 1971, Records of the RMC Administration, "B & B" files. The means by which this should be carried out are detailed in Pariseau, Etude No. 9, Annex B.
27. Richard A. Preston, "Ethno-cultural Pluralism in Military Forces: A Historical Survey," in *Policy by Other Means: Essays in Honour of C.P. Stacey*, ed. Michael Cross and Robert Bothwell (Toronto and Vancouver, 1972), pp. 21-49.
28. "The Mixed Manning Demonstration," US Naval Institute, *Proceedings*, Vol. 91 (July 1965), pp. 87-103; Hanson Baldwin, "The *Ricketts*: Mixed-Manned Ship Sails Tomorrow," *New York Times*, 14 Feb. 1965; London *Times*, 30 March 1965.
29. Cynthia Enloe, *Ethnic Soldiers: State Security in Divided Societies* (Athens, Georgia, 1980), pp. ix-x, 21-22, 23-49.
30. Ibid., pp. 21-22.
31. Ibid., p. 217. Enloe's description of French Canadians as an "ethnic group" is in line with the international use of that term, but it may disturb some French-Canadian scholars.

32. Donald V. Smiley, "French-English Relations in Canada and Consociational Democracy," in *Ethnic Conflicts in the Western World*, ed. Milton J. Esmin (Ithaca and London, 1977), pp. 179-204. See also John Porter, "Ethnic Pluralism in Canada," in Glazer and Moynihan, *Ethnicity*, pp. 267-304.

33. See V. Bouvier, *Analyse de la population de la classe de milice, 1965* (Brussels: Forces armées belges: Centre de recherches, 1966), Chapter 2; and Guy van Gorp, *Le candidat officier: aspects sociologiques du futur corps des officiers belges* (Louvain, 1969), p. 199. The opinion expressed in the text is based on the author's impressions gained in a visit to Ecole militaire royale, Brussels, and may be out of date today.

34. Enloe, p. 234.

35. Canada, Royal Commission on Bilingualism and Biculturalism, *Report* 3 (Ottawa, 19 Sept. 1969), p. 340, para. 1003.

36. Records of the RMC Administration, "B & B" files.

37. Archibald Forbes, *The "Black Watch": The Record of an Historic Regiment* (London, 1896), pp. 9-10; Charles Grant, *The Black Watch* (Norwich, 1971), pp. 4-5; W. P. Paul, *The Highland Regiments: Tigers in Tartan* (Aberdeen, 1971), p. 4; R.M. Barnes and C.K. Allen, *Uniforms and History of the Scottish Regiments* (London, n.d.), p. 52.

THE UNWELCOME SACRIFICE: A BLACK UNIT IN THE CANADIAN EXPEDITIONARY FORCE, 1917-19

JOHN G. ARMSTRONG

THE FORMATION OF military units made up of black personnel is not unusual in the North American experience. There is, of course, a substantial black population in the United States, and political imperatives and increasing manpower demands brought black units into being on several occasions. In Canada, however, the black population has never composed a bloc of proportionate or comparable significance. Thus the creation of a Canadian Negro unit during the First World War, Number 2 Construction Battalion as a component of the Canadian Expeditionary Force (CEF), was therefore both innovative and somewhat surprising. Although Canada's black population at the time approximated only 20,000, nearly 700 of them (more than half from Nova Scotia) had volunteered for service before the battalion was dispatched overseas in March 1917.[1] This little known unit provided a focus for the legitimate aspirations of members of Canada's black community to serve their country. At the same time it provided a reluctant Militia Department with an alternative to enforcing their acceptance into the many white units which all too rarely welcomed blacks into their ranks.

Canada's black community was, for the most part, excluded from the patriotic and military institutions which came to the fore as Canadians became involved in the war with Germany and her allies.[2] Enlistment in the CEF, while initially voluntary, was also accepted and advocated by most elements of the social establishment as a due and rightful obligation of free citizens in a free society. Almost any fit male of good character was therefore acceptable to the prominent Canadians whom Militia Minister Sam Hughes authorized to recruit the battalions and battalion-like drafts needed to satisfy the growing manpower demands of the CEF. Some, such as French Canadians,

---

* The author is most grateful to the Royal Military College of Canada for the Arts Research Grant which made this study possible.

recent non-British immigrants, and hard-pressed farmers, were less enthusiastic. Indeed, their relative reluctance to serve generated a degree of bitterness among Canadians of which traces remain to this day. By contrast, substantial numbers of blacks, who responded to the general enthusiasm by presenting themselves for enlistment, found to their chagrin that many battalion recruiters did not want them.

This paper does not aim to right any wrongs or redress any grievances. It intends only to report on the formation and subsequent service of a unit of black Canadians, a unit that Canada's civil and military establishment only reluctantly permitted to participate in what was widely considered to be a white man's war. As far as Sam Hughes was concerned, there was no logical impediment to black enrolment in the CEF and he had issued characteristically laconic instructions "that colored men are to be permitted to enlist in any battalion."[3] The Militia Department, however, was not able to oversee the recruiting process effectively. That authority had been delegated to the favoured (and usually politically influential) individuals placed in command of each battalion being recruited. They were, in effect, free to decide who was and who was not an acceptable recruit.[4]

Many were turned away for reasons which were blatantly prejudiced. The belief in the unsuitability of blacks for military service was commonly held at the time even by otherwise humane and generous-spirited individuals. Major-General Willoughby Gwatkin, the British officer who served as Canada's Chief of the General Staff (CGS) typified such views. A highly educated and intelligent man, he was much respected not only for his ability but also for his objectivity, tact, and kindliness. Gwatkin, nevertheless, viewed the "civilized negro" as "vain and imitative," lacking in any high sense of duty to serve, and unlikely to make a good fighter. If this were not enough, Gwatkin also saw little likelihood that the average white man would associate with him on terms of equality.[5]

There were other concerns as well. "I have been fortunate to have secured a very fine class of recruits," the Officer Commanding the 104th Overseas Battalion intimated when he was asked to explain turning away a body of fourteen blacks: "and I did not think it was fair to these men that they should have to mingle with [N]egroes. I might state further, that some of these [N]egroes arrived here very much the worse of liquor. . . ."[6]

Not all commanding officers were so adamant. Some professed no serious objection to accepting coloured recruits *per se*. Yet most felt impelled to consider the possible detriment that the presence of blacks in their battalions might have on recruitment. Others felt that the black citizen lacked in soldierly qualities.[7] At least two battalions, raised to reflect the Highland heritage, felt no need to justify the exclusion of blacks beyond the contention that they "would not look good in kilts."[8] A battalion raised in Simcoe County refused to accept blacks from outside the county, yet it said that it would accept them if they were from the same locality. A different battalion from the same county reported simply that there were no Negroes to be found there.[9]

Some black recruits were in fact accepted into various CEF units, although with so little fanfare that the actual numbers were not known at the time.[10] It was by no means enough though for those blacks who sought both recognition and service. Indignation at the rejection of their recruits mounted wherever black citizens were to be found in any numbers. There were complaints from Ontario — particularly the southwest and Toronto — and the prairies, but the frustration and resentment was particularly keen in Nova Scotia where the coloured population of approximately 7,000 (close to one-third of the total black population in Canada), was significant, long-established and not without ability to make its weight felt morally and politically. There were federal politicians in the government who were not only sympathetic but ready to help. They included Prime Minister Sir Robert Borden, who represented Halifax, John Stanfield from Truro and, most particularly, Fleming B. McCurdy, MP for Shelburne and Queen's who was Parliamentary Secretary to the frequently absent Militia Minister. McCurdy was probably instrumental in the formation of No. 2 Construction Battalion.[11]

It became increasingly clear that the government was not going to be able to prevent battalion commanders from refusing black recruits without generating even more controversy. It also became clear that, for many blacks, the prospect of service in such a potentially hostile environment would be unappealing and intimidating. Thus the idea of a black unit (or, at least, one or more units with substantial black components) became more and more attractive not only to the military establishment but also to the black community. Such prominent and articulate black leaders as J.R.B. Whitney of Toronto, editor of the Negro journal, *The Canadian Observer*, and the Reverend William A. White of Truro, Nova Scotia, led the call for such a solution.[12] As a result, pressure on the government was intensified.

Sam Hughes was opposed to units of any particular ethnic or physical stripe other than as recruiting gimmicks, with the unit being broken up for reinforcements later. For Gwatkin, however, there were other practical aspects to be considered. In particular, there was the inescapable fact that the black population of Canada was simply insufficient to maintain a separate combat unit of any size in the field for any significant length of time. There did appear to be enough manpower to support a platoon or two attached to white battalions, and at least one battalion commander had indicated a willingness to consider such an arrangement.[13] Nevertheless, the idea's detractors were in the majority. Not one of the forty-five battalions being recruited in central Ontario during the spring of 1916 expressed a willingness to accept a black platoon, despite strong pressure from Militia Headquarters to do so. "I am sure every Commanding Officer would have a very strong objection," the area commander concluded in his report on the matter.[14] The situation was becoming an embarrassment to all concerned. Indeed, by this time coloured leaders in both Ontario and Nova Scotia, acting upon Sam Hughes' assurances that platoons of coloured recruits would be welcome in the Militia, had already recruited a number of prospective members. The failure of Hughes' embarrassed officials to find a unit which would readily accept the arrangement, however, also led to a major indiscretion when a junior officer in the Toronto area headquarters bluntly advised Whitney that no unit would accept the proposed coloured platoon that he had been actively campaigning for and that the whole idea would have to be dropped.[15] Whitney expressed his outrage to Sam Hughes:

> through the columns of the "Canadian Observer" (the official organ of the Colored [sic] Race in Canada) I have published a call for recruits for the Colored Platoon. Many has [sic] responded to the call, and are eagerly waiting to be uniformed in the King's colors. The race as a whole is looking forward to the outcome of the Colored Platoon. I trust that you will see to it that the Colored Platoon will be placed with some Battalion, otherwise their [sic] will be a great disappointment with the Race and ill feeling towards the Government, which would be justifiable, as they have been authorized to go ahead and recruit, but now cannot be accepted. Believing this matter has not come before you and when acquainted with facts you will see that we receive a square deal.[16]

There was a possible means of compromise. In February 1916 the Colonial Office had sounded out the Canadian government on the possibility of raising one or more labour battalions "of the navvy class" for service overseas.[17] Such a unit would carry an establishment of 1,038 from all ranks, but would not normally be subjected to the harsh attrition rates associated with service at the front and would therefore not require constant reinforcement. The first of these was authorized in early April as No. 1 Labour Battalion but hastily renamed as No. 1 Construction Battalion when Lieutenant-

Colonel Blair Ripley, the prominent railway construction engineer who was selected to raise the unit, complained that the labour designation was not popular "with the class of men with which I would try to make up the Battalion."[18]

The possibility that a second construction battalion could be recruited from the Negro population and officered by whites appeared to offer a feasible way out and was recommended by Major-General Gwatkin. Provision would still be made for the enlistment of individual blacks in normal CEF battalions, but only at the discretion of the commanding officer concerned.[19] The Militia Council, with Prime Minister Borden presiding in another of Hughes' absences, decided to approach the War Office to determine if a Negro construction (labour) battalion would be acceptable to the Imperial authorities. A month later, on 11 May 1916, the War Office replied that they would "be glad to accept such a battalion of Canadian Negroes," provided they were enlisted as soldiers.[20]

The government was prepared to move almost immediately to form the new unit. But a new difficulty arose. A shortlist of prospective commanding officers had been prepared and duly approved by the minister. [There would be a degree of sad truth in the Adjutant-General's sardonic observation that the posting would be "a somewhat peculiar command."] The first two men offered the post declined. Finally, after considerable further effort to find additional candidates, it was the prime minister himself who suggested a fellow Nova Scotian, Daniel H. Sutherland, of River John, Pictou County. Sutherland, who had recently been enrolled as a probationary infantry officer, was a contractor with considerable experience in railway construction. He gladly accepted the invitation to command No. 2 and was duly commissioned as a lieutenant-colonel.[21]

No. 2 CONSTRUCTION Battalion was formally authorized as a component of the CEF on 5 July 1916. It was to be raised from among Canadian Negroes recruited from across Canada. It was to be officered by white men and mobilized in Nova Scotia. A circular letter from the Adjutant-General to all districts and camps advised of this departure from the jealously guarded regional recruiting prerogatives.[22] Later on, provision would also be made to allow Negro members of other units to transfer to the new battalion.[23]

The news of No. 2's formation was cause for complaint from a new source. "This report has caused some demonstration from men in Number One Construction Battalion," that unit's commanding officer advised in a telegram to headquarters. Colonel Ripley went on to suggest that:

[there] will be difficulty in holding men now on strength and serious damper will be placed on recruiting. If not official please wire so [it] can be contradicted here.

If official recommend wisdom in changing name and having understanding as to difference in class of work to be done by each battalion.[24]

Lieutenant-Colonel Ripley eventually had his way insofar as a change of name and "class of work" for his unit was concerned, but not before it went to France. Indeed, the Adjutant-General's initial reply had barely concealed his annoyance and it contained a closing reminder that the new construction battalion would

be composed of men who are British subjects and Canadians. Coloured troops, including Africans and West Indians, have done good service at the front, and are recognized as comrades in arms both in France and England. It is for you therefore, to inspire your men with correct ideas on the subject.[25]

Lieutenant-Colonel Sutherland set out to organize his new command with the enthusiastic support of those who had championed black participation in the war and with considerable assistance from the Negro social institutions that existed in various communities. This was particularly true in the case of the well-established black community and church groups in Nova Scotia.

No. 2's white officers were generally drawn from the ranks of the construction or civil engineering professions and had occupational backgrounds comparable to that of the prestigious Corps of Canadian Railway Troops. Another particularly prominent construction manager and entrepreneur, Henry Falconer McLean, who had shown particular interest in the unit, was named honorary colonel. McLean was a colourful man remembered by many for his eccentric acts in later life, such as throwing vast sums of money from the roof of the Royal York Hotel in Toronto. He was also well known, however, for his genuine humanity and his great empathy with the common labourer. His generous financial support aided the unit's recruiting efforts and provided instruments for the battalion band.[26] A particularly noteworthy member of No. 2's roster of officers was the pastor of the Truro, Nova Scotia, Zion Church, William A. White, who was enrolled as the unit's chaplain with the rank of honorary captain. As such, he was probably the first Negro to hold commissioned rank in Canadian military service.

Recruiting had begun almost at once in Nova Scotia and, by mid-August, close to two hundred men had been concentrated in the Town of Pictou, where their formation was greeted with considerable favour by the local press. The unit was soon being praised by the

Pictou Advocate as "the coloured man's opportunity to show his loyalty to the flag that has stood so long for equal rights for the men of his race." Simultaneously, the paper remarked, perhaps with some surprise and certainly with some condescension, that the conduct of the men was "exciting favorable comment in the town. All are well behaved and carry themselves like true soldiers."[27] But the local paper also called for "more than ordinary pains" to enforce the Nova Scotia Temperance Act. Indeed, it was pointed out, one of the reasons Pictou had first been selected as a location for troops was its reputation as a dry town.[28] A newspaper in Halifax reported that some of the men were calling themselves "the chocolate soldiers."[29]

There was insufficient space to quarter a full battalion in Pictou, particularly when recruits from Ontario and the west arrived later. Accordingly, Sutherland asked for and got permission to relocate the unit to Truro where there was more space and where he hoped the presence of a "coloured settlement" near the unit's headquarters would prove a further stimulus to recruiting.[30] The move was duly accomplished but not without some difficulty with a landlord, who declined to provide accommodation for the black battalion's headquarters even though other military organizations had previously used his facilities.[31]

As the battalion gradually shifted its centre of gravity from Pictou to Truro, recruiting activities intensified further afield. Recruiting offices were opened in Montreal and Toronto. One officer, Captain A.J. Gayfer, was assigned the job of attracting recruits in the west. Notwithstanding the relatively sparse Negro population on the prairies and in British Columbia, and some further difficulties in obtaining office space and persuading white doctors to examine black candidates, fifty men were eventually mustered.[32]

For reasons of not only space and economy but also probably the desire to avoid giving offence to whites by concentrating too many black men in one location, it was intended to bring the entire battalion together in Truro only immediately prior to its dispatch overseas. Accordingly, the men recruited in Ontario and the west were stationed for a while in Windsor, Ontario. Eventually, about four hundred had gathered there under Captain Gayfer's command.[33]

Not much is known about the day-to-day life of the Windsor detachment or of its impact upon the local community. The city had a population of close to 18,000 and the black sub-unit was one of several (and larger) formations being raised in the area.[34] Nevertheless, the local press did make occasional references to the black soldiers. Disciplinary infractions and such things as disorderly conduct and strong drink in a "blind pig" were mentioned. But there were also reports of recruiting fund concerts, testimonial religious services and the donation of funds from the city to help with recruiting expenses. The Women's Christian Temperance Union presented gifts of socks and handkerchiefs, and a local music store glibly contributed 225 song books "containing words and music of many of the popular songs and plantation melodies."[35] When an initial draft of fifty-four men left the city to join the parent unit in Truro, close to one thousand citizens and senior military officials are reported to have gathered at the Grand Trunk station to see them off.[36] The departure of the main body a few days later was admittedly quiet and unheralded, but this was no doubt a reflection of increasing government sensitivity to the publication of military movements. As the (Windsor) *Evening Record* observed:

> by their good behavior while here, members of the battalion won the respect and admiration of all Windsor citizens. They earned the reputation of being a sober, well-disciplined and hardworking company of soldiers.
>
> The removal of the battalion on such short notice came as a great surprise and expressions of regret that the citizens of Windsor were not afforded an opportunity of giving them a rousing farewell on their departure were heard on all sides Tuesday morning.[37]

Truro had only one-third of the population of Windsor, thus the parent body of No. 2 Construction Battalion was much more visible in that centre. The local press gave the unit frequent and complimentary coverage in its editions and the unit itself proved an attractive focus for the sorts of patriotic activity on the part of both black and white citizens which typified the times. The brass band, funded by the battalion's honorary colonel, actively participated in local events as well as those elsewhere in Nova Scotia. Recruiting committees were formed to support the new unit and a Ladies Patriotic League was organized. Concerts, parades, skating parties, religious services and recruiting meetings were held and mayors and members of Parliament lent their support to (and, no doubt, occasionally took the credit for) the campaign. A mobile recruiting station was set up in a Canadian Pacific Railway sleeping car with a cooking caboose attached. In this way battalion recruiters, accompanied by the unit band, went on a well-publicized tour of the major towns of the Annapolis Valley and the South Shore.[38]

An undoubted high point in the life of the battalion occurred on the morning of 14 November 1916 when F.B. McCurdy, Sam Hughes' parliamentary secretary, suddenly elevated to acting ministerial rank by his minister's much publicized and controversial resignation, descended from the Ottawa-bound "Limited" to inspect his unique responsibility.[39] The Truro *Daily News* proudly reported that he:

expressed his great satisfaction on the splendid appearance of the Battalion, and the good reports he had received on their excellent behaviour and pointed out that in this great struggle for Humanity and Freedom the coloured citizen had shown the world that he was ready to stand side by side with his white comrade and brother and do his "bit" and help win a glorious victory for the Allies.[40]

Unfortunately, beneath the façade of patriotic enthusiasm, all was not well with the unit. As early as September, 1916, Major-General Gwatkin expressed the concern that No. 2 "would be a troublesome unit to put up in winter quarters," and he was pressing the Adjutant-General to have it sent overseas as soon as possible.[41] The unit was subsequently warned that it could expect to be sent overseas at the end of February 1917, whether up to strength or not, having had by then seven months to raise the necessary manpower.[42]

More seriously, the battalion's recruiting campaign had not fulfilled expectations. The numbers enrolled fell drastically short of the authorized establishment of 1,038. Authorization to accept Negroes from the United States and the British West Indies had added substantially to the total but it was still not enough.[43] In all, some seven hundred Negroes were recruited but only 598 proceeded overseas, a number which included 171 men born in the United States (twenty of these, interestingly, had served in the United States Army) and sixty-six in the British West Indies.[44]

It should not be surprising that the unit did not attract as many recruits as had been hoped. While some no doubt were attracted by the prospect of serving with the company and having the support of other blacks to draw upon, there were obviously others who felt that such a form of segregation was not acceptable. Also, one recruiting officer had remarked that considerable difficulty had been experienced in recruiting: "due to the rough manner in which they have been previously turned down. . . . It is this style I think that is making the recruiting of colored men very difficult especially as they are perhaps super sensitive."[45]

The prospect of service in a labour battalion must have seemed a poor second to the prestige of active service in a combat unit. Colonel Sutherland did what he could to "remove suspicion that exists in certain quarters, that colored men will only be used as trench diggers," when he bypassed his chain of command and wrote directly to the new minister, Sir Edward Kemp, to ask that his unit be redesignated a Railway Construction Battalion.[46] He had already arranged, with ministerial approval, for a detachment of some 230 of his men to assist the Canadian Government Railways in lifting track in New Brunswick for emergency shipment overseas. News that his battalion would be engaged in building railway lines along with the other Canadian railway construction troops would be "gratifying . . . to the colored [sic] people and give a decided impulse to recruiting."[47] Any redesignation must be a British decision, the Adjutant-General advised the minister in late January 1917, and no change was forthcoming.[48] Sutherland continued to press his case but to the increasing annoyance of his superiors.[49]

The unit was beginning to be an embarrassment and the matter of employment and designation had the potential to cause political problems. The Militia Department accordingly wanted to ship its black contingent overseas as quickly and quietly as possible, but not without regard to what General Gwatkin referred to as "the susceptibilities of other troops."[50] The proposal was to dispatch the unit on its own by ship. One could be available as early as 10 March if it was not required to await the next naval convoy. "Do you object to that vessel sailing without an escort," Gwatkin inquired of the Navy Department, "the shipping Company concerned is prepared to take the risk."[51] The submarine threat in the North Atlantic was then at its height. Happily it can be reported that the Royal Canadian Navy did not agree to this heedless request.[52]

No. 2 SAILED for England on the troopship *Southland* on 25 March 1917, in company with 3,500 other troops and in a small naval convoy which arrived in Liverpool on 8 April. They remained in England for less than two months, being held at Seaford, where they were employed in general labour duties.[53] "Military training was subordinate to agricultural labor, mostly planting potatoes," the unit's War Diary somewhat glumly reports.[54]

The presence of a unit of Canadian blacks in England now presented something of a problem to the Imperial authorities and the headquarters of the overseas military forces of Canada. To begin with, it was understrength for a battalion and overstrength for a company. Serious consideration was therefore given to breaking it up and absorbing it into either the Railway Troops or the Canadian Forestry Corps, but it was not considered advisable for substantial numbers of black personnel to be absorbed into white units. Also, British policy towards troops composed of the subject races of the Empire involved such practices as confinement to camp, denial of leave, and active discouragement of fraternization with white people — especially white women. There was some concern that to do otherwise might undermine the British position in their native land when the troops returned. No such policy was acceptable to the Canadian authorities.[55]

One solution to the foregoing was to redesignate the unit. It became Number 2 Construction Company with a specially drawn up establishment for a reinforced company of 9 officers and 495 other ranks. There was no room for a lieutenant-colonel in this new establishment, however, and the commanding officer was obliged to accept reduction to the rank of major as the price of remaining with his unit.

The possibility of any inconsistency or injustice arising from British policies towards native troops was neatly side-stepped by posting No. 2 to the Jura Group of the Canadian Forestry Corps near the town of La Joux, which was in the French Army's lines of communication. The French did not draw legal distinctions between the privileges of their metropolitan and their Oriental and African soldiers. Even so, there may have been some opposition from French military and civilian officials in this relatively remote locale to the prospect of having black Canadians there. At least women in the district were said to be upset. If there was any resistance, however, it was promptly overridden and disavowed by the Ministère de la Guerre.

The Canadian Forestry Corps (CFC) had, by the end of the war, come to represent a contribution of considerable magnitude. Over 22,000 Canadian lumbermen-soldiers served in its ranks. The Corps' task involved the full spectrum of logging operations in the carefully managed woods of England and France aimed at bridging the gap between the military's insatiable appetite for wood products and the scarcity of shipping space to transport them from the usual source regions in Canada and elsewhere. Most of the Canadians were skilled lumbermen but there were others involved in the task who were considered unskilled, bringing total manpower to over 31,000. The latter included expatriate Russians no longer trusted to bear arms, prisoners of war, Chinese coolies and No. 2 Construction Company, CEF.

The unit arrived at La Joux to become part of No. 5 District, Jura Group, CFC, early on the morning of 20 May 1917, after a four-day journey by ship across the English Channel and by rail across France. The black troops were comfortably encamped in tents that same night. They appear to have been cordially received and to have been pleased with their reception. They found that their arrival had been well prepared for with water supply laid in, latrines provided, and buildings erected for an infirmary and an officers' mess. The company was ready for work the following day but a suspected case of measles resulted in their camp being placed out of bounds for ten days.

The report by the Jura Group's commander on the construction company's arrival also gave some indication that there were a few trouble-makers in the new unit. "One Company of this Battalion [*sic*]," coming from the group recruited in Windsor:

has caused considerable trouble through lack of discipline, since they left Canada. This Company was immediately taken in hand and a detail of about 50 of these men were immediately put to work this morning (Monday) building a log cabin jail. This ostentatious display is intended to impress these men at the start that ill discipline will not be tolerated. I have no doubt that they will eventually shape down and will be of considerable service.[60]

No. 2, with its 500 men, was the largest unit in No. 5 District. The 11 forestry companies, which made up its skilled labour strength, were each usually established for 6 officers and 164 other ranks. As an entity unto itself, however, the unit did not play a direct role in No. 5 District's operations. Its primary function was essentially that of an administrative holding unit. Thus, while No. 2 Construction preserved its identity and operated its own camp, the bulk of its officers and men were requisitioned for employment wherever their services were needed by the various forestry companies. Those with skills to offer, however, appear to have been effectively used.[61] It was also not unusual in the CFC to move men around from unit to unit, depending on shifting workload and needs.[62] Thus the arrangement can be viewed as fair under the circumstances and as perhaps the most effective use of the skilled and unskilled manpower available.

The work in the Juras was arduous and labour, skilled or otherwise, was in short supply; but, judging from available photographic evidence, the atmosphere seems to have offered far more of the informal camaraderie of a Canadian logging camp than that normally associated with the military. Still, Major Sutherland saw some need to maintain his own troops' military bearing. "It is believed that this is the only unit in the District complying with the order that parties are to march to and from work in an orderly fashion," the unit War Diary records with barely concealed pride.[63]

No. 2 also acted as an administrative holding unit for various groups of Russians whose presence was often less than welcome. Now that their country was out of the war, they were not considered trustworthy. As the War Diary complains of one group of forty Russians, "they not only stay in camp idle all day, but spread socialistic doctrines among the others."[64]

Days were long. Reveille was at 0500 hours and by 0700 the men were at work. Normally they laboured ten hours a day, six days a week. Work at night and on Sundays was not unusual. The employment was very diverse. Of 257 "other ranks" in the camp on 1 February 1918, the War Diary records that 30 were working as teamsters, 50 in various mills, 50 in the bush operations of the various companies, 30 in the shipping department, 15 as cooks, 35 on the roads, 20 in "other District employ" and the balance on "Miscellaneous Labour."[65] In time many of the men became quite skilled.[66] Many of Sutherland's officers were also employed outside the unit lines. One was made responsible for road maintenance throughout the forestry district. Another supervised district shipping operations. Still another ran the water supply and pumping system, and another built and operated a two-mile logging railroad.[67]

Life in the Juras, for both black and white troops, was lacking in the amenities, particularly in 1917. Later on, constructing YMCA facilities was considered (a separate one, of course, was proposed for the Negro troops) and provision was made for a cinema.[68] War diaries also reflect occasional social and recreational events, later much enhanced by the rejuvenation of No. 2's band, once their instruments were shipped over from England.[69]

No. 2's chaplain, William A. White, was also active in taking care of both the spiritual and material needs of his unit. At first he was the only chaplain in the district and his labours were on behalf of both black and white. A church was erected and the chaplain reported that his services had attracted a number of white men from the other companies.[70] Not all whites were so inclined, however. Initially the military religious establishment overseas appears to have neglected this remote corner of Canadian endeavour. But eventually it was decided to dispatch a white chaplain because, as the senior Canadian chaplain in France claimed, "the Negro chaplain is not acceptable to the white units."[71]

From the standpoint of the overall state of discipline within No. 2 Construction Company, a review of Routine Orders for No. 5 District, Canadian Forestry Crops (CFC), shows that unit personnel were awarded a small proportion of the minor punishments which were handed out.[72] However, there continued to be a very troublesome element in No. 2's membership. Its presence gave some credence to the earlier apprehensions of the local French population. In the opinion of the Paris headquarters of the CFC, the problem did not involve all of the black troops:

> a number of American negroes, — about seventy-five — who have proven most difficult to discipline. There has been already one case of rape; also one of indecent assault. The civilian population have lodged other complaints against these men, and we have come to the conclusion that they are a menace to the civil population of the neighbourhood.
>
> They are good workmen, however, strong and willing. It is suggested that they might be used to advantage in the forward Army Areas, where they would be sufficiently remote from the civilian population to prevent their getting into any further trouble.[73]

Senior French military authorities were less sanguine: the black soldiers were beyond redemption and should be removed. But labour was in short supply. Thus, the solution was to move 50 of the worst offenders out of the French zone in November 1917 into the rear area of the British Third Army near Peronne, attached to No. 37 Company, CFC.[74] This proximity to the fighting failed to have the desired effect. By August 1918 the local district commander had accumulated a long list of complaints:

> the thirty-seven men now attached to No. 37 Company, Canadian Forestry Corps, for the past fifteen months, have done a total of 2,029 days Field Punishment No. 1, during that time [54 hours/man!]. They have been charged with sodomy, attempted murder, stealing from French Civilians, and nearly all the other crimes on the Calendar. Can these men be returned to their Unit. They are demoralizing the white men of this Company. When they are doing Field Punishment No. 1 they take up the time of guards, etc. and are certainly a nuisance at all times. O.C., No. 37 Company has certainly had his share of trouble with them. On account of the men being colored, the Army will not accept them in the ordinary Field Punishment Compound. Do you know of any place where we could send them to undergo their Punishment if they cannot be returned to their unit?[75]

No. 2 had been purged of its less desirable elements but another rather absurd issue was about to remove 180 more valuable men. With the onset of colder weather in November 1917, the Company Medical Officer exercised his social conscience by recommending evacuation of the black troops to warmer climes for the winter, due to the preconceived notion that the race could not withstand its rigours. This doubtless sincere expression of humanitarian concern picked up a bureaucratic momentum of its own as it rose through the chain of command. "It seems to me that Canadian Negroes should be able to withstand the Jura Climate," the CFC's Paris headquarters advised the Director General of Timber Operations in London. "It may be, however, that the West Indian Negroes . . . may find it too severe."[76] There was considerable deliberation. Meanwhile the rain, mud and fog of November gave way to colder and dryer weather in December. The unit's West Indians and Americans from southern climes adjusted to it, and the authorities realized that their concern was unfounded. But by this time higher decisions had already been made. Orders were issued to move 180 men of West Indian or southern United States origin south to Alençon, near Bordeaux, where they were to remain. No reprieve was possible, said the Paris headquarters when they were asked to have the orders changed:

it is extremely unfortunate that you did not arrive at the decision earlier that it would be unnecessary to remove a portion of No. 2 Construction Company. The application for the move is already before
the Quartermaster-General, and we cannot very well withdraw it without making both ourselves and the Medical Officer ridiculous. The
move will take place as soon as the authority is forthcoming from the
Quartermaster-General. There are no men available to replace this
labour.[77]

No. 2 Construction Company once again became a fragmented
unit, but there were happier developments as well. Despite the shortage of manpower, members of the unit began to receive leave passes
(four or five per day) previously unavailable to them, which allowed
for travel to Paris and London. These privileges continued throughout the war, although they were withdrawn for a time after 13 of the
first 74 to return from leave arrived with venereal infections.[78]

Life in La Joux settled into a relatively uneventful but not
entirely unpleasant routine punctuated by occasional entertainments
or parades and characterized by a general improvement in quarters
and facilities. Major Sutherland still campaigned for the unit's
employment in construction work at the front, but without success.[79]
He and other members also hoped for enough reinforcements to per-
mit its reinstatement as a battalion. Efforts in this regard, which were
generally encouraged by a labour-hungry Forestry Corps, included
attempts to recover personnel who earlier had been left behind at
Bramshott. Some of these were eventually allowed to rejoin the unit
in April 1918.[80]

The Forestry Corps might well have been content to absorb the
black troops of No. 2 into their different units. Certainly Captain
White feared such a possibility sufficiently to ask a Nova Scotia member of Parliament to intervene: "the colored people are proud that
they have at least one definite Unit representing them in France.
Should we be absorbed and scattered . . . , the source of pride would
be taken away."[81]

The situation had become contradictory. A campaign which had
developed from the refusal of CEF units to accept black recruits had
become a campaign to retain the identity of Canada's only black unit.
When F.B. McCurdy heard of the matter, he was also concerned that
the black soldiers might end up "among unsympathetic strangers,"
and perhaps he was right.[82] Perhaps, indeed, a degree of apartheid
still seemed to be in the best interests of all concerned.

It was hoped that the recent introduction of compulsory military
service in Canada would enable No. 2 Construction Company not
only to retain its identity but help the unit to recover its battalion status. Probably at F.B. McCurdy's instigation, authority was granted for

the formation of a depot organization in London, Ontario, as part of the 1st Depot Battalion, Western Ontario Regiment. This was established for the purpose of collecting any black recruits brought in under conscription. A recently returned officer from No. 2, Lieutenant L.B. Young, was named its commanding officer.[83]

Young set about with considerable zeal to search out suitable recruits, particularly in the United States, but was brought up short by the Militia authorities who did not wish the new depot to perform any function beyond the collection of conscripts. There was no support for the idea of raising a sufficient number of recruits to fill a labour battalion at this point. A small draft of black reinforcements, however, was dispatched overseas.[84] No. 2 was to retain its identity, but it would not be restored to battalion status.

WHEN THE WAR ended, No. 2 Construction Company was one of the early units sent to England for processing to return home, leaving La Joux on 4 December 1918. This processing involved the breaking up of units into regionally based drafts and spending some time at Bramshott and Kinmel Park Camp. An ugly incident took place at Kinmel Park which provided an early indication of the inadequacy of Canadian provisions for troop demobilization and the inability of the authorities to maintain the necessary discipline among the impatient soldiers awaiting repatriation. The report dealing with this incident indicates that a black sergeant-major accompanying a group of some 275 members of No. 2 placed a white soldier under arrest for insubordination and placed him in the charge of a coloured escort. A "General Melee" (*sic*) ensued and the black troops produced razors. After "much trouble" someone succeeded in forming up the black troops present and moving them to a vacant hut. Five white men had had their faces slashed and several black soldiers had been injured by rocks. Subsequently, while the latter were absent, white troops raided their hut, broke all the windows and rifled their kits. Some frantic organizational work was needed to re-equip the men before their imminent departure for Canada.[85]

All the separate drafts of No. 2 Construction Company left England to return home in January 1919.[86] They were fortunate to miss the serious demobilization riots which later took place at Kinmel Park.[87]

And so ends the history of a military unit which earned no particular distinction during the war other than that it was composed almost entirely of black men. Nor were they given much opportunity to earn any distinction, notwithstanding their general readiness to serve. There is no question, however, that they played an important role in the labours of the Canadian Forestry Corps, a service which was formally recognized by a letter of thanks to their commanding officer from Major-General MacDougall, the corps commander, but sadly omitted in the semi-official history of the corps published shortly after the war.[88]

The black community's offer of sacrifice was unaccepted in some quarters, unwelcome in many, and unremarked in most. Still, Canada's blacks learned that there were sympathetic men in the political power structure prepared to consider their represented concerns to the extent that they brought about the formation of a black unit in the CEF. While perhaps all ambitions for the unit were not realized, its identity was preserved until the end of the war, and as such was a source of pride for many of those who served in it. While segregated in their own camps, the black troops appear to have mixed freely with white troops both on duty and at occasional social events. It seems reasonable to assume that many men, both black and white, profited from the interaction. It also seems fair to conclude that this otherwise unpublicized and minor component of Canada's remarkable contribution to the Allied cause represented not only a substantial willingness to share the obligations of citizenship but it may have given both impetus and legitimacy to later black claims to a more equitable share in civic rights and obligations, particularly in Nova Scotia.

Notes

1. M. Stuart Hunt, ed., *Nova Scotia's Part in the Great War* (Halifax, 1920), pp. 148f.
2. See Robin W. Winks, *The Blacks in Canada* (Montreal, 1971), pp. 313-20.
3. The National Archives of Canada (NAC), Department of National Defence, RG24, Vol. 1206, HQ 297-1-21, Hughes to Richards, 25 Nov. 1915.
4. For an analysis of Sam Hughes' performance as wartime Minister see Ronald G. Haycock, *Sam Hughes: The Public Career of a Controversial Canadian, 1885-1916* (Waterloo, Ont., 1986).
5. NAC, Sir Robert Borden Papers, p. 16587, "Memorandum on the Enlistment of Negroes in the Canadian Expeditionary Force, 13 April 1916." For a contemporary assessment of Gwatkin see Colonel C.F. Hamilton, "Lieutenant-General Willoughby Gwatkin: An Appreciation," *Canadian Defence Quarterly*, II (1925), 226-30.
6. NAC, RG24, Vol. 1206, HQ 297-1-21, OC 104 O.S. Battl. CEF to AAG 6th Division, 25 Nov. 1915.
7. Ibid., *passim*.
8. NAC, RG24, Vol. 4387, 2MD 34-7-141, OC 173 Battalion (Hamilton) to AAG MD No. 2, 14 Apr. 1916.
9. Ibid., OC 177 Battalion to AAG 2MD, 5Apr. 1916 and OC 157 Battalion to AAG 2MD, 6 Apr. 1916.
10. In fact, at least 1500 blacks saw service in various elements of the Canadian forces during World War I. Mr. Thamis Gale of Montreal has painstakingly traced the names of all of these veterans. Approximately 400 served in CEF

infantry battalions. Some were professional soldiers from the West Indies. As many as seven held commissioned rank. Those who were not full-blooded or who could pass as whites were more likely to be accepted, however. Interview with Mr. Gale, 23 Jan. 1985.

11. See NAC, Department of Militia and Defence, RG9 III, Vol. 81, HQ 10-9-40, McCurdy to Harrington, 16 Jul. 1919.
12. See NAC, RG24, Vol. 1206, HQ 297-1-21, *passim.*
13. Ibid., OC 106 Battalion to 6 Division, 14 Dec. 1915.
14. NAC, RG24, Vol. 4387, OC 2 Division to Secretary, Militia Council, 10 Mar. 1916.
15. NAC, RG24, Vol 1206, HQ 297-1-21, Capt. Trump to J.R.B. Whitney, 15 Mar. 1916.
16. Ibid., Whitney to Hughes, 18 Apr. 1916.
17. NAC, RG24, Vol. 2030, HQ 1812, v.1, War Office to Colonial Office, 25 Feb. 1916.
18. Ibid., Ripley to Militia Council, 19 Apr. 1916.
19. NAC, Borden papers, p. 16587.
20. NAC, RG24, Vol. 1206, HQ 297-1-21, War Office to Governor-General, 11 May 1916.
21. NAC, RG24, Vol. 1206, HQ 600-10-35, Adjutant-General to Minister of Labour, 10 June 1916; A.E. Blount to Hodgins, 12 June 1916 and Sutherland to Hodgins, 4 July 1916.
22. Ibid., Adjutant-General Circular Letter, 5 July 1916.
23. NAC, RG24, Vol. 4393, 2MD 34-7-171, Adjutant-General Circular Letter, 16 Aug. 1916.
24. Ibid., Ripley to Secretary, Militia Council, 7 July 1916.
25. Ibid., Adjutant-General to OC No. 1 Construction Battalion, 10 July 1916. No. 1 Construction Battalion eventually became the 1st Battalion Canadian Railway Troops. See G.W.L. Nicholson, *Canadian Expeditionary Force 1914-1919* (Ottawa, 1962), pp. 485-90.
26. *Pictou Advocate*, 18 Aug. 1916; Hunt, p. 149, and, NAC, MG30 B131, H. Falconer McLean, Papers, *passim.*
27. *Pictou Advocate*, 11 Aug. 1916.
28. Ibid.
29. Ibid. (reprint), 25 Aug. 1916.
30. NAC, RG24, Vol. 4558, 6MD 132-11-1, Sutherland to HQ 6 Divisional Area, 20 Aug. 1916
31. The battalion eventually obtained satisfactory office space in the Cummings Building, Truro, Nova Scotia. Ibid., MD No. 6 to OC No. 2 Construction Bn., 8 Sept. 1916.
32. NAC, RG24, Vol. 4486, 4MD 47-8-1 and Vol. 4599, 1OMD 20-10-52, *passim.*
33. Hunt, p. 149.
34. Arnold W. Thomas, ed., *The Canadian Almanac and Miscellaneous Directory for the Year 1916* (Toronto, 1915) p. 380.
35. *The Evening Record* (Windsor), Sept. 1916 to Mar. 1917, *passim.*
36. Ibid.
37. Ibid., 6 Mar. 1917.
38. *Pictou Advocate*, 4 to 18 Aug. 1916 and *The Truro Daily News*, 14 Nov. 1916 to 24 Feb. 1917.
39. Ibid., 14 Nov. 1916.
40. Ibid.

41. NAC, RG24, Vol. 1469, HQ 600-10-35, v.1, CGS to Adjutant-General, 18 Sept. 1916.
42. Ibid., Adjutant-General to OC No. 2 Construction Bn., 22 Dec. 1916.
43. See NAC, RG24, Vol. 1550, HQ 683-124-2, OC No. 2 Construction Bn., to Secretary Militia Council, 27 Nov. 1916.
44. NDHQ, DHIST, CEF Sailing Lists, Vol. XIII. The roster also indicates that two men were born in Mexico and one each in Holland, Cuba, South Africa, Malta and Arabia.
45. NAC, RG24, Vol 4599, 10MD 20-10-52, Capt. Gayfer to Col. Gray, 22 Nov. 1916.
46. NAC, RG24, Vol. 1469, HQ 600-1-35, v.1, Sutherland to Kemp, 18 Jan. 1917.
47. Ibid. and Vol. 1472, HQ 600-10-50, Bell to Fiset, 11 Jan. 1917.
48. NAC, RG24, Vol. 1469, HQ 600-10-35, v.1, Adjutant-General to Minister, 22 Jan. 1917.
49. Ibid., Sutherland to Militia Council, 15 Feb. 1917 with handwritten minute by A.E. Kemp.
50. Ibid., Minute, Gwatkin to Quartermaster-General (QMG), 19 Feb. 1917.
51. Ibid., Gwatkin to Naval Secretary Interdepartmental Committee, 21 Feb. 1917.
52. Ibid., Stephens to Gwatkin, 23 Feb. 1917.
53. Hunt, p. 150.
54. NAC, RG9 III, Vol. 5015, No. 2 Construction Company, War Diary, 17 May 1917.
55. NAC, RG9 III, Vol. 81, 10-9-40, Adjutant-General Canadians to Private Secretary, Minister Overseas Military Forces, 20 Dec. 1917. For a discussion of how the British dealt with the subject races in France, see Jeffrey Greenhut, "Race, Sex and War: The Impact of Race and Sex on Morale and Health Services for the Indian Corps on the Western Front, 1914," *Military Affairs*, 45 (1981), 71-74.
56. Ibid.
57. NAC, RG9 III, Vol. 1608, E. 186-9, Forestry Directorate Paris Mission to Directorate of Forestry, 9 May 1917.
58. Nicholson, pp. 499-500.
59. NAC, RG9 III, Vol 1608, E-186-9, Maj. Johnson to Col. White, 21 May 1917. Also see Vol. 5015, War Diary, No. 2 Construction Company, May 1917.
60. Ibid.
61. Ibid.
62. See C.W. Bird and J.B. Davies, *The Canadian Forestry Corps: Its Inception, Development and Achievements* (London, 1919), pp. 41-2. For a photographic view of the life shared by black and white soldiers in No. 5 District see NAC, National Photography Collection, Thomas H. Bacon Collection.
63. NAC, RG9 III, Vol. 5015, War Diary, No. 2 Construction Company, 2 Apr. 1918.
64. Ibid.
65. Ibid., 1 Feb. 1918.
66. NAC, RG9 III, Vol. 1608, E-186-9, Director of Forestry to QMG, 10 Jan. 1918.
67. NAC, RG9 III, Vol. 5015, War Diary, No. 2 Construction Company, June 1917.
68. NAC, RG9 III, Vol. 1608, E-186-9, Director of Forestry to Senior Officer, YMCA, 9 June 1917.

69. NAC, RG9 III, Vol. 5015, War Diary, No. 2 Construction Company, *passim*.
70. NAC, RG9 III Vol. 4965, C-W-23 White W.A., White to Director of Chaplain Services, 26 May 1917 and 20 June 1917.
71. NAC, RG9 III, Vol. 4616, C-B-8, Beattie, Wm., to Director Chaplain Services, 20 Feb. 1918. Actually, White seems to have been respected by the senior chaplains. They simply assumed that coloured chaplains were unemployable with white troops. See NAC, RG9 III, Vol. 4965, C-W-23, W.A. White, *passim*.
72. NAC, RG9 III, Vol. 3819, No. 5 District CFC Routine Orders, *passim*.
73. NAC, RG9 III, Vol. 1608, E-186-9, Assistant Director of Forestry to QMG, 12 Sept. 1917. Several courts-martial were convened. One of them led to a sentence of death which was later commuted to life imprisonment by Field Marshal Haig. NAC, RG9 III, Vol. 5015, War Diary, No. 2 Construction Company, 2 Oct. 1917.
74. Ibid., HQ l. of C. Area (Lieut.-Gen. J. Asser) to Adjutant-General, 11 Oct. 1917 and Director Timber Operations to HQ Jura Group, 4 Nov. 1917.
75. NAC, RG9 III, Vol. 1608, E-186-9, OC No. 9 District to Director Timber Operations, 1 Aug. 1918.
76. Ibid., A/Director Timber Operations to Director General of Timber Operations, 22 Nov. 1917.
77. Ibid., A/Director Timber Operations to HQ Jura Group, 17 Dec. 1917.
78. NAC, RG9 III, Vol. 5015, War Diary, No. 2 Construction Company, 4 Feb. 1918 and 17 Apr. 1918.
79. Ibid., 3 Apr. 1918.
80. Ibid., 9 Apr. 1918.
81. NAC, RG9 III, Vol. 81, 10-9-40, White to Frank Stanfield, M.P., 18 Oct. 1917.
82. See ibid., McCurdy to Perley, 14 Nov. 1917.
83. NAC, RG24, Vol. 1469, HQ 600-10-35, v.1, McCurdy to Mewburn, 17 Jan. 1918 and Shannon to Militia Council, 13 Feb. 1918.
84. Ibid., Young to Milligan, 13 Mar. 1918 and Adjutant-General to GOC MD No. 1, 30 Apr. 1918. Also see White to Sir Robert Borden, 11 Aug. 1918.
85. NAC, RG9 III, Vol. 1709, D-3-13, v.6, OC Camp 19, MD6 to OC Cdn. Troops, Kinmel Park Camp, 10 Jan. 1919.
86. Hunt, p. 151.
87. See Desmond Morton, "'Kicking and Complaining': Demobilization Riots in the Canadian Expeditionary Force, 1918-19," *Canadian Historical Review*, 61 (1980), 334-60. As Professor Morton points out, the account in Winks, *The Blacks in Canada*, is misleading.
88. Hunt, p. 153. See also Bird and Davies, *The Canadian Forestry Corps*. This bulky work contained no references to either No. 2 Construction Company or to black soldiers.

INDEX